THE BLIND GUARDIANS OF IGNORANCE

COVID-19, SUSTAINABILITY, AND OUR VULNERABLE FUTURE

A handbook for change leaders, young and old

Mats Larsson

ia

imprint-academic.com

Published in the UK by
Imprint Academic, PO Box 200, Exeter EX5 5YX, UK

Distributed in the USA by
Ingram Book Company,
One Ingram Blvd., La Vergne, TN 37086, USA

ISBN 9781788360487 Paperback

A CIP catalogue record for this book is available from the
British Library and US Library of Congress

Contents

"It is a curse to have ideas that people understand only when it is too late."
— Nassim Nicholas Taleb,
The Bed of Procrustes

Mikael Höök

Foreword

One of the most important questions one can ask relates to current society and its sustainability over time. Literature is increasingly filled with books questioning past or present societies — and also attempts to highlight new visions for more sustainable paths — as the rapidly growing body of literature on sustainability indicates. Modern society uses a number of inputs to keep the wheels of our global economy turning as well as to satisfy the demand for increasing welfare and prosperity by a growing population. Economic growth and increased consumption are seen as politically important goals and have helped to build up the wealth of the western civilization. Emerging economies in Asia are now pursuing similar development, with increased demand for natural resources and fuels.

Hans Carl von Carlowitz studied *"sustainable management"* as an idea in 1713, and reflected upon the connections between prospering human activities and careful management of required natural resources. Others, such as Carl Linneus, also contemplated the organizing principles of nature and its surrounding administration that seemed to provide abundance for life in many forms. Since those early days, sustainability science has evolved much and branched out into several diverging schools of thought and diverging views on the best paths towards sustainability.

The realization that many societal challenges involve interconnecting sectors has been popular in the last decade. This includes everything from globalized trade and industrial supply chains to new frameworks for management of risks and the organization of transformation. The Sustainable Development Goals formulated by the UN in 2015 contain many such intersecting issues like poverty alleviation, climate action, and clean/affordable energy for production.

Industrial supply chains are essential for our modern society and they are not given as much contemplation in public discussions as they should. Inputs of raw materials flow from all over the world to manufacturing centres and are transformed into consumer goods—containing embodied energy, emissions, and materials—to be traded in the globalized economy. This direct and indirect transfer of energy and material via international trade results in material flows that span multiple economies across the globe with the need for international perspectives. This gives rise to a complex interconnectivity between sectors and also complicated power structures rarely given the attention they deserve.

Climate change is increasingly regarded as one of humanity's greatest collective challenges, which threatens to permanently alter the foundations of life and societies across the world. In response to this threat, the international community has outlined ambitious goals for the reduction of greenhouse gas emissions in the 2016 Paris Agreement. These goals can only be reached by simultaneously implementing a number of comprehensive measures, including the transformation of the energy sector and a decrease in energy use with significant impacts on many supply chains and societies.

A third of known global oil reserves, half of gas reserves, and over 80 per cent of coal reserves should remain unused from 2010 to 2050 in order to meet the target of limiting warming to 2°C—regardless of what is potentially available for exploitation. The need to reduce global emissions coincides with economic and population growth in the Global South and transitioning countries. Consequently, global energy demand is projected to grow by more than a quarter to 2040. Efforts to curb climate change thus face a double challenge: to rapidly and fundamentally transform the energy sector while preserving opportunities for increased well-being, economic development, and social stability as stipulated in the Sustainable Development Goals.

This challenge is hardly trivial, and how to even formulate sensible transformation pathways are far from easy. Historically, sustained and equitable economic growth, facilitated by ample access to cheap energy, has been a major source of welfare improvements and an important explanation for the remarkable decline in conflicts and wars among developed states. To the extent that climate change mitigation threatens the trajectory and distribution of future income and well-being, political turmoil and conflict are conceivable outcomes. In countries where fossil fuel production is a major source of income, a rapid global shift to low-carbon economies could have destabilizing effects. At the same time, effective shifts towards more sustainable systems will reduce loss and the damage of global warming and, in the longer term, generate benefits that extend beyond the climate system.

Transformation in societal systems is complex and can include everything from large changes in the state of the system, to substitutions of one technology to another, diffusion of completely new technologies, to new and consumer preferences or systemwide events with dramatic and unanticipated effects. For example, whale oil was—technically—an energy source in the nineteenth century, despite the fact that the overall economy was chiefly based on coal at the time. Whale oil was used only for very specific purposes (primarily illumination), and the transition to kerosene was easy and occurred very rapidly. Bardi[1] explored this in more detail and made several important remarks that pinpoint how difficult it can be to substitute energy sources. In particular, he showed that resource scarcity often dramatically increases the amplitude of price oscillations, which often slow an energy transition. Businesses and governments struggle with alternating circumstances of insufficient cash flow to handle price spikes and plummeting prices that do not cover their existing cost structures. Long-term planning in this ever-changing environment becomes extremely difficult, and investment—even highly needed investment—can drop precipitously.

Over longer timespans events occur that are simply unforeseeable or at least unpredictable with any certainty, for example the oil shocks, environmental concerns, or opposition to nuclear power. Projecting the outlook 20—let alone 40—years into the future is a far too long period for maintaining validity of many assumptions and achieving accurate predictions. Currently, the lockdowns associated with the Covid-19 pandemic are estimated to affect around 40% of global energy demand and have drastically impacted travel, politics, and society. Who would have expected such a radical shift in energy consumption trends to suddenly occur? Transformative visions need to embrace explorative and normative projections as a better way in order to illustrate possible and preferable paths for the future.

The links between transformations and sustainability remain underexplored, but are clearly gaining traction with academia, industry, and policymakers. Sustainability may easily be a key issue for the long-term survival of society. However, the important questions and answers are increasingly mixed with ideological, political, ethical, and other

---

1   Bardi, U. & Lavacchi, A. (2009) A simple interpretation of Hubbert's model of resource exploitation, *Energies*, 2 (3), pp. 646–661.

viewpoints. As Engelmann (2013)[2] daringly stated "we live in an age of sustainobabble". In such a conflux of vague concepts and chaotic differences that may arise when drawn to extremes, Larsson daringly paints pictures of the future and of transformative paths that differs from many mainstream narratives.

Against this backdrop, other important trends affecting humans are the ever-present march of technological development as well as shifts in geopolitical power with the emergence of new actors and the current challenge of Covid-19. All this is fused into a thought-provoking mixture by Larsson in his attempt to inform and discuss these issues and stake out possible paths forward for change leaders.

---

2   Engelmann, R. (2013) Beyond sustainobabble, in *State of the World 2013: Is Sustainability Still Possible?*, pp. 3–16, Washington, DC: Worldwatch Institute.

Part 1:

The Age of Ignorance

Chapter One

The Blind Guardians
of Ignorance

Globalization on a Massive Scale

In the present global society, we have taken an idea to an extreme, without considering the consequences. This is the story of how the majority of the population of the western world came to believe in market-based development to such an extent that the roles of foresight and collective action were repressed and largely forgotten by experts, politicians, and the general public. It is the story of how the governments of countries came to not observe the risks of the lack of thoughtful consideration and planning and left the fate of their countries in the hands of blind irresponsible forces. This is also the story of the territories of ignorance that have developed as an entire generation lost the vocabulary and the concepts needed to talk about collective activities that most people from an intellectual perspective can recognize as necessary, but that for almost three decades have been designated as politically incorrect. In this landscape of forgetfulness, blind guardians of ignorance have taken it upon themselves to purge the political landscape of the forbidden ideas. Surprisingly, the blind guardians have not always been aware of the consequences of our collective blindness, but the current in society has been so powerful that it has become almost impossible for individuals to resist and go against it. The advantages of going with the ever more powerful flow has been so much more rewarding than trying to stop or divert it—a seemingly futile and meaningless activity.

With the Covid-19 pandemic this situation is rapidly changing. People are becoming aware of the risks that have mounted for countries, due to the increasing dependence on production in far-away countries, transportation around the globe, and an endless flow of raw materials. While citizens have not experienced all the risks that have built up, minds around the world open to the idea that conscious decisions need to counterbalance the action of free markets. The market is clearly the most efficient tool for allocating resources in a wide range of situations, but there are also areas where the power of the market needs to be balanced and enhanced by analysis and decisions to manage risk and drive development in directions the market is not able to support. For, as we shall see, political decisions, when wisely made, do not stop the market from doing its magic, they boost its power. This book is an attempt to discuss some of the territories of blindness and how people in general, politicians, and governments need to regain influence. It is not about taking away the power of the market and creating command economies but enhancing it by helping development on its way in areas where the market is too blunt a tool to be effective.

To many people this is probably one of the most surprising pieces of news that they could imagine. The idea that free markets cannot drive technology and economic development in all situations probably seems like a suggestion reminiscent of the 1980s and a chill may go down their spine, but there is nothing to fear. It is like in the early days of sound films, when film producers said that cinema audiences did not want to hear actors talk. But movies with sound brought an entirely new dimension to experiencing a film. In the same way, conscious contributions to the development of markets will bring a new dimension to people's understanding of economic development. There is a dimension of intelligent decision making, timing, and nuance that will bring market-based development to a new level. Once people have seen how decisions influence the development of markets, they will realize that technology development has never been an automatic process, it has always been almost like an art form — art that forms society and improves peoples' lives. It is social engineering at its best.

A lack of understanding of the interaction between markets and high-level decisions may at worst destroy societies and the lives of people, not once, but many times over. The only scary thing is that many people, the public as well as politicians, experts, and business leaders, will have to learn about aspects of reality that have been forgotten for three decades and supressed for longer than that. Public financing has, for a long time, supported markets and made them function better. Through the pages of this book we will learn how markets are usually unable to drive technology development through the early phases, and how governments, in different ways, through large-scale financing and critical decisions have driven the development of the technologies that have in turn driven economic growth in recent decades. Most people know that this is true. The computer, the internet, space technologies, power technologies, telephony and mobile phone systems are all technologies that in their early phases of development were to a large extent financed by governments. We will come back to this later, not once, but several times.

Most of us have not been aware of the large territories of ignorance that have been building up behind our backs. Many will recognize that they have, in one way or another — mostly unwittingly — contributed to moving interest away from the issues discussed in this book by drawing interest to areas we have felt comfortable discussing and where people have been more knowledgeable. While we cannot change the past, we all have a choice for the future. We can choose to spend time and learn about the important subjects that have been neglected and draw attention to the challenges that mankind is facing. The future is built by conscious decisions of governments in combination with the invisible and automatic hand of the market. In the past three decades the role of collective action has been forgotten and powers have been ascribed to the market that it has never had.

As the development of the Covid-19 pandemic unfolded in the early months of 2020, an increasing number of people had reason to ask themselves how modern society could have become so vulnerable to unexpected shocks as our present society turned out to be. How could it be that countries had no emergency supplies of critical medical equipment? And how could companies in Europe indiscriminately outsource all kinds of production to China, India, and other far-away countries without any debate of the fact that the production of everything from medical equipment to pharmaceuticals, and parts for society's critical infrastructure, are produced in countries where western governments have no control of resources, processes, or priorities? In the early months of 2020, countries were in the midst of very expensive mitigation activities of a pandemic that could perhaps have been avoided — and that definitely should have been planned for. Epidemiologists have in numerous books described how pandemics have killed millions and warned that it is only a matter of time until the next pandemic strikes our increasingly entangled society.[1] A few weeks into the pandemic it became known, for example, that 97 per cent of all

---

[1] In *The Pandemic Century: One Hundred Years of Panic, Hysteria, and Hubris,* medical historian Mark Honigsbaum relates the pandemics of the twentieth century, from the Spanish flu to SARS, and ebola.

antibiotics used in the United States were made in China and that Europe has also become highly dependent on China and India for its supply of pharmaceuticals.[2] Some of the drugs that are only sourced from China and India are critical to patients for their daily treatments and many patients would die if supplies were interrupted for a longer period.

The outsourcing has been driven by seemingly good reasons. Asian countries, with low wages and salaries, have over decades been able to offer more competitive prices and production costs, and the dependence between sellers and buyers was seen to provide enough of a guarantee that governments and suppliers in the world's manufacturing countries would remain loyal to buyers and maintain supplies. The penalty of not transferring production would have been too great as lower production cost and prices contribute to economic growth, and the access to cheap oil has made transportation across the globe so inexpensive that the cost of transportation is far outweighed by the reduced cost of production. What nobody had calculated was the possibility that factors outside of the control of human decision makers could cause a breakdown of global supply chains and force countries across the world to close down production and other business activities in an effort to fight a virus pandemic of a type that had been successfully dealt with a number of times before. First of all, China closed down companies in the province of Hubei and a few other regions that were most severely hit by the virus. By the time Chinese workers were starting to come back to work, Italy, Spain, the United States, the UK, and other countries that were the most severely hit by the pandemic had closed down the entire countries, or parts thereof, in order to combat the disease.

As a second wave after the fear of becoming infected, the consequences for the economy became obvious. The business for airlines, hotels, restaurants, and other service companies dried up almost completely in the wake of travel bans and recommendations to avoid travelling. The demand for many products shrunk dramatically, sometimes close to zero as people were kept from shopping for everything but the absolute necessities like food and pharmaceuticals, as governments in many countries closed shops. A month into the crisis,

---

2   In an article titled "U.S. Dependence on Pharmaceutical Products from China" of the 14 August 2019 the Council on Foreign Relations, an independent membership organization for foreign policy, provided this information.

companies started to file for bankruptcy and governments had to start up mammoth programmes to come to the aid of ailing companies and entire industries in large sectors of the economy.

Nothing similar had happened before, and the scale of the shutdown was dramatic. Few had anticipated that a disaster of this scale could happen to a modern society. The sudden demand for ventilators and medical supplies that was caused by the need to put infected persons in intensive care emptied available stocks of these products, and production resources had not been dimensioned to replenish stocks across the world when demand in all countries soared at the same time.

Nobody could have foreseen the sudden outbreak of the coronavirus pandemic, and nobody could foresee the rapid spread of the virus from China to other parts of the world in January and February of 2020. Yet, many epidemiologists had warned of the risk of a pandemic, due to the modern lifestyle enjoyed by people travelling for business and pleasure across the globe in the global and affluent economy. One factor that exacerbated the disaster was the slow but steady outsourcing of production to Asia that had been going on for more than two decades. The share of global production that was done in China in 1990 amounted to a few per cent of global manufacturing and by 2018 the share had risen to 28 per cent. This included production in most industries. An additional share of manufacturing was done in other Asian countries, taking the total of goods produced in Asia well above 30 per cent. All types of mass and speciality production had been moved to far-away countries — and the opportunity for governments to order face masks and other critical supplies was limited. From 2004 to 2018, the share of global production by the United States went down from 22 to 17 per cent, while at the same time the share of manufacturing that was done in China went from 9 to 28 percentage points. At the same time, the share of manufacturing that was done in Europe declined from 28 per cent in 2004 to around 18 per cent in 2018.[3] And the outsourcing has been indiscriminate in the sense that it has been entirely driven by price considerations. Governments have seen no reason to become involved, neither in assessing the risk involved in the outsourcing of the production of certain industrial sectors that may be particularly sensitive for the economy, nor in considering the

---

[3] Marchinski, R. & Martinez Turegano, D., "Reassessing the Decline of EU Manufacturing: A Global Value Chain Analysis", *JRT Technical Report 2019*.

dependence that arises from outsourcing production to far-away countries, some with totalitarian political systems that are not as open as western democracies.

When facing the disaster, companies in western countries did what they could to produce to the needs of governments. In the United States, the president ordered General Motors to produce ventilators, using the Defence Production Act that authorizes the president to order companies to manufacture products that are considered essential for the nation. In other countries, similar measures were taken by governments to secure the supplies of medical supplies and equipment.

Blind Guardians of Ignorance

How could governments and their citizens sit idly by and watch how increasing shares of production were moved to low-cost countries? Did nobody reflect on the risks connected to abandoning all control of production, even of some of the most critical emergency supplies?

Perhaps, but probably to a lesser extent as time went by. In the 1970s, during the Cold War, governments kept large stocks of oil, food, and other necessities in the face of the threat of a new war. Internet technologies were developed to make American research centres and universities less vulnerable to military strikes. Through electronic communication classified documents could be sent between centres and they could be stored electronically in places out of reach of enemy bombs and missiles. Governments all over the world had the Second World War fresh in their memories and there was a strong sentiment in the population that security of supply should be a high priority and that critical supplies should be produced within the borders of a country, or in allied countries. It was also a fact that poor countries did not have very many manufacturing companies that could compete with those of the more developed countries in the world. For a long time into the 1980s, Japanese products had an inferior image, compared to ones that had been made in Europe and North America, and many experts held the belief that Japanese industry would never be able to achieve the same level of quality as western firms. At that time South Korea, China, India, and Eastern European countries had not even emerged as exporters of any importance. A further factor was that computer technology was in its infancy and communication was conducted via letter, phone, and telex. Even the fax machine was only launched on a global scale in the late 1980s. The dominance of the west was not in any way in question.

At this time, a number of new trends emerged, and a sequence of events took place that gradually changed the global economy. In the mid-1980s Chinese exports made up only 2 per cent of world exports. China was still a minor player in the economic landscape, but double-digit growth had started that was about to take the country up to the leading position it has today. By the end of the 1980s the use of fax machines had spread so that even small companies had one — a development that greatly facilitated world trade as detailed messages and drawings could be faxed at a low cost. With the fax, any document could be put into the machine and immediately sent to be read by the recipient. Telex messages had to be brief and it was difficult to convey complex ideas or instructions in such messages. In the 1990s the internet and e-mails increased the efficiency of communication even further. In the 1980s the Japanese industrial wonder eclipsed the Chinese rise in global markets. The Japanese had for a long time been an exporter of second-rate industrial products, toys, and components, but in the 1980s they emerged as a developer and manufacturer of world-leading electronics, and Japanese companies like Sony, Mitsubishi, and Hitachi flooded world markets with highly competitive consumer electronics. People in western countries gradually realized that Japan would become a force to contend with in the future.

In 1989 the iron curtain fell, and the countries of the former Soviet bloc became free. Western European companies started to invest and build networks of stores in these emerging markets, and manufacturing companies started to notice that the location close to Western Europe and the low wages made these countries ideal suppliers of industrial products of all types. However, it was soon noted that workers lacked the experience of working with demanding customers and that the cost of doing business was sometimes higher than the low prices indicated. Nevertheless, a number of new competitors had emerged on the scene that would change the landscape of manufacturing for the long term.

The fall of the Soviet Union and the conversion of China to a capitalist economy made capitalism the only remaining ideology, and proponents of socialism had to admit that capitalist principles were the only ones that brought affluence and economic growth to an economy. It became the only ideology that could be applied by democratic countries. Government intervention in economic and technology development was to be kept to a minimum. At this time, socialist and communist parties changed their argumentation to become more open to market-based development, and some left-wing activists instead became environmentalists and started to advance the green political movement, founded parties, and started activist organizations like Greenpeace. Gradually, environmentalists abandoned activism to instead embrace the market as the tool for change. When the white goods industry developed alternatives to Freon as the primary cooling medium in refrigerators and freezers, it showed that industry could reform itself and abandon outdated products and practices. The automotive industry went through similar developments as engines became more fuel efficient, lead-free petrol replaced leaded, and catalytic cleaning of exhaust fumes reduced emissions dramatically. Few had a reason to doubt that technology advancement could solve environmental challenges. These changes, however, could be achieved through modest alterations of supply chains and production and they were neither as big nor as complex as the changes that lie ahead of countries at present.

From the 1990s and onwards these trends contributed to form the political, economic, and social landscape of the present day. The fall of the Soviet Union and the failure of other communist systems to provide the same quality of life that the capitalist economies of the west had done effectively stopped people from discussing important aspects of economic development, a close-down of the attention to important aspects of collective action that the world now is experiencing some of the consequences of. The failure to prepare society for unforeseen disasters is only one aspect of the blindness that has developed. The stigma that has precluded all constructive discussions about government involvement in technology development and industrial transformation has created not only blind spots, but substantial blind territories that have been guarded by vocal individuals with the purpose of cleansing public debate from certain ideas and topics that have been designated "politically incorrect".

As conversation in society has been purged of the unacceptable ideas for almost thirty years, development has been going on for this period of time almost unnoticed, without the checks and balances that are available in many other areas of society, where there is scope for open discussion of all important aspects. Development is monitored via key performance indicators of economic growth, joblessness, and investment. The growth of Chinese and Asian production and the volume of products that are imported to Europe and the United States have been monitored and discussed. The rise of China as an economic superpower has been noted, but the increasing dependence on China for loans and supplies has not been widely discussed as a risk to western economies. Instead, the supply of low-cost products has been noted as a driver of economic growth. The world has now started to experience some of the consequences that are caused by the transferral of more than one quarter of all manufacturing to Asia. Companies in China produce more than 90 per cent of the antibiotics used in the United States and many of the active ingredients for drugs are imported from China and India. A large part of other critical supplies, such as medical equipment for Europe as well as North America, is also produced in Asia, together with parts and components for all kinds of industrial products.

Why has this move come about and why has nobody reacted? Human society has functioned like the proverbial frog in the pan of water that is slowly coming to the boil. In the tale about the frog, often told in order to illustrate how gradual change can be lethal to species that are not observant of their surroundings, the frog is so stupid that it does not jump out of the pan until it is too late. In reality, frogs jump long before they are boiled, but human society is organized in such a way that we are unable to notice important changes until they hit us in the face and threaten to kill us. Only aspects that have been identified as risks are regularly monitored and discussed. In the case of economic growth, experts develop a very detailed knowledge of growth in different sectors of society, growth in different countries, the level of investment and its potential to drive growth, and a number of other factors related to this subject. Issues that have not been recognized as important are not discussed in the same way. Development may be noted and discussed but, for example, in the case of the growth of China as a large exporter there are no indicators that are monitored and no discussions of risks that need to be avoided.

Moving production to China has given people the opportunity to increase consumption and buy all kinds of products at lower prices. At the same time, it has provided western companies with the opportunity to purchase raw materials, parts, and machinery at rock-bottom prices, which has improved the competitiveness of European and North American companies. Altogether it has reduced cost across industries and contributed to propel economic growth. All have benefited from this and few have had a short-term incentive to criticize globalization. Those who have done so have been environmentalists, or left-wing supporters, and they have been a minority. The opponents of globalization have carved out a niche in the economic landscape where they have been able to thrive by researching emissions, working as politicians in green parties, lobbying, and driving small-scale transformation projects. A balance has been struck between the sides and no party has had any strong incentive to shake that balance. Environmentalism has found a role in society, proponents occupy seats in parliaments, governments, and supranational organizations, and the ranks have grown over the decades, making it a viable career path for people with a variety of skills. But environmentalism has not attracted many experts on business development and change management and the ones who have tried to build support for business development strategies and change management, such as the author of this book, have met with strong but silent opposition. The only threat that has been noted from globalization is the environmental threat stemming from emissions, and that has seldom been traced back to its primary sources. The amount of resources used for global transportation has seldom been noted and the risks connected to large-scale imports of key products have not been widely discussed either.

Even Greta Thunberg and other activists and sustainability experts, who have argued that governments have done too little to combat climate change, have not specified the changes that need to be made to reduce emissions. When the different sources of emissions are compared, it becomes clear that global trade accounts for a large share of emissions, since global trade gives rise to many different activities that in different ways contribute to emissions that supposedly cause global warming. Some of the obvious sources are shipping, air transport, and transportation by truck. The manufacturing of transport vehicles, ships, and airplanes should also be included and so should a share of the building and expansion of ports, airports, and distribution centres. There are many different types of activities that emanate from the growth in transportation. Some of the sources of emissions could be removed through the transformation of vehicle fleets to electric alternatives, but this will take a very long time. A reduction in global transportation through an increase in local production is one measure that has the potential to reduce emissions, but large-scale changes to supply chains, such as the establishment of supply chains for local production, takes many years and requires large investment.

The focus on market-driven economic development has closed the eyes and minds of people to the discussion of the role of government investment and collective action in innovation. In economic development, the focus on environmental aspects of the transformation to sustainability has in a similar way closed the eyes and minds of decision makers and experts to the exploration of the magnitude of the changes and the activities that will become necessary to alter the world's production and distribution systems to sustainable flows.

Throughout this process, sustainability experts and activists like Greta Thunberg, the former Vice President of the United States Al Gore, and Sir David Attenborough have put forward the environmental consequences of our present lifestyles, but they have not offered any clues regarding what the solutions might be. They have mentioned the implementation of renewable fuels, but they have not started to discuss the large-scale transformation of production and distribution systems that would become necessary in order to manufacture and use the new fuels or the investment this transformation would require. In her book *No One is Too Small to Make a Difference*, Greta Thunberg does not discuss what type of activities will have to be involved in the transformation, and the same is true for books by Al Gore and the BBC production from 2019, *Climate Change – The Facts*, featuring Sir David Attenborough. Other sustainability experts have also not put forward any plan for the transformation to a sustainable society.

The development of the new technologies has instead been driven by technical experts and technology companies, but they have focused on the technical aspects of the new systems that need to be implemented and on the marketing of sustainable products while giving the impression that the transformation to a sustainable society is well under way, not on the transformation challenges or the investment that will become necessary. Through their arguments they have given the impression that the transformation will not be very complicated, that the technologies already exist, and that politicians have the power to decide about their large-scale implementation, but they have avoided discussing the process of implementation and the investment needs and cost altogether.

In the same way that the proponents of market-driven development of the global economy have been blind to the vast territory of ignorance that has developed when it comes to the need for government involvement in this process, the proponents of the transformation to a sustainable future have become blind guardians of ignorance regarding the activities that will be necessary in order to drive the transformation forwards. With the protection of these two groups of activists, empty territories have developed, territories built on un-knowledge about important aspects of the development of society that have been impossible to discuss, and it has been designated as politically incorrect to even acknowledge their existence or talk about them.

The Changing Geopolitical Landscape

Through the blind belief in market-driven development the world has become increasingly dependent on global trade, which itself is entirely dependent on a steady and growing flow of oil to fuel economic growth and globalization. The implementation of electric transportation is at an early stage of development and the coronavirus crisis threatens economic growth and global cooperation. The increasing vulnerability of countries to supply-shocks like the coronavirus crisis highlights the need to build more production within the borders of western countries, in Europe, and North America, but in order for this expansion of local production to result in a favourable economic development it has to be done in a spirit of cooperation.

During the presidency of Donald Trump, the United States has started to withdraw from its position as the leader of the free world. International affairs have become less a matter of strengthening global trade and promoting open market policies and increasingly become a matter of being friends of Donald Trump—or being admired by him. Even in domestic politics President Trump has openly declared that he will primarily support states with governors with whom he is on good terms, and on the 2 April 2020 in a speech he told Vice President Pence, responsible for the coordination of federal activities to combat the coronavirus crisis, that it would be a waste of time to talk to the governors of Washington and Michigan and that their states should not be given the support afforded the other states in the union.

In Europe, there are similar tendencies towards isolation. In 2019 the United Kingdom left the EU—the first country to leave the union. The Hungarian President Orban is openly nationalistic and critical of EU collaboration, while at the same time his country is dependent on funding from the union. In the EU, countries in Central and Northern Europe have to a large extent financed the development of countries in Southern and Eastern Europe, a support that has benefited development across Europe as markets for products from the technically advanced countries have opened up and purchasing power has increased. At the same time, the support has weighed heavily on the national budgets of the supporting countries, and to uninitiated observers it has appeared as if the benefits of EU collaboration have gone in one direction only, from the strong economies to the weaker ones. With the coronavirus crisis, the weak countries received another blow to their economies and, despite strong efforts to stop transmission of the virus, it continued to spread for months, increasing the death toll in some countries to more than one thousand per day.

The cost of combatting the pandemic and the financial effects of fighting the disease create an increasing burden on already weak economies, and the need for support from the financially strong countries increases to previously unseen levels. At some point there is a risk that the majority of voters in the strong economies lose their patience and find that too much money is being spent supporting the weak and that the domestic costs for battling the pandemic are high enough. This increases the risk that more countries will exit the EU and work to become increasingly self-sufficient.

The weakening of global collaboration and the need to build domestic supply chains in order to reduce the risk of future disruptions of trade will increase the need for political decision making and speed up a development that is also necessary for other reasons. With decreasing oil production, a need is created to reduce the dependence on Chinese production and take back an increasing share of manufacturing to Europe and to each individual country. The same need will arise if cooperation within the EU is weakened and countries decide to reduce collaboration within the union or exit the union altogether. Through the coronavirus crisis, unemployment will also increase and a need will arise to create many new jobs. An incentive will then arise to promote the establishment of production and distribution companies that sell to local and domestic markets that can replace production resources in Asia and other low-cost countries. This book provides some of the tools for countries to strengthen the development of domestic production, while at the same time supporting the continued international collaboration that has formed the basis for advancement and economic growth in the post-war era. It cannot be denied that international trade has benefited humanity in ways that would not have been possible in its absence. Technologies like electricity, automotive technologies, ICT, aviation, space technologies, and new materials have created opportunities that could only be dreamed of by previous generations. But it would also be futile to deny that the fruits of this process of internationalization are now threatened by developments that have been going on for a long time without being noted and that are likely to become more pronounced through the development in the near future.

Present generations need to learn how to live well and at the same time use fewer resources, and we need to develop the sustainable systems that sustainability experts and proponents have failed to design or describe. In the present situation we need to build a sustainable society that preserves as much as possible of the values and benefits that have been created through the post-war period and create as much affluence as possible for future generations. This means that countries need to embark on a new path of local development in combination with international collaboration.

Choosing Battles

With increasing support for a few key ideas that cannot be discussed, barriers arise. These barriers make it increasingly difficult to discuss ideas that are not covered within leading ideologies and paradigms, and researchers, politicians, and business leaders gradually adapt. As this process continues it becomes increasingly uncomfortable for ambitious individuals to discuss matters that touch on the boundaries. Arguments in support of leading ideas are considered politically correct and it soon becomes vital for decision makers and experts, in their work and argumentation, to stay clear of grey zones and definitely not go against any of the tenets that are seen as approved. A few years into the development, people who speak or write in ways that are seen as incorrect find it difficult or impossible to make a living, they risk getting ridiculed by individuals who adhere to the politically correct ideas, and avoid discussing matters that are sensitive or seen as impossible to touch upon, or they attract a small following of dedicated individuals who read books and maintain a dialogue outside of the views of mainstream experts.

Wise individuals choose their battles and an increasing number avoid discussing matters that may blow up in their faces and damage their careers or those of their supporters. Few have the strength to go against the current in areas where they risk attracting opposition. Most important for the majority of researchers is to find an area of expertise where they can work and build knowledge and respect for their expertise. As long as experts avoid using certain combinations of words and expressing particular ideas, they avoid criticism and it becomes a matter of tactics and experience to be able to do constructive work that is seen to contribute to the development of society and ignore the risks that build up and that emanate from the forbidden territories.

As the process continues, fewer take an interest in the areas of un-knowledge, and the uncontrolled development accumulates risks that become too large to handle and discuss, because of the risk that blame will be shifted to the groups who brought up the argument in the first place. In that way, the outsourcing of production to China — a country governed by a totalitarian regime — has granted the country almost 30 per cent of global production, and through this development production resources have been built up in China at the same time they have been dismantled in western countries, making it both costly and time consuming to reverse the trend. In a similar way, the debate on sustainability has made many people aware of the need to change and many are asking themselves and their friends and colleagues why more is not being done to accelerate the transformation. To answer this question, people need to examine the forbidden area of industrial change to sustainability, investment, and financing of this process, and the answer to the pressing question, for this reason, remains undiscovered and undiscussed. Covid-19 has provided some insight into the dependence and the need to change, and it is important to use this ray of light into forbidden territories to create an interest in the adjustment that will be needed in the years to come.

Territories of Ignorance

Over decades, huge territories of ignorance develop and it becomes increasingly dangerous for individuals to put forward ideas that do not resonate well with the key ideas in society. So far, we have identified three territories that are fiercely guarded by leading proponents of the faiths:

– Market-driven growth, exclusively;
– No important risks arise;
– Sustainability focus on the transformation.

In each of these territories a number of different issues get suppressed and the discourse makes it impossible to elaborate on the topics and to integrate key aspects of the development into the debate in society, and for this reason subjects that need to be seen in combination to create a holistic picture have to be treated separately, as if they had nothing to do with each other. As an example, in the Swedish government administration the Ministry of the Environment is dealing with the transformation to sustainability and they are discussing mainly the reduction of emissions and initiating small-scale projects and activities aimed at creating circular systems. The Ministry of Industry, on the other hand, works to create and maintain economic growth with a focus on making Swedish companies more competitive in global markets. The attempts to reduce emissions and the use of resources by the Ministry of the Environment are of a small scale compared to the resources used and the emissions caused by the growth of the global economy. No dialogue is going on about how the country's industry can be transformed to sustainability or about the investment that will be needed to build sustainable production and distribution systems. While the EU has set the goal of making the union carbon neutral by 2050, this has not yet boiled down to the realization that carbon neutrality involves the reorganization of industry into more resource-effective supply chains and distribution systems. The process of healing discourses and patterns of thought will be difficult and take a long time. The following sections provide a discussion of the territories of ignorance. The latter part of the book will be dedicated to the discussion of how we as citizens, from the present situation, need to work to build a sustainable society that becomes more resilient than the current situation.

Forbidden Territory 1: Market-Driven Growth, Exclusively

Market-driven growth has become the paradigm in society that cannot be questioned. In our present economic system growth and growth expectations play key roles, not primarily because present generations need to experience more affluence, but because growth expectations are the forces that maintain the value of resources and maintain and increase the affluence of developed countries. Ultimately, it is the increasing affluence of developed countries that spills over and helps poor countries rise out of poverty. Without growth expectations, the demand for shares in the stock market would dwindle, the propensity of investors to invest would be reduced, and consumption would decrease as well. This would create a vicious circle that would increase unemployment, reduce consumption, and make poor countries even poorer.

While these are facts related to the present economic system, the elaboration of ideas becomes impossible because economic discourse is dictated by economists and politicians from all parts of the political spectrum who do not have the incentive to constructively discuss these matters, neither amongst themselves nor in public. Thus, the hegemony of the market in all areas becomes unquestioned and all debaters who want to be taken seriously need to acknowledge this as a fact. Politicians, experts in areas other than economics, and members of the public in private discussions find it difficult to contest the idea that the market needs to be the sole arbiter of decisions about production and distribution. Most of the critics of the market economy argue that economic growth and globalization lead to increasing resource consumption, an argument that is usually countered by the statement that the market economy may have some drawbacks, but there is no other system available to replace it. The idea that market-based development needs to be combined with government decisions in areas where the market has no power to drive development has not occurred to most experts or politicians.

People who want to discuss alternative economic systems need to do this on their own, without the contribution of economists and people who understand how an economy needs to be designed, which means that, in the absence of expertise in economics, research papers often lack a foundation in reality and fundamental aspects become forgotten or denied. One example of this is a project driven by six prominent Swedish universities and research institutes to develop ideas for economic systems that are not based on economic growth.[4] In the project, four different scenarios were developed with the titles "Collaborative Economy, Local Self-Sufficiency, Automation for Quality of Life, and Circular Economy in the Welfare State". While the idea is commendable, the scenarios lack broader reasoning of how these ideas of sustainable economies are going to be developed into fully-fledged economic systems and made to work, how incentives for investment in development are to be created, and how the systems could be realized. The report becomes a meaningless contribution to a discussion that is not likely to generate any viable ideas that can be implemented, because the ideas lack a foundation in an analysis of how the present economic system works and a discussion of how a new system needs to be structured, organized, and actualized.

The situation outside of academia does not look better. While the development of a political system is an issue that should engage large swathes of the population, there is little debate in parliaments and few ideas presented in the media of how the transformation can be achieved. This gives rise to a curious situation where an increasing share of the population agrees that countries need to reduce resource consumption, but no work is being done developing or implementing a new system. During the coronavirus pandemic, people as rapidly as possible want to get back to the normal situation, because no vision has been developed of a new system that could replace the global economy and create the sustainable and resilient societies that an increasing share of people seem to want.

These are only some of the critical issues that need to be dealt with that are never mentioned in visionary publications about sustainability.

---

4   Report: "Scenarier för hållbart samhällsbyggande bortom BNP-tillväxt" (in English, "Scenarios for a Sustainable Society Beyond GDP Growth").

It is necessary to transform the existing economy to a sustainable one, but the solutions that are developed need to fulfil the basic requirements of well-functioning economies. Any imaginative author could dream up a splendid Shangri-La, but developing an economic system that can work in practice is a much more demanding task. Unfortunately, most sustainability experts seem to not have realized this.

Market-based growth has been accepted as the leading principle also in the sustainability area, and it is firmly believed that the development of promising new technologies and business concepts can be driven by the market from start to finish, something we will come back to below.

Forbidden Territory 2: No Important Risks Arise

Market-based growth has been accepted as the only principle to drive the development of society and few have dared to point out the threat this creates to European and North American countries as they have become increasingly dependent on imports from China. The belief in the market as the sole arbiter of resource allocation has led to an inability to discuss important issues like the preparedness of society for disasters like Covid-19. Admittedly, nobody could have foreseen this exact pandemic, but epidemics and pandemics have occurred regularly throughout human history and the risk has increased, rather than decreased, with urbanization and the growth of cities and urban areas — and the development of lifestyles where hundreds, thousands, and tens of thousands of people get together on a regular basis. Epidemiologists have for many years warned of the high risk of epidemics and pandemics owing to the modern lifestyle.

The outbreak and rapid transmission of the Covid-19 pandemic illustrates the vulnerability of the world to rapidly spreading pandemics and demonstrates the lack of preparedness in most countries for a disaster of this magnitude. The disease has rapidly created a need to scramble to procure or produce ventilators, face masks, and other equipment and consumables. Pharmaceuticals are bought from sources that could offer some supplies. In Sweden in 1995 there were 2,100 extra ventilators held in store for emergency situations, but this supply had been eliminated and the number in 2020 was zero. In a similar way, there used to be gas masks for all citizens, but this supply was also destroyed in the 1990s because of the assumption that the probability of a conflict or disaster was close to zero. The country's county councils were on paper responsible for preparations, but they had not taken the responsibility seriously and neither had central government, as there has been no follow-up of the precautions. The preparations for such situations have been left to the market and market-based players have seen no reason to keep stock of emergency supplies. As Covid-19 spread, governments across the world had to scramble to find suppliers and order as many necessities as they could.

At this point in time the cooperation between countries was negligible. In early April of 2020 countries seized supplies on their way to other countries, to secure material for their own population. The United States seized shipments of face masks and other materials destined for Europe and the actions were described by officials in Europe as piracy. The EU did not initiate or support cooperation in any visible way. The union was founded to foster collaboration among member states, but the main purpose was to reduce barriers to trade, and cooperation had apparently not extended to collective preparation for disasters. Still, Covid-19 was not an unexpected event. Epidemiologists had for many years warned of pandemics and, considering the mobility and lifestyles of modern society, it was an event that could have been anticipated. In the case of earlier epidemics like ebola and SARS, the spreading of these viruses could be contained, but the coronavirus was brought from China to South Korea and Europe through tourists and visitors. Also, the celebrations of the Chinese New Year, which started on 25 January 2020, may have contributed, as this is an occasion when many Chinese travel to visit friends and relatives at home in China and abroad.

The reliance of the entire world on market-driven development closed the minds of politicians, public officials, and company managers to ideas related to the need for government intervention in preparations for large-scale catastrophic events and even for the consequences of wars. Politicians may have suggested that countries should prepare for unexpected events, but as decision makers have become increasingly convinced that the market is the best tool for allocating resources, and the growing belief that global trade will reduce the risk of military conflicts to almost zero, the less interest such proposals have attracted.

The market mind-set has kept most people from questioning the relevance of the idea that the market can take care of complex tasks, such as helping society prepare for an emergency. Few experts in areas where countries rely on the market for resource allocation realize that the only thing that a market does is to determine the price of goods and services that are traded in that market. The price is momentary and subject to change based on supply and demand. Expectations for the future are considered, but only expectations that people are aware of, and expectations only influence price. No market mechanisms have been observed that induce players in a market to start to build stores of resources in the way that governments did during the Cold War. In a situation where the scope of information and debate becomes increasingly narrow, few players in the market take important risks into consideration, regardless of how serious the consequences would be in the case of an emergency. As the bold and daring accumulate profits and preparations for the future do not bring any significant rewards short term, few take an interest in preparing for disasters. But as the belief in the hegemony of the market spreads, the less likely it becomes that politicians, the media, or the general public start to ask questions about preparations that may reveal the truth about the situation.

One example of how difficult it is to discuss aspects of development that call the supremacy of the market into question in areas where other forces are necessary in order to drive development in the expected direction would be my own experiences of trying to inform about the need to prepare for the future decline of oil production, something that may happen in the next few years. When, in 2004, I started to inform people about the need to prepare countries for a reduced supply of oil, I naïvely thought that experts on sustainability and technical experts involved in the development of electric vehicle technologies, with whom I was talking, would understand that the market could not drive change in a phase of development when only a very small number of electric cars were sold in a year. I thought that they, as I described the magnitude of investment and the small revenue that car companies were earning from electric cars, would rapidly see the need for government financing of innovation projects, just as governments in the past have done in other technology areas at early stages—investment that hase made our present lifestyles possible. At that time, oil production was predicted by independent experts to reach its peak in the next few years and it was obvious that the transformation to electric vehicle systems would take decades. The prediction of the peak has not been borne out. The production of conventional oil has been flat, and the production of shale oil and other forms of unconventional oil has increased to 7 per cent of global oil production. I found that the people I discussed this topic with could understand my arguments on an individual basis, but the people I spoke to, being professors, business managers, and MPs, had no incentive to bring the issue into the debate in society. I realized this as I started to discuss with decision makers and experts in 2005 and I intensified this work when my first book on the need to develop national and global strategies for the transformation to electric transport systems was published in 2009.

There was some discussion of the peak in oil production up until about 2010, but this died away, and when the production of shale oil started to take off in the United States and Canada fears of shortages soon dissipated, despite the fact that shale oil could only push the peak a few years forwards. Those years should not be used to continue to increase our dependence on global transportation by moving an increasing share of global manufacturing to China; it ought to have been used to reduce the dependence on transportation by building resources for the production of key supplies in western countries. But even the people who warned of declining oil production—such as retired oil geologists, professors studying oil production, and some investment bankers, who understood the challenges[5]—did not bring up the aspect of what needed to be done in order to prepare for a situation when oil, the most important fuel and the most important industrial raw material, would start to go into decline. When I launched the argument that market-driven transformation would not be enough, some people, in private conversations, seemed to agree and understand that the advancement of renewable fuel technologies was at too early a stage of development to be driven forwards by the purchases of cars by the small number of early adopters that were using them. But I received few followers who were prepared to go public with the idea that governments would need to invest large sums of money to drive the development of electric vehicle technologies to the level where they started to become competitive against petrol- and diesel-based systems. I even worked together with a publicist in Washington DC, who helped with communication on the issue in the United States, and I went there to meet with investors and company managers but could not get through with the ideas. Now that it is becoming obvious that the

---

[5]   A small number of oil geologists wrote books and initiated the debate on Peak Oil in the early years of the twenty-first century. Kenneth Deffeyes wrote *Beyond Oil* (2006) and *Hubbert's Peak* (2008), and Colin Campbell collaborated with Professor Kjell Aleklett of Uppsala University in starting the Peak Oil movement and coined the phrase Peak Oil together with Aleklett. Professor Aleklett wrote *Peeking at Peak Oil*. Investment banker Matthew Simmons wrote *Twilight in the Desert*, discussing the coming peak in Saudi Arabian oil production.

capacity of market forces to drive development in areas where there is little opportunity to make a profit is weak, it is becoming easier to explain that the market is not the omnipotent force that can drive any imaginable development and set everything right in society that needs to be put in order. The market works well mainly when it comes to allocating resources in mature industries, where business models are competitive, and technologies have become inexpensive enough to be used in many different areas.

A few decades of development and debate when the free market has been the only tool of development that could be discussed takes away the vocabulary and imagery of collective action from people's minds. Young people, who have never experienced a situation when governments have had more important roles in development than they have had in the past decades, have never needed to talk about or consider any form of innovation driven by the government, whether it be through subsidies, preparations for crises, or other areas in which governments used to be active.

Even perfectly necessary and obvious aspects of government-financed development have been impossible to discuss and get people to understand, as people have assumed that the situation with respect to the need for government financing has been changed fundamentally. Most, perhaps all, of the present technologies have, in their early phases of development, been financed or supported by governments. Some of the largest government-financed development projects in modern history have been bankrolled by the government of the United States. The late professor of economics Vernon W. Ruttan of University of Minnesota analysed six technology complexes that have to a large extent been financed by the US government. Those were the American Production System, airplane technologies, space technologies, nuclear power, computer technologies, and internet technologies. In his book *Is War Necessary for Economic Growth?* Ruttan concludes that large-scale and long-term government investments have, in all cases, substantially sped up the advancement of these technologies, and that in one case, nuclear power, the technology would not have come into existence at all without government financing. The development of all these technologies has been strongly supported by the American government, almost from the time when the technologies were first invented. In the case of airplane technologies and the development of a system of air transportation, the United States government started to finance development during the First World War, and financing continued at least until the time when Ruttan did his research in the late 1990s.

In many other countries, government investment has contributed to driving technology development in the early stages. Railways, electricity grids, sewage and water systems, telephony, and mobile telephony were developed and launched by governments and financed through public investment. Governments were in many cases the only players in the economy that could mobilize the resources to build, maintain, and operate these systems that have been important for sanitary and strategic purposes. Governments have also always been the only parties that have been able to apply a long-term perspective on investment, not having the need to get short-term payback from their financing. Technologies were not, at early points in their development, affordable enough for everybody to use the services on a daily basis or to attract large enough volumes of business to make profits short term.

This is even more true today in the transformations to e-mobility and the circular economy because the new technologies have a very weak competitive position against incumbent offerings and technologies. When politicians and experts in the past few years have wondered which investors will be the ones that make the large-scale investments in charging infrastructure for electric vehicles, they have been at a loss for words that point out the only realistic party that could make most of the large-scale and long-term investments that will become necessary to electrify road networks — national governments. In the case of electric vehicles and charging infrastructure, including investment in expanding power grids and turning them into smart grids that can handle the charging of millions of electric vehicles, the only realistic financing party in most cases is likely be governments. In the early phases investments have been small and the systems have been unassuming. It has been enough to install a small number of charging posts for electric cars, but when the majority of drivers drive electric vehicles, large-scale investment in power generation, distribution, advanced control systems for smart power grids with battery storage, and controls to manage effect utilization will become necessary.

One Week Without Trucks

In 2019, the Swedish industry organization for road transport companies, Åkeriföretagen, in collaboration with the Swedish Emergency Management Agency, conducted a survey to assess society's dependence on transportation. They asked the question to executives in a number of industries what consequences it would have if all transportation by truck stopped on Sunday without warning and identified the following consequences:

Day 1:
- Milk and factory-baked bread runs out in food stores.
- Waste removal immediately becomes a problem.
- Hospitals run out of food and there is a shortage of bed linen, etc.
- Letters and packages cannot be sent.

Day 2:
- Only emergency care can be offered at hospitals.
- Fruit and vegetables run out in food stores.
- Food can no longer be supplied to elderly care.
- Household and restaurant waste piles up in the streets.
- The stores at pharmacies rapidly run out.

Day 3:
- No snow removal in the winter.
- Almost all restaurants close.
- Petrol and diesel run out at petrol stations.
- The shelves at off-licences are empty.
- Hotels run out of food and bed linen, etc.

Day 4:
- Food supply becomes critical at hospitals and in elderly care.
- Waste piles become sanitary hazards.
- District heating ceases to work.

Day 5:
- No clean drinking water due to shortage of necessary chemicals.
- Vital medicines run out at pharmacies.
- Almost all food runs out, critical shortages of other types of products.
- Sewage sludge that has been temporarily stored has to be released without cleaning into water reservoirs.

A gradual reduction in the supply of oil is not likely to have such dramatic consequences, but disagreements between countries regarding supplies may, in a situation of declining production, lead to supply problems. If the reduction is approached in an orderly fashion with collaboration between countries and the transformation to electric mobility is driven with force, the process will be gradual and countries will to some extent be able to adjust and prioritize. If, on the other hand, conflicts arise, some of the above consequences may appear rapidly and without warning, in a way similar to how Covid-19 surprised the global community.

The investment necessary to develop and implement autonomous vehicles will come later and add significant costs on top of the ones that will be necessary for the implementation of systems for electric mobility. The communication needs between autonomous and ordinary vehicles and traffic control systems will grow exponentially compared to the present situation. But, in the political environment of the early twenty-first century, government financing has been an impossible thought and most governments have not seen a need to investigate the full extent of the development activities that will become necessary to implement electric transport systems on a large scale.

Of all new fuel alternatives, electric cars and trucks are the only possible option for the future, but, in order for governments to make such a move, it must first be proven that the area of electric mobility represents a case of market failure and that, for this reason, governments need to step in. To implement electric transport systems on a small scale, there is no need for government financing. There are enough affluent individuals and families in the world to create some demand for innovative transport technologies, just like there was an early demand for cars in the nineteenth and early twentieth centuries. The big breakthrough of cars came when vehicles started to become affordable for ordinary citizens, which happened after armies became mechanized. During and after the First World War, governments ordered large numbers of identical vehicles, which brought prices down. A few years before that, in 1913, Henry Ford built his first factory with an assembly line that reduced the time for building a car by almost 80 per cent. The invention of the assembly line has for a long time been recognized as an important event in the advancement of manufacturing, but the motorization of armies was as important.

An innovation that was necessary to make both these developments possible was the development of the American Production System by the US government during the nineteenth century. The American Production System evolved as a reaction to the more advanced production systems used in Britain and other countries in Europe and involved the development of production methods based on identical and interchangeable components. In the preceding system, every product was made from start to finish as a unique individual product. The parts of a number of damaged guns could not be used in battle to put together one or two functioning ones, because the parts of each gun had been individually crafted. Two guns may have looked identical, but their parts had slightly different measures and could not be transferred to other weapons of the same make and type. In a series of projects from the mid-nineteenth century, the government financed the development that paved the way for the implementation of the assembly line. This illustrates the fact that it has been necessary before for governments to finance system changes that have been required in order to prepare their countries for the challenges of the future. In the case of the United States government, they have financed a long sequence of large-scale development projects that have contributed to forming present society. Investors are always looking for promising business opportunities, and many realize that the winners in the long term have to enter the market at an early point, but so far a few large business failures have resulted from the early investments of optimists about e-mobility.

At the present time, even though many of the prerequisites for the transformation to electric transportation are already in place, many innovations need to be driven to make electric cars and hybrid trucks competitive against petrol and diesel alternatives, and car buyers have the opportunity to choose the tried and tested petroleum-based alterna-tives. The guardians of ignorance have monopolized the debate, and how incumbent technologies slow down the transformation has not to any significant extent been explored or discussed. Thus, neither researchers nor practitioners have observed the immense competitive disadvantages that electric transport systems will face if they are going to be implemented on a large scale. The development will not only require a change of vehicles—several other large-scale investments will be necessary as well. Under current circumstances, it is likely to take one or two more decades until economists agree that market forces cannot finance the development and large-scale implementation of e-mobility and clear the way for governments to make the necessary investment.

At present, different investment needs are discussed in reports and discussion groups, but if the investment needs are not compiled in one report the extent of the challenge to implement the new systems will not become widely known. In the case of the progression of the inter-net, which carries a large part of all digital communication in the world, this was financed by the United States government from the first day, and the same government made a large share of the investments in the development of computers—and before that it took a key role in the financing of the development of the punch-card machines that pre-ceded computers. It was a series of large-scale investments made over almost a century that made the present digitized society possible. In the development of computers and punch-card machines, the United States government bought a large share of the early machines of companies like IBM and its competitors. As long as governments continue to be happy to buy most of their cars in the form of petrol and diesel vehicles, the transformation to electric mobility is not likely to speed up significantly. When described in this way, the role of public investment becomes clear, but without the full picture of the challenges that lie ahead it is impossible for experts, governments, and business leaders to see the writing on the wall, especially since the coronavirus crisis has forced governments to spend large amounts of money mitigating this problem. If we look at the sequence of investments in technology development that have been made in past centuries, we will find that the technologies we use today and the production systems that make them have been developed through more than a century of investment that to a large extent has been made by governments. Through this type of analysis, people will understand the extent of investment that needs to be made in the development and growth of new technologies. In the absence of efforts to learn how advancement has been financed through history, the blind guardians of ignorance will be able to maintain focus on the comparatively insignificant details of development, such as the slow progress that can be made without large-scale government financing.

Without government financing of the establishment of the most important technologies of present society, people would not have been able to enjoy the present level of affluence. Yet, few experts, politicians, and business leaders have been able to realize that technologies that are at an early stage of development need large-scale and long-term government financing to become viable and competitive against incumbent technologies. Many are likely to doubt that government involvement will be necessary on a large scale, but we need to consider that governments were making investments in large public works projects already in the nineteenth century, for example in the sewage systems of London and other big cities. When looked at in detail, the situations with regard to the transformation to e-mobility and the circular economy are not very different from these situations more than one hundred years ago.

Forbidden Territory 3: Focus on Sustainability – Not Large-Scale Transformation

In 2018, Greta Thunberg became famous overnight for going on a school strike and for arguing that political leaders had not done enough to combat climate change. Over recent decades an increasing number of sustainability experts have put forward the same argument, but none of the experts or the politicians that have tried to turn the arguments of environmentalists into policy have provided a credible explanation of what needs to be done to transform the industrial systems of present society to sustainable production and distribution systems, or mentioned the magnitude of the investment and transformation efforts that will be necessary to succeed with the change.

Several professors and experts in various disciplines of sustainability argue that the technologies that will need to replace the unsustainable technologies of the present are already available, they only need to be implemented. They say this as if all governments need to do to transform society to sustainable flows would be to press a button and thereby start a systematic transformation. In some countries there are even reports by experts where the authors argue that the transformation can be achieved without any significant cost to society. When these documents and the arguments therein are scrutinized, the analyses are made without investigating and discussing the very large investment that will be necessary to drive the development forwards and the speed of market penetration of the new fuels is vastly overestimated. The analyses are entirely based on the assumption that the only aspects that matter are technical details and that there is no need to take into account the fact that the new fuels—and the technologies that are needed in order to utilize them—are at early stages of development, and that there is a need to build entirely new systems for the production and distribution of the renewable fuels and for large parts of the cars and other vehicles that are needed in order to use them.

The report, by Professor Thomas B. Johansson, *Fossil Freedom on the Way* was written based on an investigation ordered by the Swedish government in 2011 and is a case in point.[6] Most books and reports are not so explicit about the assumptions and conclusions. Most authors on sustainability matters approach their subjects from an entirely technical or environmental perspective and often manage to entirely avoid the discussions of any financial aspects of the transformation. In the case of the almost 1000-page report by Professor Johansson, the shortcomings are obvious to anyone with an interest in technology development and innovation. One of the conclusions is that a number of new biofuels need to be implemented in parallel, something that is hardly realistic when you consider that the new fuels—and the cars and other vehicles that will use them—rapidly need to become competitive against petrol and diesel and this is hardly realistic if a number of new systems are going to be built up in parallel. The investment needed in each system in production capacity for fuels, new vehicles, and distribution systems for fuels would be very high and none of the systems would become

---

[6]   The investigation continued for two years and published its report in 2013 with the number SOU2013:84 (SOU (Statens Offentliga Utredningar) = The Swedish Government's Public Investigations).

competitive. The fact that the implementation of the new fuels will require entirely new fleets of vehicles in every country and systems for the production and distribution of the new fuels is not mentioned, and no costs or investments for the transformation of vehicle fleets are included in the calculations. A more realistic analysis would conclude that the most promising new fuel needs to be identified and all resources need to be invested in the development and marketing of this alternative.

The technical and environmental focus and the arguments by sustainability and technology experts have created a vast territory of un-knowledge about the magnitude of investment and transformation activities and the nature of the coordinated and collective efforts that will become necessary to succeed. The proponents of sustainability— Greta Thunberg, Sir David Attenborough, Al Gore, politicians belonging to green parties, and technical experts at universities and at companies large and small around the world—have become blind guardians of ignorance. They have been very successful in their efforts to turn the attention of politicians, other experts, and the public towards climate change and the increasing concentration of carbon dioxide in the atmosphere that is supposed to be the cause of global warming, and at the same time turn attention away from the measures that need to be initiated in order to drive the transformation forwards. If the radical change is going to succeed, the focus needs to switch from emissions to the activities that need to be initiated to drive the transformation forwards. Now that it has become obvious that present society has become blind to the needs to prepare for the current pandemic, it will perhaps be possible to understand that a similar blindness has developed in other areas as well.

From Insight to Action—Building Resources

In order to build the stable and sustainable society of the future, change leaders need to start to explore the areas of ignorance that have developed in the absence of insight from the blind guardians and the rest of humanity that, as bystanders, have listened to the rallying cries of market evangelists and sustainability experts. The market economy rests on a set of very sound principles. The market is the most efficient allocator of resources in many situations in society, but there is a need for government involvement in the preparation for future disasters, for the financing of innovation at early stages, as well as for the transformation to sustainability. The severe consequences of a lack of preparations and government involvement have come out into the open through the spreading of the Covid-19 pandemic and more bad experiences are likely to follow, unless people pay attention to and support the entire range of activities that will become necessary in order to form the future and build the resources necessary to do this. Change is always to a large extent uncertain, but this change will be necessary and the sooner it starts, the higher the probability that it will be successful.

It will not be enough for people and experts to start to learn about the transformation process and discuss the facts related to this. The acquisition of knowledge and the development of a new way of speaking about an issue do not lead to change. For change to take place, transformation resources need to be built. These resources are sometimes referred to as "orgware", organizations consisting of individuals with the right background, knowledge, financing, and tools to start up and lead large-scale change activities. In the area of national security and preparedness for a war or some other disaster there used to be organizations in many countries that built and maintained supplies of oil, food, and medical equipment, and that developed routines that would be applied in these emergency situations to initiate activities, start rationing and other necessary measures, and distribute supplies. These organizations and the supplies have to a large extent been dismantled and reduced to the bare minimum that is considered necessary in a society where resource allocation is handled by the market—and where there is little need for foresight and planning.

In the case of sustainability, countries have built orgware for the research of environmental issues and small-scale mitigation on the national, regional, and municipal levels. There are government authorities that monitor pollution and set limits to the levels of emissions that are allowed, there are authorities responsible for the preservation of nature, and there are many NGOs that work with small-scale activities to promote the implementation of electric mobility on a small scale or run projects to implement circular business models, also on a small scale. In municipalities in many countries there are environmental strategists with the task of implementing more sustainable routines in the organizations. These organizations are formed around knowledge about sustainability and sustainable technologies. I have had the opportunity to work with researchers from a sustainability institute connected to a major university—an institute that trains masters students from across the globe to become environmental strategists or take on similar roles in companies and public organizations—and what has struck me is the almost exclusive focus in the curriculum on environmental subjects and the total lack of subjects related to business development. The students learn a lot about pollution and waste management, but very little about how new sustainable products and business practices are developed and marketed and how change processes need to be driven to become effective. On a few occasions I have had the opportunity to be the opponent on the masters theses of students and I have had the chance to discuss the business aspects that have been almost entirely absent from their theses. These discussions have been very brief and neither the students nor their teachers have had very much to say about business related questions.

In recent decades an awareness of the issues that humanity will have to deal with has spread among people, but at the same time almost no resources have been expended on working out how the transformation will be driven. Students have not been taught anything about how the revolution will be organized, financed, or how the most important change activities will be identified and how resources will be prioritized for large-scale change to be initiated. Instead of contributing to the development of relevant measures and debating the nature of these, green parties and sustainability experts have argued that all renewable fuels will have to be used, and the same view has permeated the debate in other areas of transformation as well.[7] In the areas included under the umbrella concept of the circular economy – the development of production and distribution systems within which resources will be used and reused in never-ending cycles – government agencies and the EU have financed pilot projects in different areas, assuming that the market will be able to determine which technologies and business models are the most promising and most worthy of receiving further financing. At early stages of the development of a new technology or concept the customers are, however, so few that the small revenue created by sales cannot finance the development in a number of areas that are necessary to rapidly move the transformation to the new technology forwards. Individual companies may be built based on new concepts, but for large-scale change to take place there is a need to invest in the transformation of entire production and distribution systems, a change that will require many billions of euro in

---

7　In the book *Biofuels for Transport*, published by the Worldwatch Institute, all available biofuels are discussed, without mentioning any need to focus on the most promising new transport systems. This is similar to how the subject was treated by Professor Thomas B. Johansson in his investigation *Fossil Freedom on the Way*.

investment and a systematic approach to the transformation process. In the case of the development of existing technologies, the early phases of innovation and implementation have been financed by governments or by government agencies.

The forms of financing have varied depending on the challenges. In the early decades of the twentieth century, the American government financed the development and expansion of commercial air travel, and goods transportation subsidies were used to incentivize airlines to also make room for a few passengers. In the case of space technologies, NASA co-financed development projects and competitive bidding was used to hand out contracts to the most competitive bidders. In the case of the advancement of computers, financing of development projects was used in combination with the purchases of the early generations of computers by the IRS and other authorities. In a similar way, European governments financed the development of railways and producers of engines, cars, railways, and signalling systems, electricity and phone networks, and the technologies included in these, and they built sewage and fresh water systems and contributed to the development of many other technologies. The fact that many of these systems have been privatized in later years does not mean that the market in the twenty-first century can finance the development of new technologies from the early stages or that the market can drive a rapid and focused transformation process. Despite the fact that there are entrepreneurs that express an interest in building electric road networks, the large-scale roll-out is likely to take very long and the way forwards is likely to become fraught by bankruptcies and failures of companies that underestimate the risk and overestimate the willingness of customers to buy electric trucks, and their ability to make profitable use of them. The belief in the power of the market has made even experienced and knowledgeable individuals believe that the market can work wonders, but it cannot, and it will not.

Despite the evidence that market-driven development needs to be complemented by financing from governments, little research has been done into the relationship between these two necessary sources of financing and how they need to be used to assist each other. As we can see from the examples of the past that have already been given and those that will be provided later in the text, government financing does not detract power from the market. On the contrary, it strengthens the market and contributes to its ability to work its magic. The blind guardians of ignorance have been at work defending their convictions, and through their activities they have managed to maintain focus on the areas that are related to sustainability knowledge, and avoid that the focus be directed towards the change that is becoming increasingly pressing.

We may hope that suppression of the advancement of knowledge of the transformation has been unintentional, an unfortunate by-product of the fact that green politicians and sustainability experts happen to have expertise in areas related to the environment, but that they lack an understanding of business and the transformation of production and distribution that will be necessary to achieve their ambitious change goals — but this does not seem to be the complete truth. As I for more than 15 years have been trying to inform people about the magnitude of the transformation challenge, for example by highlighting the size of oil production and the need to replace all of the world's 1.2 billion cars and some 100 million heavy vehicles with electric vehicles, and about the need to start large-scale transformation efforts involving large investment programmes financed by companies and governments in collaboration, many sustainability experts with whom I have spoken have clearly understood the message. Few have, however, contributed to informing others or to letting me present these issues in front of their peers.

This inability of sustainability professors and experts to act on their insight puzzled me for years when I started to discuss the need for transformation. With such strong support for the idea that countries need to transform production and transportation systems to sustainability, the interest in how to do it should be high as well. I was also puzzled by the same inability to take my message further that was shown by the business leaders and journalists that I talked and wrote to. It took me several years and the publication of five books and a similar number of reports to realize that individuals have little incentive to stand up and support ideas that have not yet become mainstream, even if they realize that those same ideas need to be implemented in order to save society from calamities. I realized that people perceive it as too risky and too much of a challenge to carry the torch for someone whose ideas they cannot fully explain or relate to and ones that their peers may look upon with suspicion. When I talk to someone and relate the facts behind the transformation need, from a business and resource perspective, many can understand the reasoning. But understanding the arguments when someone else is relating the facts and connecting the various dots to a description of a very complex and threatening situation is a far cry from being able to relate the same reasoning yourself, and an entirely different thing compared to explaining and defending the conclusions that someone else has drawn.

In our modern society, individuals have full working days and most do not want to spend their evenings reading books on unfamiliar subjects that relate arguments that they feel little spontaneous connection with, regardless of how important the books and ideas may be for the future of society. Thus, for a long time, in the absence of media coverage of the aspects of large-scale change, the few experts who happen to have taken an interest in these things are on their own when it comes to communicating and spreading knowledge about the transformation. An increasing share of individuals instead help with purging from public debate ideas that challenge the politically correct views of market-driven change, and it becomes increasingly difficult to get people to discuss other aspects of change than the ones that are accepted by most people as gospel—which means increasingly naïve descriptions of how the transformation is going to progress. When, at some point in the development, an activist like Greta Thunberg enters the scene, she receives publicity across the world, because she relates facts and arguments that most people have become comfortable with. They do not perhaps understand or agree with all her views, but they have heard the arguments so many times that they feel familiar. She gets perceived as a rebel, but there is nothing in her argumentation that is designed to threaten the status quo, as she does not say anything about the solution to the predicament she describes.

Then, unexpectedly, like lightning from a clear blue sky, comes the coronavirus pandemic, which suddenly makes it clear that neither national governments nor the EU have made preparations for a disaster that has been foreseen and warned of by experts for a number of years. As governments scramble to buy the medical supplies they desperately need and get domestic companies to change production to manufacture everything that can be produced locally, people may start to realize that some aspects of development have been forgotten in recent decades. When the lack of preparations for disasters becomes apparent, information is uncovered that stockpiles of products that were in place up until the 1980s have been sold, used up, or burned, and not been replaced by new inventory. And it becomes increasingly clear that a different mind-set is needed in order to prepare for future shocks.

On 25 March 2020, the economist Klas Eklund appeared on Swedish television. He is one of the country's most well-known experts on economic development, who used to be chief economist and sustainability expert of one of the largest Swedish banks, SEB. During the early phase of the pandemic in Sweden, this prominent neo-classical econo-mist predicted that companies after the crisis would focus on reducing risk by procuring an increasing share of supplies in their home market or closer to Sweden, forecasting a paradigm shift in the development that has accorded China almost 30 per cent of global production.

Soon governments, experts, journalists, and the population at large are likely to realize that countries have done far too little to prepare for disasters that could have been prepared for. As people take in the numbers related to the transformation to a sustainable society, many are also likely to realize that the transformation to a large extent will have to be financed by governments. A certain share of the prepara-tions needs to be the building of organizations that will be necessary to manage the change, in the way that NASA has managed the space programmes and other space-related activities in the United States. Similar to how NASA has financed development projects for space technologies and systems, the organizations will have to finance the development of the business models and technology solutions that will be needed to build the circular economy and electric mobility. When countries start to build up their economies and production systems again it is important that governments change their mind-sets com-pared to the situation before the crisis. Supply chains and production systems need to be designed in a different way compared to the earlier situation, and they need to increasingly rely on local production. Development in the coming decades will need to go forwards on that path, instead of embarking on a new journey towards unbridled globalization.

Chapter Two

The Truth about the Future

In the next few years, focus and resources will have to be dedicated to the restructuring of society's supply systems and we will need to decrease resource consumption and create new jobs that can replace the ones that have been lost in the coronavirus crisis. This reconstruction of society's vital systems cannot primarily focus on rebuilding the supply chains of the global economy. For different reasons we need to reduce the reliance on global supply chains and resource intensive production and distribution systems and increase local self-sufficiency in many areas. Yet, it will not be possible to go back to local production of everything in the way that production was organized in the 1950s. China and other Asian countries perform altogether more than 30 per cent of the production activities in the global economy and it would be impossible to rapidly build up production resources in Europe and the United States that eliminate imports from far-away countries. This would also have unfavourable effects for the economies of all countries. Many high-tech products need to be produced in a small number of locations, but the number of locations may have to be increased. In the cases of critical supplies, a larger share must be produced nationally or in closely cooperating neighbouring countries. The share of groceries that are produced locally needs to increase substantially. Governments are the only entities that can take the lead in a rapid restructuring of key aspects of production. They need guidance from citizens that rapidly build the necessary knowledge to participate in these discussions. Countries need to increase the sustainability of production and distribution systems and regions and nations need to become more resilient to the effects of pandemics and other disasters.

Less than a year ago, in 2019, Greta Thunberg became world famous for scolding world leaders, arguing they had not done enough to combat climate change. The young founder of Fridays for Future was awarded the title "Person of the Year" by *Time Magazine*, she has spoken at a number of international conferences, and she has been received for private meetings by heads of state. But what exactly has to be done to combat climate change and create a sustainable society? Greta did not say. And was climate change really the only, or even the most pressing, challenge that humanity needs to meet to prepare for the future? Events have shown people around the world that there are other threats and, even among the entirely foreseeable events, climate change was just the most discussed topic that countries had failed to prepare for. The world has for thirty years applied an entirely market-based approach to development that has deprived countries of fore-sight. By focusing on the problem of climate change and entirely avoiding discussions of the solutions, Greta has taken the role of a blind guardian of ignorance and, in this role, she has been supported by her followers and the leaders that invited her to one-on-one meetings. By applauding her audacity, people endorsed the fact that she, on behalf of the climate and the ailing planet, dares to speak up against the people in power and admonish them to do more to combat climate change, but her tearful anger disguises the fact that neither she, nor any other sustainability expert, has a clue as to the measures that need to be taken in order to transform the global economy to sustainability and resilience.

The answer to the question of what needs to be done is complex and, to understand the nature and magnitude of the activities that need to be initiated to create a sustainable future, the discussion has to be taken into uncharted territories. The discussion is made more complex through the coronavirus pandemic, but this is also likely to open the minds of people to the need for change. It is no exaggeration to say that there are vast areas of ignorance that are guarded by sustainability experts that want neither the public nor decision makers to find out that some of the most important questions about the course towards the future have no ready-made answers. There are no simple and straightforward solutions to the excessive use of resources, nor any defined way of reducing the emissions of our present society that are ready to be implemented. There are no plans waiting in the top drawers of the desks of heads of state. The complex of challenges has not been described in a way that is understood and shared by most leaders and some of the most pressing issues have been confined to the undergrowth of public debate and policy development. Few citizens and leaders are aware of the lack of solutions, and that the ones that exist are not well understood, not even by the experts who are most active in the debate on sustainability and technology development. This is because the solutions must involve government action, large-scale investment in the development of new transport systems, and the creation of economic systems that are substantially more resource efficient than the present global economy. The new systems need to be resilient and there are many building blocks available, but the large-scale global systems of production and distribution need to be made more local and regional, instead of national and global—a change that will require large amounts of resources and an entirely new mind-set among most people. This truth hurts, especially since present generations have to a large extent renounced the vocabulary and the concepts that will become necessary to rediscover to develop solutions. For many people it will be hard to accept that governments need to have a role in this transformation, simply because they cannot envision what that role may be. How could governments achieve results that the free market is not able to accomplish? Preposterous!

Individuals who take on the challenge of scouting the path forwards can take the role of change leaders, a role that will be very important to show the way into the future. Change leaders will need a handbook to lead them down the road of change, but the handbook cannot at this point consist of a list of simple dos and don'ts, because no simple solutions have been developed. Closing coal-fired power plants will not be enough, and the transformation of transportation to e-mobility has only just started. The leaders of the transformation need to become leaders in the most genuine sense. They need to first lead society through a phase of analysis and debate, when the strategies for the transformation will have to be made and when the technologies and the change tools will have to be selected and packaged, and then lead society into a transformation phase, when an increasing number of citizens can start to participate and become part of the change.

Developing the sustainable society of the future will be a task more complex and challenging than the task that governments were facing in their efforts to procure supplies to combat the coronavirus pandemic. As will be explained throughout the text, the transformation of society to sustainability and resilience will ultimately involve the reorganization of all industries and all aspects of society. The goal of the transformation to a circular economy is that human activities in the future will not produce any waste or emissions, and that everything people use will be re-manufactured or recycled. None of these changes will provide a rapid enough transformation. There will also be a need to reduce consumption, something that is likely, to some extent, to come naturally in the wake of the Covid-19 crisis, but the reduction will have to be larger than anything most people can imagine and much more significant than the limited effects of the coronavirus pandemic.

The change will require the development of entirely new philosophies of production and distribution and new supply chains. It will also have to involve major lifestyle adjustments. While it is possible to deny this, turn a blind eye to the complexity of change, and simply say that it needs to be done and that it will not pose any major challenge, this approach would turn us into blind guardians of ignorance and confirm the relevance of the theme of this book. But it will not be possible to change everything at the same time. Countries and the world at large need to prioritize and develop strategies and set aside resources to implement those strategies. The present approach of doing a little of everything in an uncoordinated manner is tantamount to starting to build the foundations of hundreds of houses at the same time and not setting aside the resources to finish any of them. The construction of each of the houses in this metaphor has only just begun by building a small part of the foundation. In no area has construction progressed beyond one or two per cent, and in most areas progress has been much slower than this. The pace of progress means that in many cases results erode before builders come back and continue the work.

If the coronavirus crisis makes people consume less, it will still not solve the problem. Reducing consumption will help to somewhat slow down the use of resources, but there will be a need to evaluate in some detail how the global community can organize production and distribution in a much more sustainable way that builds less sensitivity into the system, and there is no better time to do this than after a major crisis, like the coronavirus pandemic. At that point, people have the woes of the situation fresh in their memories and many will be dedicated to the idea of avoiding future crises that may arise from epidemics or from an expected decrease in oil production.

In order to start the analysis phase, a number of activities need to be started — many that few have thought of — but before the actual change can begin on a large scale there is a need to prioritize the most important and highly critical activities, something that neither Greta Thunberg nor other sustainability experts mention when they discuss this.

Technology development can be described through the metaphor of an airplane, where the new technologies that will be needed have been advanced only to early and rudimentary versions of products and systems. The planes representing the efforts to develop the new technologies and systems that will be needed to transform the world to sustainability have only started to move along the runway. Decades of development of technologies and system solutions will be required until the planes reach cruising altitude; that is, when the technologies they symbolize become competitive against incumbent technologies that are used today throughout the global economy and become able to drive economic growth and contribute to the transformation to sustainability. Trillions of euro in investment will be needed for key technologies and system solutions to reach maturity, and well-conceived and insightful strategies will be necessary to drive some of the most important technologies and solutions to maturity. Without a strategy and a focused investment plan, many planes/technologies are likely to never get off the ground, and most are likely to only reach low altitudes, without reaching the momentum to go all the way up to cruising altitude and maturity. Considering the amount of resources that have been necessary in the past for technologies to reach maturity, it is unlikely that, without focused development programmes, any significant new technology complexes will get there within the lifespan of present generations, which will have very sad consequences for economic growth and for the ability of the global society.

The leaders of the European Union have set the goal for Europe of becoming climate neutral by 2050, but this has also been done without actually investigating which development and transformation efforts will be required to achieve the goal. Few are likely to have realized that a complete reorganization of the economy will be needed in order to do this, and few are likely to have seen the significance of the fact that the transformation to electric mobility that has been going on for more than a decade has so far resulted in a share of electric cars of 0.5 per cent of global car fleets.[1] Seen from this perspective, there are also no leaders that are ready to drive the transformation into the future, only decision makers who make judgments without understanding their real implications. Politicians simply take it for granted that 2050 is a reasonable target, but there are no experts who have looked into the details of the transformation of production and distribution systems and who are able to verify the possibility or contradict the idea that climate neutrality can be reached by that year. Greta Thunberg and many

---

[1] I met a retired manager from the Swedish Ministry of Environment who has been involved in the development of e-mobility since the 1990s and who had one of the first Volkswagen electric cars in the early 1990s provided to him by his employer for test purposes.

others seem prepared to take on the role of leaders of the transformation, but they are as blind to the challenges as the politicians who have made the decisions. To make change possible, many will have to learn about the activities that have to form the core of the transition. Large-scale change will be impossible without a strategy that can be shared and communicated among leaders and among members of the public who will have to participate. Based on the strategy, plans need to be made. The coronavirus crisis and the fear and feelings of powerlessness that this has caused among the public illustrate what will happen when oil production starts to decline, but the rapid results of the scrambling by governments to lay their hands on as much as possible of what they need, and the efforts to transform production to cover the urgent needs of the medical system, also illustrate that much more can be done in terms of transformation than people tend to believe when there is no immediate threat at hand.

The future is not likely to pan out the way most people expect—as a continuation of the development the world has experienced in recent decades, offering citizens more affluence through, for example, computerization and greater mobility. There are far too many sources of disturbance that are not controllable by companies and governments. Governments, the media, and business have promised a world of improvements in terms of technical amenities and quality of life, and the "insignificant" issue of transforming production and consumption to sustainable processes and flows will be handled without people noticing it or having to take part in the process. Influential authors, such as the former editor of *Wired Magazine*, Kevin Kelly, have described the future many people expect, promising that computerization and increasing access to services powered by artificial intelligence will be available to almost everyone in the years to come. The title of Kelly's book speaks for itself—*The Inevitable*. There is, according to Kelly, no doubt that the future of highly automated digital services, delivered by computers that have access to information about every detail of people's lives, will form an important cornerstone of the future that our society is approaching at very high speed.

Another extreme is represented by sustainability experts who promise that the global economy is about to be transformed to sustainability by the rapid growth of circular business models and electric mobility. Michael Braungart and co-author William McDonough in their influential books *Cradle-to-Cradle* and *The Upcycle* launched the idea that products in the future will be used and reused in a circular system, before the renewable materials they are made of will be recycled and turned into new products. The transformation of society to a circular system where all products and materials will be used and reused is, according to Braungart, well under way. At a presentation in Malmö, Sweden, in January of 2017 he said, in response to a question from the audience, that the persons present would not have to do anything to make the circular economy a reality, because the change would happen regardless of what people do. This is a very confusing statement, since all changes need to be driven by individuals with determination, and the people who listened to the presentation were some of the leaders in the sustainability sector in southern Sweden— individuals who by their decisions make resources available for the transformation. In the absence of decisions from some of the persons participating at the seminar, very little would happen in the region to move the development of the circular economy forwards.

Both of the above positions are based on weak foundations. Neither can explain how their visions of the future will be realized, how the necessary investment will have to be financed, or what steps will have to be taken for their visions to be turned into reality. Neither of the arguments can be turned into a handbook that can be used by change leaders. In their world, most probably, no such handbook will be needed, because the market forces that, presumably, have formed the world we live in right now will form the future as well. The assumption that market forces are on the side of humanity and that market-driven change will inevitably lead to solutions that are favourable to the development of society does not need to be questioned or explained, at least not according to the proponents of any of the straightforward and obvious "truths" about the future that at present form some of the core beliefs in society. The proponents of the paradigm that the market can make all important decisions and that the market will set aside enough resources to mitigate disasters and drive the transformation to sustainability have become blind guardians of ignorance and effectively put a stop to all efforts to discuss decisions and activities that need to be made and initiated by human decision makers and planners. Michael Braungart is one of the sustainability experts who, deliberately or without understanding the implications of his words, denies that human decisions will be needed to drive change in the direction he himself advocates.

The title of the present book, which calls the proponents of business-as-usual and small-scale change *blind guardians of ignorance*, may seem harsh, but people need a wake-up call. Many people, without thinking, have supported the notion that the advancement that the world has experienced in recent decades can go on, with small glitches, almost for eternity, as the market economy will solve all kinds of problems without cost and without intervention by decision makers. This way of thinking is not only factually wrong, it also causes tremendous risks to the entire edifice of the global community. Voters, consumers, investors, and people as they go about their daily activities need to realize that market-driven development needs to be combined with various forms of collective action, and that countries, regions, the EU, the United Nations, and other transnational bodies need to build the competence, orgware, and financial resources to manage the process of transformation.

It is the economic development in countries and in the global economy overall that will determine which reality present and future generations will experience, and neither technical development nor the drift towards sustainability can determine the path of this process. In the situation after the coronavirus pandemic, governments will have to take a stronger role in economic development, by funding the most important transformation opportunities and by allowing less promising alternatives to perish. Many people claim that they are guided by science, but science supports many different conclusions and individual scientists are seldom in possession of the complete picture. All the knowledge necessary to drive development forwards is available to scientists, but few have attempted to put together a holistic picture and devise a viable route forwards. Above all, people who are interested in science in general are seldom interested in the fields of business and economics. The rapid progress of digitization and the slower development of electric mobility and other new transportation and production technologies are more concrete and easier to relate to than abstract ideas of how technology development only in its later phases contributes to economic growth and other similar ideas. A situation like the coronavirus crisis may open our eyes to the fact that there is a need to build a holistic view of the future and allow this to be discussed in wider circles, in parallel with the development that is going on in narrow fields of expertise. The belief that the market, left on its own, can drive development is unscientific. It has no foundation in experience. Without government financing, the world would not have seen any of the technologies that people now have access to, and we would be nowhere near the present level of affluence. The entire vision of the future that has been built in past decades relies primarily on aspects that have not been extensively discussed, matters related to economic growth, the risks of extensive globalization, and the transformation to a sustainable society. Experts in different areas cannot develop a credible vision of the future without a firm understanding of the forces that have driven economic growth in the past, because the same forces will be the ones that drive economic growth and technology development in the future.

To many, the statement that economic growth determines development in society is not very palatable, especially not for the proponents of sustainability, who argue that economic growth must come to an end. Economic growth causes overuse of finite natural resources and this cannot continue for much longer. The excessive use of resources, in combination with the emissions caused by fossil fuels, will force humanity to change track and develop a circular economy that does not depend on economic growth. As has been indicated above, this argument is also built on a blindness to the complexity of the changes that will be needed and a consequent unwillingness to deal with the task of developing strategies and tools that can be used throughout the process.

While it is true that the use of resources cannot continue for much longer — for example, the International Energy Agency, an organization financed by 30 countries, warns that oil production is approaching its peak and that a decline in production is imminent — it is also a fact that the development of circular production and distribution systems on a large scale will require very large investment. Investment in the creation of circular and fossil-free systems will have to be made in all countries and in all regions for this development to take effect. New systems that will replace the present cannot arise from nowhere and they will not come into existence without very large expenditure, and large expenditure brings with it the use of large volumes of resources. The same is true for the digital solutions of the future. Digital services that will be based on artificial intelligence and fully automated production systems that are discussed under the banner of Industry 4.0 can only come into existence through very strong financing, because these technologies are at an early stage in their development. Billions, or more probably trillions, of euro in investment will become necessary to drive these innovations to maturity. This is the magnitude of the investment that is required to drive technologies from their early movements on the runway to full fruition as mature *general-purpose* technologies — competitive, user-friendly, and applicable for a wide range of uses. It is impossible to know exactly how much will have to be invested, but determining by the development of railway technologies, telephony, ICT, internet, space, and airplane technologies the coming innovations are likely to require the same magnitude of investment as the ones that have been driven in the past. What drives the cost of innovation is that technology development on the drawing board does not lead to results. For technologies to become general-purpose, they need to be implemented on a large scale in many different environments, and this is a process that takes decades.

A handbook for the leaders of the transformation would be incomplete without a description of the investment needs and the framework that needs to be developed for this investment to take place. Investment will have to be made both by governments and private companies, and the collaboration needs to be, in each case, structured based on an understanding of the development needs. Few such structures are yet even on the drawing board, even for the most important cornerstones of the transformation. A simple example will illustrate the point.

The Development of Airplane Technologies

Many readers are likely to doubt that large investment will be needed in order for new technologies to reach maturity, but earlier development processes clearly indicate that this has always been the case, and we can safely assume that the same will be true for technology development in the future as well. In the early stages of technology advancement, it has been necessary for governments to drive the process forwards through long-term and large-scale investment. It has not been until technologies have reached maturity or approached that stage that private investment and the market can take over as the driving forces of improvement, but even at this stage governments in many cases have continued to invest, long after technologies have become general-purpose.

Over recent decades air travel has become increasingly inexpensive and the market has to a large extent driven the expansion of commercial air travel, but government investment still plays an important role in technology development and improvement, as governments finance the development of military aircraft that spills over into civil aviation. In the early stages, governments drove development for decades—almost single-handedly—made investments, and offered subsidies without which air travel and transportation would not have been able to reach its present level of advancement. But it should be noted that some initiatives turn out to be dead ends. The creation of the ultrasonic passenger aircraft Concorde, driven as a collaborative project between France and the United Kingdom, did not get any followers, at least not within the first 45 years after its first regular flight. A total of 20 aircraft were manufactured and kept in service from 1976 to 2003, but despite this and other costly misjudgments, air travel has become one of the highly successful technologies of our modern society that has contributed significantly to economic growth, at least up until the start of the coronavirus pandemic. The coronavirus pandemic could be seen as a failure of government decision making, but most of the critical development initiatives have to a large extent been financed by governments. The below examples summarize the investments made in the development of airplane technologies by the US Government.

In his book *Is War Necessary for Economic Growth?* Professor Vernon W. Ruttan describes how large-scale and long-term investment in technology development, by the US government, created the foundation for six different technologies to become general-purpose technologies. The technologies studied by Ruttan are the American Production System, airplane technologies, space, computer, and internet technologies, and nuclear power. Ruttan studied these innovations to understand the mechanisms that made them fit for use for a large variety of purposes. In the book he admits that the most important conclusion was staring him in the face for a long time without him being able to see it. When he suddenly saw what he had failed to see he realized that, in all the cases he studied, large-scale and long-term investment made by the US government had been crucial to progress, and this investment had contributed substantially to speeding up the process of development. In the early stages the government made investments for decades in development, financing a series of projects to drive development forwards and to systematically reduce production cost and innovate applications. In the case of the advancement of airplane technologies, for example, the government from the early days of the twentieth century used three principal tools in order to drive the development in the airline industry: heavy subsidies of airmail, the procurement of military aircraft, and the financing of research and development programmes. As early as 1915, the government established NACA, the National Advisory Committee for Aeronautics, and the aircraft industry became the only manufacturing industry that had a government research organization with the sole purpose of supporting the industry's research and development. As the United States entered the First World War, its European allies demanded that they increase production of aircraft. In 1916, only 411 airplanes were produced, but the industry, with only 300 companies, expanded to 175,000 workers who between April 1917 and November 1918 produced 12,894 aircraft and 41,983 engines. By the end of the war, the engines had become stronger, but no major breakthroughs had been made in the design of aircraft. At the time, the industry primarily produced military planes, but in 1918 an airmail service was opened between New York and Washington DC. By 1930 a transcontinental system had been established, and in 1925 the introduction of rotating beacons at airports made night flight possible. Companies were started with the purpose of handling mail transportation, and the services were subsidized in order to become profitable. Companies were paid by the volume of the aircraft, which created an incentive to also make room for a few passengers. As Herbert Hoover became Postmaster General, he moved to promote mergers between airlines to create regional and national carriers and increase the efficiency of the industry. This was done with the intention of building a modern aircraft industry and a national system for air transport. By 1933, four major airlines (American, TWA, Eastern, and United) were in operation, and this structure remained until after the Second World War.

In its first ten years of operation, NACA focused on two major tasks, propeller design and the construction of advanced wind tunnels, and in the coming decades research was financed to investigate the interaction between the pilot and the plane and to develop more efficient engines. The NACA facility at Langley Field was in the 1930s recognized as the leading aviation research centre in the world. In 1913, US investment in the aircraft industry was on par with those of Brazil, while the leaders Germany and France invested more than 50 times more money. In 1939, the United States built the best commercial airliners and the country had the largest airline system in the world. The DC3 airplane, which was launched in the 1930s and remained in operation until the 1960s, incorporated technologies that had been created for military aircraft and engines.

NACA management was not convinced of the necessity to develop jet propulsion, since it required new aerodynamics for flight and these technologies were not available in the US. Instead, German and British engineers and companies took the lead in this innovation. Most aircraft that were produced in the United States during the Second World War were designed before the war. A jet aircraft was developed in 1941 by the Army Air Force using a British jet engine, without informing NACA of the initiative. It was not until after the war that NACA came to master the art of building jet aircraft, and the delay significantly weakened the political position of NACA and its ability to get financing for projects. Boeing developed a military jet, the B47, innovating revolutionary technology that was also applied in the production of its first commercial jet airliner, the 707. The ability to apply technology that had been developed in military projects to the creation of commercial airliners constitutes an important basis for Boeing's success.

After the Second World War, the aircraft industry was the United States' largest industry. Large public investment had gone into the development and purchase of military aircraft. For example, 13,726 B17 bombers had been built during the war and the number of fighters was much higher. The total number of aircraft built by the US in the war was 296,600,[2] and Boeing had established itself as a leading manufacturer of military aircraft, transferring that position to become the leader in commercial aircraft too.

In the 1930s, NACA embarked on a programme to develop high-speed flight, which culminated with the first supersonic flight in 1947. This required a complete redesign of the aircraft, including the development of fundamental principles for aircraft design, leading to a revolution in design largely driven by Boeing in collaboration with the Air Force. The new principles were later used in the design of the 707, which set the standard for the design of commercial airliners.

---

[2] The number of aircraft can be found on page 353 of *An Empire of Wealth* by John Steele Gordon.

In 1958, NASA was founded and NACA was incorporated into the new organization. The driving forces of the US Army Air Force to convert entirely to jet propulsion and the need to continue to develop high-speed aviation technologies kept research and development at a high level. Investment in R&D amounted to 20 per cent of gross revenue in the aircraft industry, of which only a tenth (2 per cent) was financed through private sources.

In the 1980s, the United States' commercial aircraft industry faced strong competition from European manufacturers, which led the US Government to invest 1 billion dollars per year on an ongoing basis in all aspects of commercial aircraft development and demonstration. In his reflections, Ruttan concludes that the industry could not have developed in the way it has without the long-term and large-scale government investment that have been made since 1915.[3]

Investments in the development of new technologies and new industrial sectors must be made by governments, because they are made with a time horizon from investment to payback that cannot be handled by private companies. The primary drivers of the improvement in airplanes was the development of the country's infrastructure and investment in building military strength. Building the competitive position of the aircraft industry has been an important aspect as well, but probably not as important as the first two drivers. Private investments need to pay back in only a few years. In the cases studied by Ruttan, the US government had invested billions of dollars over seven decades, without the expectation for the investment to pay back short-term. In many cases it has been uncertain if the investment would ever be paid back.

The book's title, *Is War Necessary for Economic Growth?*, refers to the strategic aspect of the investment made by the US government and the possibility that large-scale and long-term investment cannot be mustered in the absence of a military threat. In the absence of such investment, there is a substantial risk that economic growth will come to a halt. The economic growth that has been enjoyed in the world in the past century seems almost to be a by-product of strategic investment and not something that has primarily been created for financial or commercial reasons. Politicians and economists, in policy development, have turned a blind eye to the role of governments in this respect, a blindness that has created a large territory of ignorance throughout society.

The development of space and computer technologies, and the internet, has been financed by the government in similar ways, and the same is true for the American Production System, which was developed in the nineteenth century. In the case of nuclear power, Ruttan concluded that this technology would probably never even have come into existence in the absence of government investment, as it builds on research aimed at

---

[3]   The full analysis is available on pp. 33–65 of *Is War Necessary for Economic Growth?* by Vernon W. Ruttan.

developing nuclear weapons. In the case of the automobile industry, which is not discussed by Ruttan, growth took off as countries started to motorize their armies and needed large numbers of identical vehicles that were reliable and easy to repair. This, in combination with the development of the assembly line by Henry Ford, drove the price of cars down so that the demand for cars could increase to present levels, but it was not until after the Second World War that the majority of households in developed countries could afford to buy a car.

Based on his studies, Ruttan, at the start of the new millennium, concluded that the private sector would not drive the development of new general-purpose technologies. He also thought that it is doubtful whether governments would have the incentive to invest large enough sums into the development of non-military technologies, apart from health and food, and that new general-purpose technologies may not be developed in the future.[4] Without doubt, many of the technologies that have driven growth in past decades are approaching maturity as they near full penetration of target markets, and the lack of obvious new candidates that can drive future growth should be cause for concern. The investments that have been described above in the case of the development of aviation technologies represent a magnitude and duration that most experts on specific technologies are not likely to be aware of. It will require substantial research to define the status of development of candidate technologies today, such as Internet-of-Things, artificial intelligence, autonomous vehicles, and new materials. Is, for example, the development of Industry 4.0, which is presented as the next step in the development of industrial automation, on the verge of taking industrial development with leaps and bounds into the future? The next question then will be whether it will be possible to contain the value creation in the economy in such a way that all citizens can enjoy the fruits of increasing productivity.

Economic and technology advancement is much more complex than most students of the future realize, but when reading *The Invevitable* by Kevin Kelly, and other similar forecasts of the future, the reader is given the impression that many aspects of the development are certain and unquestionable. Kelly argues that digital technologies will continue to be advanced at a pace that will move society forwards to the point where artificial intelligence, robotics, and other technologies will become inexpensive general-purpose technologies. The development he describes as inevitable can only take place in a society with significant economic growth, and it will be an important task in the near future to determine if growth can continue for much longer and stake out a strategy for development that can sustain a high pace. There is a significant risk that this will not be the case and that society will come up against unexpected challenges that have been neglected.

---

[4] Ruttan discussed the prospects for new general-purpose technologies on pp. 177–185.

Without government investment, Robert Solow would have had to wait several decades more until IT development could be seen in the productivity statistics, and it suddenly becomes apparent that, in the absence of government investment, many of the technologies that people today take for granted would not have seen the light of day, at least not yet.

In recent decades there have not been very many large-scale projects like the Apollo Programme or the investment in the development of computers and internet technologies that were financed by ARPA, the Advanced Research Projects Agency that was financed by the United States government.

In the case of artificial intelligence, this seems to be at an early stage in its development. It is used in high-value applications, such as for granting bank loans and in order to reduce credit risks, but it is clearly at a very early stage of innovation and probably decades away from driving economic growth. In the case of robotics, this technology has come further, but it is not yet a general-purpose technology. For many applications in production it is still too expensive to apply robots, and it is primarily in situations where production is highly repetitive, and identical tasks are performed day in and day out, that the technology can be applied. In situations where batches are small, the programming becomes too expensive to be economically viable. The present status of robotics may perhaps be compared to the status of aviation in the 1970s or 1980s.

When are General-Purpose Technologies Created?

It is not until a technology is used by companies and people for a large number of purposes that it becomes a general-purpose technology, and it is about that time when it starts to contribute to economic growth. The reason for this is straightforward. The amount of money and resources that are invested each year in the development of the technology is so vast that the savings need to be very great to pay back the cost of development. Even if there are companies that make good profits selling a technology or the resulting products and services, the volume of innovation that is financed by governments must be included in the equation. For society, the technology does not contribute to productivity improvement until the savings compensate for all the investment and activities that are necessary in order to develop, implement, and operate the systems each year. A technology may be profitable for the companies that supply products and services, but it may still not contribute to productivity improvement at the level of society — the effects that Robert Solow and other economists are looking for. When a technology matures, even though savings at a low level may continue for many decades, it is only for a short period of time that the technology contributes to economic growth. The reason for this is also straightforward. Economic growth is a measurement of the increase of the economic value created compared to the previous year, the growth of GDP. During a period when an increasing number of people get access to a technology, the change in productivity is likely to be significant. When most people already use the technology, improvements decrease. At this point the price of the technology may still go down, due to increasing use, which creates room for people to spend money on other things, but savings are not big enough for society to outweigh the investments.

A somewhat spooky aspect of this is that society can never reach a high enough level of affluence. New improvements in productivity still need to be made every year for economic growth to continue and for people to be able to continue to enjoy their present level of affluence. In principle, the advances that were made in the previous year become irrelevant on 31 December when the counting of the productivity improvements for the present year started. The level of GDP per capita that has been achieved indicates the level of affluence, but affluence can only be maintained through continuous growth. As soon as citizens realize that economic growth will turn into decline for the long term, affluence is likely to start to decline as well. Again, this is because of the structure of the economy. These aspects are well-known, but they are never taken into consideration by sustainability experts when they discuss the transformation to a sustainable society. If they had been taken into consideration, the highly simplified ideas that the market will be able to drive the change would not have gained the level of traction they have.

The examples illustrate how much money needs to be invested in the development of technologies for them to reach a level where they contribute to economic growth. This is probably much more than most people, and even many experts, would assume. Very large investment needs to be made over the long term, and in order to achieve this governments need determination and focus, in the way that governments have had in the past when they have invested in railways, telephone networks, and space technologies. It is not likely to be achieved if a *laissez faire* approach is applied and investment in the development of a technology is left to the market entirely. Surprisingly, and probably to a large extent without knowing it, governments and large companies have made investments that forty or fifty years later have contributed to economic growth. They did this for decades, sometimes from the nineteenth century and for a long time into the twentieth, but in recent decades they have no longer assumed that role and there is a risk that there are not enough technologies that are on the verge of becoming general-purpose technologies.

An important additional observation is the number of technologies that have contributed to economic growth in recent decades. ICT is not the only set of technologies that has driven development. New materials, improved production technologies, automation, miniaturization, the development in the automotive sector, chemicals, and a number of other technologies have together contributed to improving productivity. As the power of these technologies to do this starts to wane, it is likely to be difficult to once more drive growth in the global economy. These are only some of the aspects to which economists, sustainability experts, and governments have become blind, and the price of this blindness is being paid by the citizens of nations across the world. The blindness has extended to transnational organizations like the UN and the EU, which has further contributed to the blindness and the difficulty of opening the eyes of both the guardians of ignorance and of the general public.

When the world transitions from the present Covid-19 crisis to the post-coronavirus economy, we may ask ourselves if the above matters. Is it not enough that a small number of economists care about economic growth and allow the rest of us to continue to lead our lives as we have become used to? No, citizens cannot resign from the democratic responsibility of forming the world based on the most viable ideas. Voters need to collectively upgrade their understanding of society, not abandon the world to the impersonal forces of the market in phases of technology development during which the market does not have the power to drive that development. People cannot continue to believe in ideologies that overstate the power of random decisions over conscious development policies. Even if there are customers who buy electric cars and the products of the circular economy, they are not enough to finance the advancement and marketing efforts that will become necessary for these new technologies to take over from the business principles and technologies of the global economy. The belief that the market can drive things forwards from the early phases to the time when a product becomes mature enough to drive growth will, if it continues to be applied as the only principle of innovation, put an end to development as we know it, and it will effectively put an end to economic growth and affluence as well. We cannot knowingly allow the large territories of ignorance that have been created through the unquestioning belief in the power of markets to remain uncharted, because development is a necessary aspect of present society.

These facts are not too complicated for people to take in or care about. Should everybody just ignore the implications of this and go back to business as usual as soon as possible once the coronavirus pandemic has receded? There is a lot to be said for learning from mistakes, but where will the incentive to change come from? How can experts and decision makers build the courage to start on an entirely new path of sustainability, based on aspects of collective action, and start to explore the territories of un-knowledge that have been closed to human thought for almost three decades? It is not only a matter of building resources for the transformation—most people lack the vocabulary necessary to discuss the various aspects of public involvement in development. Few are likely to understand the concept of developing a strategy for the transformation to sustainable production and distribution systems.

Apart from the need to innovate a number of new technologies that are currently at early stages of development, a further aspect is that some of the technologies and systems that have driven economic growth in recent decades are approaching the end of the period when they have the power to drive growth. This is a further aspect that change leaders will have to consider when plans are made for the transformation. Simply put, there is a need for technologies that are positioned to drive economic growth so that countries will be able to spend the resources that are generated through growth on the transformation to a sustainable society. Thirty years ago, computers were large and expensive and there were business leaders in the computer industry who believed that it would never be relevant for people to have computers in their homes. The manager who has become famous for saying this is Ken Olsen, the founder of Digital Equipment Corporation, one of the suppliers of mainframe computers. As late as 1977 he thought that computers would never become so inexpensive that it would be possible for families to have them at home, and that for this reason it could never be justified for software companies to develop applications that cater to their needs. Now, most people have not one but several computers in their homes, and the price of computers and processors continues to go down.

Economic growth, however, depends on the improvement of productivity, year after year. The increase in productivity has been tremendous in past decades, as more people have been able to access digital services and computer programs that help them improve their productivity at work and at home. Now, most people have access to a large variety of computerized services and apps on computers and mobile devices and it will no longer be possible to improve productivity by adding large numbers of new users of existing services. The productivity improvements that will be generated by mainstream digital applications and services will gradually decline, and growth in the near future will have to be generated by other technologies, for example the ones included under the banners of artificial intelligence and Industry 4.0. The problem is that these technology complexes have not yet been advanced to a level of maturity where they have the power to drive growth, and thus the development of the technologies will have to be driven to the point where they take off from the runway and gain altitude all the way up to cruising altitude.

The improvement potential that remains in the economy is also declining, another little understood challenge. Most people assume that improvement potential is infinite, but this is not the case. The concept may seem abstract, but it will have tremendous practical implications for development. Nothing can be done in less than no time or at a cost lower than zero, and through digitization the development in many areas has been driven to a point very close to zero both in terms of time and cost. Google searches and automatic transactions in computer systems are performed in almost no time and at a cost close to zero. Only ten years ago, many services that are now digitized required hours of manual work. In many areas in administration, as well as in production and services, companies have been working in recent decades to eliminate as much waste of time and money as possible, and in many business processes very little time and cost remains to be removed through future improvements. Technical improvement can still be driven forwards, but the savings in terms of time and cost will be smaller than they have been in recent decades and centuries. Productivity improvement is an area that will experience diminishing returns on investments in existing technologies, and there are few new technologies that are on the verge of starting to contribute to productivity. Unfortunately, this means that the contributions to growth made by existing technologies are likely to soon start a rapid decline, which will create an additional challenge for present generations and for the people who aspire to lead the transformation to sustainability. When the fact that room for improvement is decreasing is mentioned, many argue that new technologies are invented all the time that start on new trajectories of improvement. This does not seem to be true. New technologies contribute to reducing the time and cost of performing tasks that have been done for centuries, or millennia. Computers speed up writing, accounting, printing, communication, and sales and marketing, all tasks that have been performed since time immemorial. The development of computers has brought the time and cost of all of these tasks close to zero, and other developments, like Lean Production and other operational improvements in companies, have taken away the better part of the time and cost of many business processes, leaving a minimum of wasted time remaining to be removed and very little productivity improvement to be achieved thereby. The momentum of technology development and productivity improvement that has been going on in recent decades is still so strong that economic growth is improved each year but, as the remaining room for improvement is reduced by progress, economic growth is likely to slow down as well, with foreseeable consequences.

When the coronavirus pandemic starts to recede, these issues may not immediately become obvious, but governments will have to take them seriously, because they are going to emerge as very concrete challenges in the coming decade. Governments and industry will have to come to terms with these problems and start to analyse how they will impact development and when they are likely to emerge as issues on the dashboards of economists, central banks, and businesses.

In order to create economic growth in the future, which will still be necessary to make room for large investment in new digital technologies, robotics, e-mobility, new materials, and the circular economy, new technology complexes have to be developed from the present early stages to maturity. It is not until late in the development of a technology that it contributes to economic growth. In the case of information technology (IT) the Nobel laureate economist Robert Solow observed in the 1990s that computers could be seen everywhere in society, except in the productivity statistics. It deserves to be remembered that it was not until the late 1990s, after more than forty years of IT development— when most large and many medium sized companies had been using computer systems for book-keeping, resource planning, and sales administration for more than two decades—that information technology started to generate productivity improvements in society overall.

In the case of the technologies included under the labels of artificial intelligence and Industry 4.0, these innovations may be at a level similar to the that of IT development of the 1960s, when thirty more years remained until these technologies would become inexpensive enough to contribute to driving growth. Nobody knows exactly when any of these technologies may start to generate productivity improvements, but it is not going to be next year or the year after. In the case of electricity, according to Ruttan,[5] investment had to go on for almost a century until the technologies started to contribute to economic growth for society overall. This was probably due to the vast amount of infrastructure that had to be built and improved before savings outweighed investment and operational cost. As already mentioned, especially tough challenges can be foreseen for the implementation of e-mobility and the circular economy. The idea is that these concepts will replace a large share of the production and distribution systems that already exist in all countries by new systems, products, and services that at this point are produced in small volumes. These offerings are not in widespread use, and they have a long period of development ahead of them to become competitive and demanded by large swathes of the market.

Neither e-mobility nor the circular economy can be expected to improve productivity. Transportation is not likely to become more efficient through e-mobility and the production of all kinds of goods

---

5   Vernon W. Ruttan, *Is War Necessary for Economic Growth?*

and services will not become more efficient through the circular economy. These new technologies and concepts are instead likely to make production and transportation more expensive, which will have the opposite effect. They will most likely reduce productivity, instead of increasing it. For change leaders, the fact that local small-scale production and biological materials will have to replace the very efficient production systems that dominate the global economy presents a challenge. In the past, economic growth has been driven by the increased efficiency that has been achieved broadly across most industries, and this improved productivity has more than compensated for any losses of productivity that may have appeared in some areas. In the future, change leaders will have to find ways to drive the transformation forwards on a broad basis in many industries, and find ways of financing this, despite the fact that the technologies that will have to drive transformation are at an early stage of development and that it will take many years until they can contribute to driving growth. From the standpoint of present generations, it must be possible to succeed with the transformation, we have only not yet found the way of doing it!

Rude Awakening

This is a different picture compared to the one provided in the media and by politicians and business leaders, and it is probably an unexpected reality for people who have been impressed by the speeches of Greta Thunberg that indicate that driving forwards the efforts to create a sustainable future will be a simple choice for politicians. Why not just do it? Sustainability has been debated for so long now that just about everybody should know what needs to be done! Leaders want to give the impression that the transition into the future will be smooth and almost seamless and that very few things will need to change, except that people will become more affluent. Instead, unexpected challenges will emerge, ones that have not been planned for, such as Covid-19. A further issue is likely to be the expected decline in oil production, which will have a negative effect on economic growth. The increase in the use of oil has temporarily been delayed, but the decrease in oil production is likely to start in the next few years after the coronavirus pandemic and it will also reduce the ability of governments to invest large amounts of money in the transformation to sustainability. Politicians have not prepared for this situation at all and will be at a loss as to how to meet the unexpected challenges. The situation is likely to become worse than most people can imagine, since declining oil production is likely to cause shortages of fuel but also of the products that are now produced and transported using petroleum-based fuels for transportation and oil as a raw material. Piling this need for change on top of the need to recover from the coronavirus crisis may seem like a bad idea. Can we not delay the transformation until countries have recovered and the consequences of declining oil production can be seen in the economy? Surely, now that countries are going through the worst recession in modern times, Greta Thunberg and other sustainability experts must understand that it is not the right time to press on for more change!

The reply to this is that neither governments nor people in general have the power to decide when to move forwards with the transformation. Changing society will take many decades, and continuing to build and rebuild structures that we know will have to be changed in the next few years is a bad idea. Despite its devastating effects, the coronavirus crisis offers an opportunity to consider the different options that mankind can choose from, and countries need to make the right choice and build more local and regional supply chains — building economies that can thrive based on an increasing share of local and regional production. Many products will still have to be supplied through global supply chains, but long-distance transportation cannot continue to form the backbone of the global economy as the situation has been in the past. Countries will have the opportunity to move in the direction of globalization or move away from it, and the choice must be to build a more resource-effective economy with less global transportation.

To build the new economy, leadership will be necessary and the leaders who aspire to take roles at the foreforont of the transformation need to step forwards. Countries cannot continue on the path towards globalization for very long, and people are not likely to afterwards understand the excuse from politicians and business leaders that they did not see the challenges coming. This may be possible with respect to the exact timing of a pandemic, but it is obvious that governments should in recent decades have taken precautions and prepared for a pandemic, considering that epidemiologists have for decades warned of a crisis with devastating effects for humanity.[6] This type of oversight, or negligence, cannot become the principle on which modern society is

---

6   In *The Pandemic Century – One Hundred Years of Panic, Hysteria, and Hubris* Mark Honigsbaum relates the story of pandemics in the past century and concludes that the question in 2019, when the book was published, was not *if*, but rather *when*, the next global pandemic would strike.

built, because if it continues there will be no modern society or global community to save. Governments and large companies have the resources to analyse the most probable development in the near future and they could, if they would, verify that the challenges described in this book are real and that it will be futile to continue to deny the realism of the description, at least without having carried out a thorough investigation. While it is most likely that an investigation would render the same results as those presented here, a sense of urgency among decision makers and joint efforts to develop solutions can open up opportunities that can be realized through large-scale collaboration within and between countries. Again, the progress that was made in a few weeks to build new production resources for a small number of products after the start of the Covid-19 pandemic illustrates that it is possible to achieve changes that most people would deem unrealistic. The Apollo Programme, the Marshall Plan, and the trans-formation of the industry of the United States to war production in 1942 are examples that show what is possible when resources are focused on achieving important goals. Transforming society to sustainability and resilience will require larger efforts than the men-tioned programmes combined, but it will still be possible to make significant progress using a structured approach.

The situation described here is not a hypothetical situation that may arise in case oil production, against all odds, goes into decline and if economic growth should happen to slow down. It is not like a pan-demic, something that is unlikely to happen in any year and something that can be avoided through proper actions by governments. The probability that oil production will start to go down in the next few years is very high, and the consequences of declining oil production can only be mitigated through a reduced reliance on oil — and this, in its turn, can only be achieved through a large-scale transformation of society.

There is no way forwards that does not include sacrifice. The only reason why the transformation has become so pressing without anyone observing it is the blindness that has spread, and the cause behind this is the widespread belief that the market will drive the transformation process and that no human decision makers need to become involved in the process. The organization International Energy Agency has for more than a decade warned of the imminent decline in oil production, but, just like the warnings of pandemics, politicians have not heeded them or started to learn about the consequences and what needs to be done to avoid a disastrous situation in the near future. And forward-looking economists, such as the late Professor Vernon W. Ruttan of University of Minnesota, have for years warned that the growth driven by technologies that are mature at present will come to an end and that no new technologies have been developed to the point where they can take over the role of driving growth. Instead of taking warnings seriously, governments have continued to drive development forwards along the beaten paths, and important insights have been lost as people have become blind to the need for precautions against pandemics and change to make the global economy less vulnerable against the declining production of scarce resources. Voters have been more interested in supporting economic growth, short term, than in investing in a sustainable future. We prefer not to think or to build resources to avoid disasters, but we need to wake up to the fact that we have created a very sensitive global economic system that is expensive and resource-consuming to maintain and change.

Why worry about declining oil production? It goes without saying that at the beginning there will not be a shortage of everything all the time. At the beginning of the decline, most transportation will be able to run, and it is likely to be the least important goods and journeys that will not be prioritized highly enough when oil production starts to decrease, so initially people are not likely to experience much discomfort. There will more likely be shortages of some things some of the time. But, as there will be no new transport systems that can replace petrol and diesel for a number of years, people will realize, with the help of media and experts who at that point will be willing to share their knowledge, how precarious the situation will become. In the same way that governments and the general public at present experience the consequences of a lack of preparations for the spreading of diseases, decision makers and people in general will rapidly see the consequences of not having prepared for a decline in oil production. At present we are told that it may take more than a year until countries can go back to business as usual and leave, for example, social distancing behind. When oil starts to become scarce, experts are going to tell us all that it will take decades to rebuild production and distribution systems that can function in a situation of only half of the present oil production, and that countries will have to endure shortages for a very long time into the future. While the experiences of the coronavirus pandemic are important as examples of a total lack of preparations, the starting up of production of face masks and ventilators and supplying them to hospitals and other care units are much less complex than the transformation to electric transportation, which involves developing and producing competitive electric vehicles and selling them to authorities, households, and companies on a large scale — and expanding power production and distribution to facilitate the charging of large numbers of cars, buses, and trucks. The latter transformation will take decades, even if it becomes strongly supported by governments.

Europe, a continent almost without its own production of oil, will be particularly vulnerable to the situation that will emerge. At that point, governments will have to start activities to build new transport systems that will have to be built on available technologies and be based on the current status of innovation. Building new systems, however, will be difficult under the financial circumstances, at the beginning of a severe recession. Society will also have to build production systems that do not rely on plastics — as oil, together with natural gas, is one of the feedstocks for plastics production — and find alternative feed-stocks for the production of lubricants, pharmaceuticals, and other products that oil is used for at present. This will represent a further challenge, as plastic is a highly cost effective material, much less expensive to produce and form than wood or metal. As these challenges seem too abstract and difficult for decision makers to grasp, the issues related to the imminent decline in oil production go unnoticed, just like the lack of preparations for a pandemic had done before the outbreak of Covid-19.

Decline in Oil Production — Surely, There Must Be Enough?[7]

Could oil production really go into decline? Oil reserves must be huge, and largely untapped sources of shale oil are available in the United States, Canada, and in many other countries around the world.

Yes, this is true, but it is important for change leaders to understand some of the intricacies related to the hugely important topic of oil production. The problem is that most experts on sustainability or new technologies have not taken the time to read up on the facts about oil production and most politicians simply assume that renewable fuels can replace oil once the price of oil increases to a high enough level. The first thing that will happen when oil becomes scarce is not that companies start to invest in electric trucks, because there are no competitive systems for electric long-

---

[7]   I regularly calibrate my knowledge about oil production and the prospects of a decline through phone conversations with Mikael Höök, Assistant Professor and Senior Lecturer at Uppsala University and head of a department there that has access to one of the world's richest databases for oil production. Professor Höök is the successor of Kjell Aleklett, the expert who coined the term Peak Oil.

distance transportation that are ready to be implemented. Apart from that, the situation related to oil is very sensitive and interesting. There are many aspects to take in that are necessary to grasp in order to understand the challenges of declining oil supply and the transformation of transport systems to electric mobility.

The high demand for oil is built into the structures of the global economy, and large investments in new production and distribution systems and new patterns of production, distribution, and travel for leisure and for work need to be developed. If more people continue to work at home and more people decide to take their holidays in their home countries, this will have a small effect on oil demand, but large volumes of goods and large numbers of people will still have to be moved every day.

There are vast sources of oil remaining in the ground, in the area of 1,000 billion barrels of conventional oil. The problem is that people and companies around the world use 36 billion barrels per year. If current production could continue at the same rate into the future, reserves would be entirely depleted in about 30 years. The volume of new discoveries is, despite the high price level, at an all-time low. Only a few billion barrels are found every year, less than 10 per cent of the volumes that are used in a year, and the volumes are declining on average. New discoveries may at most add two or three years of production to the forecast. As of early May 2020, the Covid-19 pandemic had reduced oil demand by about 20 per cent, and previous experiences from recessions indicate that demand is likely to bounce back to previous levels soon after the pandemic has ended.

The production of unconventional oil, like shale oil and oil from tar sands, is still at an early stage of development and further growth is problematic for several reasons. The resources are huge, maybe twice as large as the amounts of conventional oil, but wells have a very short lifespan. Eighteen months after production has been started, volumes are down to 30 per cent of peak levels and large amounts of heat, generated by the burning of natural gas, and the use of large volumes of chemicals are necessary to facilitate production.[8] In 2018, the production of unconventional oil accounted for around 7 per cent of global oil production and most experts doubt that it could increase to the levels necessary in order for this production to take over a large share of oil production once the decline starts.

It is highly likely that conventional oil goes into decline in the next few years. Independent oil experts, like the Swedish Professor Emeritus Kjell Aleklett[9] and the International Energy Agency, which is related to OECD and financed by 30 countries, and an increasing number of others have been warning of this for close to two decades, without really getting the attention of heads of state and their governments. They have pointed out

---

[8] Richard Heinberg — *Snake Oil*.

[9] Professor Kjell Aleklett describes his work to inform about Peak Oil in *Peeking at Peak Oil*.

that oil production cannot be expected to continue for much longer at the present rate and that there are signs that the peak is imminent. The main reason for this is that oil is produced from underground wells. In the past, the bulk of production has come from large wells that have contributed very large volumes to global production for several decades. The largest of them all is the Saudi Arabian oil field Ghawar, that has been producing at a rate of four to five million barrels per day since the 1980s.[10] A number of other very large oil fields, so-called *elephants*, have also contributed large amounts. Presently, there are six fields in the world that produce more than one million barrels per day, and they jointly account for more than 10 per cent of global oil production. As the big oil fields go into decline, they need to be replaced by many much smaller wells that produce smaller volumes for a shorter period of time. This adds cost, and over time it will be increasingly difficult to keep volumes at a high level. At the same time, as the amount of oil in conventional wells decreases, the pressure in the wells also decreases. Rock that contains oil is like a Swiss cheese, full of holes, and as the amount of oil decreases the pressure goes down and the volumes produced decline as well. At this point, large volumes of water need to be pumped into wells to maintain pressure, which results in large volumes of water being pumped together with the oil, which also contributes to a decline in the volume of oil.

Smaller fields and wells and an increasing share of water being pumped will lead to a decline in oil production, which many experts expect will happen in the next few years. Many oil producing countries have experienced declines for more than a decade, such as Norway and the United Kingdom that have seen their volumes halve, and the increase in production emanates from volume increases from a small number of large producers, like the United States, OPEC, and Russia. According to recent figures, OPEC are expecting a decline in production by two million barrels per day in the next few years, and the growth in the United States is expected to slow down. It is impossible to say exactly, beforehand, when the decline in global production will start, but once it does it is likely to lead to a decline in production of some 1.5 or 2 per cent per year in the first years and then accelerate to higher annual percentages of decline.[11] Once transportation systems are up and running again and the use of oil as an industrial raw material goes back to normal levels, the consumption of oil in general will be back at similar levels to those that were reached before the crisis. Oil demand is built into the systems structures of the global economy, and volumes can only be reduced through large investment in the building of new systems, not through a temporary shutdown.

---

[10]   Matthew R. Simmons—*Twilight in the Desert*.
[11]   This process has been described in several books on Peak Oil, one of them being *Peeking at Peak Oil* by Kjell Aleklett.

The big news is not the amount of knowledge countries need to build around the challenges themselves, but the understanding that needs to be developed about the measures that must be initiated. Change leaders should not primarily emulate Greta Thunberg or other experts and spread a message based on environmental arguments. They need to understand how countries need to transform production and distribution in order to secure supply of goods and services in a future when oil and other resources are likely to become scarce and other challenges will contribute to making life, and economic development, increasingly difficult. Once more, this is a complex picture of the future that decision makers should not simply ignore. If citizens ignore it, there will be no pressure on politicians to start to take measures on a large scale. If consumers ignore it, business leaders have no incentive to change the practices of companies on a large scale. Then companies can continue with business as usual, investing only small amounts in the transformation to sustainability. When all parties, including sustainability experts, politicians, and business experts, ignore the fact that the methods for transformation need to be developed before they can be set in motion, the territories of ignorance grow and it becomes increasingly dangerous to discuss the activities that will be necessary.

If nobody acknowledges the magnitude of the challenge, nobody will have any legitimate reason to lament the fact that too little was done — not politicians, not Greta Thunberg, and not the general public. If too little is done, it is likely to be because nobody bothered to develop a plan for the transformation that included a specification of the activities that needed to be performed in order to succeed with the transition, and that nobody bothered to observe that neither Greta nor anyone else knew what actions were needed.

When the challenges become apparent to most people, it is likely to be obvious that many changes need to be undertaken to prepare for a new phase in the development of the global society. Despite the urgent need, under such circumstances few citizens will be prepared to buy new electric cars as this is likely to seem like a very large and risky investment. Governments can study the sales of new vehicles during the coronavirus crisis. People reduce investments and save money for more urgent needs. It will also be difficult for citizens to start new businesses based on circular business models and fewer can afford to buy the more expensive products of the still very small circular economy.

When a new development is starting to set in there will be a need to save money for many other eventualities and companies, in the harsher business environment with declining revenue and profit that is likely to emerge, will find it difficult to finance investment in fleets of electric vehicles. It will rapidly become apparent how large the investment will have to be that will be necessary to drive the development of e-mobility and the circular economy forwards in order to as rapidly as possible reduce the dependence on oil.

Governments will find that only they control the resources necessary to build the new systems and, after the coronavirus crisis, the opportunity for governments to finance the transformation will be lower than before. Still, the transformation will be necessary. Governments need to find a way of driving the transformation forwards in the face of weaker financial circumstances. At that point it will also become apparent that large investment will be needed to drive digital development forwards to create the future that Kevin Kelly and many others see as inevitable. It will become clear to all that the advancement that people have become accustomed to is a hard-earned result of wise political decisions to invest heavily, and for long periods of time, up until the 1980s in technology development, something that governments have not done to the same extent lately, at least not in the development and implementation of new technologies. The EU and national governments finance innovations at early stages by small amounts, but there is no awareness that sustained government financing is necessary to drive the advancement of individual technologies to maturity. The result of the aversion to public investment in technology development and implementation is that there are no technology complexes that are on the brink of maturity and that it is less than clear how economic growth can be driven forwards in their absence.

Whose Fault is it?

At this point many people will look around to try to find the persons or groups who are responsible for the oversights that have led to the calamitous situation. Greta Thunberg has identified heads of state as the ones that have failed to invest in the sustainable future that many young people now demand. When people find out about the number of areas that need to change and the magnitude of the investment that is needed to drive development forwards, many are likely to use harsher language to describe the lack of awareness that has led to the critical situation.

Clearly it is easy to state that politicians, sustainability experts, and business leaders should have asked more penetrating questions regarding the consequences of not doing enough to reduce the dependence on oil. It will most likely be identified as one of the main errors that most groups and individuals in society have kept their focus on the wrong issues. Instead of discussing how society should plan and take precautions for the spreading of disease and how the transformation to sustainability should be approached, financed, organized, and which areas need to be transformed first, the focus has been on climate issues and the discussion of by how many degrees the temperature will increase and whether emissions of carbon dioxide were responsible for the change. An expectation has been built up by believers in the free market that the market should divert large enough sums of money for preparations for the future — without planning by politicians — and their followers and voters have not asked questions. Has the focus on environmental and climate issues, and the decisions to not interfere with markets, been conscious decisions rather than an unfortunate oversight, and did some groups benefit so much from that focus of the debate that they avoided leading discussions into the important, but uncharted, territory? The proponents of increased measures have, by not investigating the investment and change efforts that will become necessary, turned into blind guardians of ignorance, but have they ignored the transformation need on purpose, or have they simply not realized that the power of the market will have to be supported by political action?

One explanation would be that the blindness to the actual development needs has been caused not by conscious decisions, but by a process that is often called "groupthink". This has been observed even in teams with high competence, but where all members have similar backgrounds and share the same political views and background knowledge. In such situations, members of teams sometimes become overly confident in their own abilities and in their conclusions and forget to question the soundness of reasoning and decisions. One often-cited example was the lines of thought of the team around President John F. Kennedy during the planning of the invasion of Cuba in 1961. It has been suggested that the decision to go through with the Bay of Pigs invasion — the failed attempt in 1961 by the United States to invade Cuba — was to a large extent due to the similarities of the views and the patterns of thought of the persons in the team. They had all been trained at the same schools and were part of the same political establishment, and they were so strongly convinced of the superiority of the United States and its military forces that they were unable to foresee the risk that the Cuban army would be able to strike back and force the American troops to retreat.

Even though present society and political and social life comprises people with many different types of educations and backgrounds, a small number of very strong ideas have penetrated the minds of most people, regardless of their political views, and the concept of political correctness has been introduced in order to clear the political landscape of outrageous ideas, such as ones suggesting that the leading ideas may be wrong, or incomplete. Two of the strongest ideas that permeate present-day political thinking are that the market in all situations is the most efficient tool for allocating resources and that all resource allocation can be achieved by market forces unaided by human decision making. The market would, according to this line of reasoning, allocate appropriate resources for fighting epidemics and pandemics and manage the transformation to sustainability when the need becomes critical at a relatively low cost and while society continues to function in the way people have become used to. In the past, most successful technologies have, in the early phases of development, been developed in projects financed by governments. Companies are more apt at operating the systems, but the financing and programme management of early development and implementation has been performed by public organizations. As it has become increasingly difficult to discuss the public financing of new technologies, a substantial part of the complexity of the development of new technologies has been forgotten about, and people have assumed that the market can finance technology development and the creation of new businesses and industries from day one, something that has seldom been the case in reality.

Different Aspects of Government Involvement

In the debate about free markets versus a government-controlled economy, there are several aspects of government control that are possible. Investment in technology development and implementation in the early phases of growth have been necessary for the maturation of technologies, and without it present generations would not have enjoyed the level of affluence that we are now able to. The question is, of course, which technologies to support and how much should be invested. History shows that very large sums are necessary to invest for lengthy periods of time and that only governments can afford to take the long-term perspective on development that is needed to fund growth for such long periods of time.[12]

---

[12] Ruttan draws this conclusion in *Is War Necessary for Economic Growth?*

The ownership of companies and control of product development and production in mature industries is an entirely different matter. Few people would see any benefits of having the government own companies and control how many shoes are produced, or the development and production of cars. In order to drive the development of electric mobility forwards, the government may need to buy large volumes of cars to replace vehicles used by authorities and the military, and finance the development of smart power grids, the expansion of power production to cover charging, and the implementation of electrified motorways and highways. The products and services that will be necessary to drive the transformation should be procured from the most competitive bidders, in the same way that has been the case in most government-financed programmes up until now.

Another area that is much debated is the reallocation of income through taxes, grants, and subsidies. This is also not a matter of discussion in this book. Different countries have different approaches to this.

When people make assumptions regarding the power of the market to drive the development of new fuels in virtually no time and at no cost, or assume that the transformation to a sustainable society can be achieved rapidly and at very low cost, they reiterate statements that have become part of the lore of our times that most people believe do not need to be scrutinized. The sustainability experts, who in different ways express what most people believe to be true, are probably not aware that they contribute to justifying the inertia that Greta Thunberg argues against. Michael Braungart and many others argue that no decisions will be needed by human decision makers to drive the transformation forwards. This is clearly wrong. Many decisions will need to be made in many different areas for the transformation to gain momentum and take off, and the same is true for preparations for disasters.

The human mind has evolved over millennia when humans have been forced to perform the same tasks in the same way, day in and day out. Most people are not prepared to engage in complex thought processes in areas where they have no or little experience. The most common response to how people believe the future will develop is that they think it is going to be similar to the present. People will have access to some more of the digital services that we have had access to in recent decades and many anticipate that everyone will soon use electric and autonomous vehicles, without mentioning the very large investment that will be needed in order for this to become a reality. It is not surprising that books that proclaim this sell well, and that some of the authors get elevated almost to the level of prophets. Few are likely to consider the possibility that development will come to a standstill, only because technology development has reached a new phase or that oil production is about to go into decline. Despite warnings that a pandemic would strike hard against humanity any time soon, few anticipated that this would happen and that countries would need to prepare for it. Apart from the complexity of the chains of reasoning that have to take place, the outcome of which depends on access to bodies of information that are not readily available to most people, due to the focus on the continuation of the development of the past, people also calibrate their own state of mind against that of others and if few people seem to be worried this has a soothing effect on others as well. It is always easier to go with the flow and not take in novel ideas until they have become accepted by most citizens. People have done it this way in every new development through history. The new ideas of human rights and women's liberation were held and discussed by a small number of activists before they became politically correct and shared by most people. The difference now is that the future of our society depends on many people being able to learn about the activities that will become necessary to drive change for a sustainable society to be created. A small number of experts cannot drive the change themselves. People need to get involved in their various roles as voters, consumers, and investors to drive development in different areas forwards.

Despite the difficulty of drawing the relevant conclusions, there are experts and academics who one would assume should have the resources and the motivation to describe the future in a truthful way, but even for these individuals it seems difficult, or well-nigh impossible, to break out of the confines of established thought patterns. Many may perceive that they are restricted by unwritten or, sometimes, written agreements with peers and superiors to adhere to beliefs that they have held for a long time. One example of this may be Professor Thomas B. Johansson, who, together with a team of experts, spent two years from 2011 to 2013 analysing the time frame and cost of transforming Swedish road transportation to systems based on renewable fuels. He and his team analysed the issue, based on the higher cost of the renewable fuels, assuming that the transformation could progress without building up new vehicle fleets and without large investments in infrastructure for charging or for the production and distribution of biofuels. The experts did not include the need to replace Sweden's more than four million cars and 500,000 heavy vehicles with vehicles that can run on the different renewable fuels that were discussed in the analysis, and they did not calculate the cost or time of developing competitive vehicles based on the early and substantially more expensive varieties that were on sale at the time when the study was made.[13] As the focus at the time was firmly on the transformation to biofuels, the team did not spend much effort investigating the opportunities related to electric and hybrid vehicles. Maybe there was nobody present who could make them consider the aspects mentioned, but when the investigation started, I sent an email to Professor Johansson, offering my assistance with analysing the business-related factors and contributing a high-level business perspective to the investigation. I never received a reply. The final report lacked these aspects and did not provide any clear advice to decision makers regarding which decisions needed to be made to drive the development forwards. The sustainability expert Professor Johansson through his report also contributed to the inertia that Greta Thunberg criticizes. If the transformation is described as straightforward, and if it can be achieved at almost no cost to society, why should decision makers and experts learn about it, start to make decisions, and allocate resources on a large scale?

The minister who gave the professor the assignment was Annie Lööf, the Industry Minister at the time. She is the leader of the environmentalist and liberal Centre Party and she wanted an investigation that proved that the transformation of transport systems to sustainability could be achieved before 2030 without significant cost to society. She probably thought she was doing a service to the cause of sustainability by assigning the task of investigating the matter to Professor Johansson, and she probably did not consider the consequences of playing down the time frame and the cost. She may have thought that it would be easier to get the process started if it were described as a simple matter of taxing petrol and diesel and subsidizing renewable fuels, rather than a complex transformation of two sectors of society — the automotive and fuels industries — and a development that also would have to involve the large-scale digitization of the transport sector, in order to efficiently charge vehicles around the clock when spare electricity is available. Most probably she was not aware of the mistake, and Professor Johansson was probably not aware that he did sustainability a great disservice by accepting the assignment, lacking an understanding of the transformation as a whole and the financial and operational aspects of the systems that he was about to investigate. He

---

13 The report by Professor Johansson was published in 2013 as one of the government's public investigations with the number SOU2013:84 with the title in Swedish "Fossilfrihet på väg", which translates to "Fossil Freedom on its Way".

clearly lacked the ambition to leave no stone unturned in the analysis that calmed everybody down who may have believed that the transformation would demand large resources and tough decisions. Now, more than seven years later, Greta Thunberg criticizes politicians for doing too little. Other experts who have misrepresented the complexity and magnitude of the required changes, such as Michael Braungart, have also contributed to playing down the need for resources and decisions by arguing that no political or financing decisions need to be made.

Experts in other fields, such as authors of books about the future, Kevin Kelly, and Youval Noah Harari, and many, many others, have failed to see the inevitable relationship between the different developments. They have failed to see the need to make large investments in the development of new technologies in order to realize their potential, and they have drawn the conclusion that the advancement of digitization and that of new materials and other resources that contribute to economic growth will continue also in the absence of political decisions and strong financing. These experts have simply used their lack of understanding of technology development and social progress to project the present trajectories of development in different areas forwards, seemingly without realizing that the factor that will ultimately determine the future of society is economic growth and investment in the development of new technologies—none of these analysts have included this aspect.

The study of economic growth is the realm of economists, and economic analysis is a complex science that requires specific training and access to data sets that describe relevant aspects of economic progress, such as interest rates, investment, employment rates, and company profits. Most economists who work at banks, government agencies and ministries, and public organizations primarily focus on forecasting the development of the business cycle, short term, and suggest what measures central banks and governments need to take in order to get more people into jobs and maintain a high investment level, without risking that the economy overheats. The long-term development of technologies, the stages of innovation of mature technologies, and the technologies that will succeed them as drivers of economic growth are not things that occupy the thoughts of most present-day economists. After all, the last time that a stagnation or recession was ascribed to the status of technology development was during the "stagflation" period of the 1970s and 1980s. In those days, years were spent by economists and business experts analysing the situation to understand the causes and develop solutions. After almost a decade of stagnating economic growth and high inflation, growth once more increased and inflation went down. This was probably in part due to policies of opening markets and increasing investment by companies that were followed by the maturing of information and communication technologies. It was probably also due to investment in the development of better and more efficient materials and production technologies and principles that have contributed to increasing productivity, and somewhat later to the opening up of previously closed markets in Eastern Europe and Asia that have driven growth to date.

As has been noted above, economic growth is necessary within the confines of the present economic system, and the creation of a new system is a very large undertaking. It would have been necessary to involve both research in business, economics, and heavy political lobbying and debate. In order for this process to even start, politicians and business leaders need to be aware of the precarious situation that present generations have put ourselves in, largely because of the inability of the same categories of decision makers to understand the factors that drive the long-term growth of the economy. To stop economic growth, as sustainability advocates often argue we should, it is not enough for people to become satisfied with what they already have and stop buying goods and services. This would cause a recession and a dramatically reduced standard of living across society and the globe, something that most advocates of a no-growth economy do not seem to anticipate. In order to reduce the need for growth, new mechanisms need to be implemented into the economic system that can keep the economy stable without growth, and the development and implementation of such a system would be a very complex and delicate task.

Complex Systems, Abstract Reasoning

It has taken my entire working life to build up the knowledge and have the experiences that have made it possible for me to write this book and describe the situation and the actions that need to be taken. I started out as a business consultant in 1990 and before that I had registered as a doctoral student with an interest in business strategy, economics, and marketing. As I edit the pages of this book, I see how the literature I have studied can be traced through the pages and the projects I have worked on have made their mark. Reasoning about economic growth requires substantial amounts of knowledge about different aspects of business, politics, economics, and society, and researchers as well as practitioners need the ability for abstract reasoning. Without the relevant knowledge it is difficult to come to correct conclusions. I believe that the ability to follow lines of thought to a large extent depends on experience, and experiences build over long periods of time. In this book, I have not only tried to gather the ideas that will be necessary for future change leaders to use, but also present them in a straightforward way that makes it possible for readers with all kinds of backgrounds to understand them. Most people who have lived a few decades in our modern society have a general understanding of many of the subjects that are brought up in the text—they only have to connect the dots in a way that is different from the way the dots are connected by most present-day politicians and experts. The simple metaphor of the airplane that has to travel to cruising altitude came to me after thinking of many metaphors that did not work as well as this one.

In my case, the first fifteen years of reading books and collecting experiences were random, primarily determined by my activities as a business consultant with a strong interest in economics and technology development. Together with my colleague David Lundberg, I wrote two books about e-business at an early stage of my career (*The Transparent Market*, Palgrave Macmillan 1998, and the Swedish *Den transparenta ekonomin*, SNS Förlag 2000). They were among the first books in the world to analyse the development of e-business from a business strategy perspective. Then, in 2004, I sent the manuscript of my book *The Limits of Business Development and Economic Growth* to the publisher, I googled the title of that book, and found references to books about Peak Oil. It was then that I started to dig into the consequences of Peak Oil and how humanity needs to prepare for the decline in oil production. I interviewed numerous experts on oil production and sustainability. Change leaders need to develop principles for how governments have to prepare for the peak in oil production and explain to decision makers what needs to be done. A number of times during 2019 and 2020 I called up Professor Mikael Höök, the successor of Professor Kjell Aleklett as head of the group of researchers on Peak Oil at Uppsala University, whom I have talked with many times in recent years. The group has access to one of the most extensive databases on oil production in the world and I wanted to update my knowledge about the prospects of oil production in order to present accurate information about it in this book. The discussions with Professor Höök have helped me confirm that my picture of the decline of oil production is correct and he has helped me fill in details that I did not previously know.

The insight into the consequences of Peak Oil goes above and beyond the arguments of Greta Thunberg, although she is making an important effort by making people aware of the lack of action to mitigate climate change. But the peak in oil production, and the subsequent decline, will have an immediate effect on the global economy and the willingness of consumers and investors to continue to consume and invest, while climate change is likely to have more gradual consequences over decades. Peak Oil will not mean that oil production will come to an immediate stand-still, but a decline will from an early point in proceedings lead to shortages of petrol and diesel at petrol stations, and after that the situation will get worse. The coronavirus pandemic and the speeches of Greta Thunberg pave the way for spreading information about challenges other than climate change. Greta and other sustainability experts inform us about one of the challenges that humanity must look forwards to, but someone must fill in the gaps in the picture. The Covid-19 pandemic illustrates weaknesses of present society that few were aware of, and the question is left dangling if there are other weaknesses that governments have not prepared for. People have a right to know. The blind guardians of ignorance are not likely to inform us of the topography of the territories we have learned to not acknowledge the existence of. From the time I started as a doctoral student and a business consultant, I set out to learn about business in order to be able to reveal aspects of the market economy and capitalism that other people are not able to see.

Since I started to study the preparation needs for Peak Oil, I have spent fifteen years investigating the challenges related to financing and organizing the transformation, I have interviewed key people in business and politics, and I have worked to inform politicians, researchers, business leaders, and experts about the need to develop strategies for the transformation. Warning about this has, however, been difficult as I've had to discuss the topic with one decision maker at a time and it has proven difficult to get them to take the message further. It is time for change leaders to step forwards and acknowledge that the challenge of the future is not to understand the facts of climate change, but rather it is about understanding the complex set of threats that humanity will be facing—and the really difficult task will be to develop solutions. Many different solutions will be needed, and they need to be implemented in many different areas to transform production and distribution systems to alternatives that are less dependent on oil and other resources. To prepare for such a large-scale transformation, a change strategy must be developed, and it will become the most important task of change leaders to drive the development of the strategy and the plans that need to be based on it.

What Can We Do About It?

People may discuss whether experts like Professor Johansson or politicians like Annie Lööf (who assigned him the task of analysing the time frame and the cost of transforming transport systems to fossil-free alternatives) are partly responsible for the lack of investment in mitigation efforts that Greta Thunberg criticizes. It may be understandable that people who are unaware of the need to invest heavily in the transformation underestimate the need, like Jeremy Clarkson or Donald Trump, but it is not so easy to understand why people who have dedicated their lives to the promotion of sustainability play down the magnitude of the required investment and argue that the largest transformation the world has experienced can be achieved over the course of a few years and at almost no cost to society. As the change leaders of the near future arrive at increasingly accurate estimates of the investment and resource needs it is likely that many will express strong opinions and try to shift the blame to particular groups and decision makers, in a way similar to how Greta Thunberg blames politicians for having stolen the future of the children of today. Instead of blaming decision makers and experts who, because of a lack of insight, narrow political or financial incentives, or a lack of pressure from peers, expect analyses and reports to be in line with the views of supporters, we may consider what change leaders can do to start the development that Greta Thunberg and her allies advocate.

Because of the complex set of challenges that humanity is facing, and the very large investment that will be needed to go through with the transformation to sustainable and carbon neutral production and distribution systems by 2050, governments cannot only focus, for example, on banning coal-fired power plants and petroleum fuelled cars and trucks. A wide range of activities will need to be undertaken to reduce the dependence on resources, because the replacement of carbon-based power production and petroleum-based transportation will not be a swift or cost-neutral affair. The types of activities that make up the backbone of the tool-chest of sustainability experts are small-scale activities that have little or no impact on emissions, because it is not until systems become developed to a large scale that they become cost effective, and there are currently no strategies for large-scale expansion. The global dependence on oil and other resources will have to be reduced substantially in just the next few years. This will have to be done regardless of whether countries experience a shortage of resources in this precise period. Countries will not be able to reduce dependence on resources rapidly enough after the peak in oil production, so it is necessary, even though perhaps counter-intuitive to many, to start to reduce resource dependence ahead of the beginning of the decline. As most of us, people in general, and virtually all sustainability experts are blind to the magnitude of the transformation and thus feel no intuitive fear of resource shortages in the near future, people cannot build up the urgency to act. Experts and politicians have told us to fear climate change, a problem that may not be caused by emissions of carbon dioxide, but many have accepted this as a fact.[14] At the same time, most people do not fear a reduction in oil production, because this issue has not been widely debated in the last decade, despite the fact that this is likely to be a larger and more immediate problem for humanity to deal with.

Replacing coal-fired power production with wind and solar power will involve extremely large investment, and at the same time developing the technologies, products, and systems that will be needed in order to transform transportation will involve investment of a similar magnitude. Coal-fired power plants account for 38 per cent of the global production of electricity and the number of coal-fired plants is growing every year. The installed base of capacity was, in 2018, 2 TW of effect. There is no sign that coal is about to be replaced by renewable fuels on a global level and there is no strategy in place for how this can be done on a large scale or in a short space of time. The power infrastructure consists of very large investments in all countries, and power plants are expected to be used for fifty years or more. Global car fleets are made up of 1.2 billion cars and fleets of heavy vehicles amount to some 100 million units. At present there are less than 6 million electric and hybrid cars and a similar share of heavy vehicles that can run on electricity, and there are no systems for heavy long-distance transportation that are starting to become competitive and ready to be implemented. The efforts that will be needed to go through with these transformations will be more demanding in terms of resources and manpower than the Apollo Programme. If the transformation is going

---

14 In their book *The Chilling Stars* climate physicist Henrik Svensmark and science writer Nigel Calder argue that the sun and cosmic phenomena have a stronger impact on the climate on our planet than carbon dioxide emissions and they support their argument with diagrams and facts about the climate over the past millions of years.

to succeed, European countries with a high level of awareness of the problems as they have been described up until now and a high level of support for political measures will have to march in front of other countries and show how the lofty goals are going to be achieved, but there is no insight into the complexity of these changes. The reliance on global supply chains in virtually all industries is a major source of resource consumption and emissions of carbon dioxide. The development of a carbon-neutral society has to involve less global transportation, and this is definitely a requirement if countries want to mitigate the peak in oil production — but decision makers and people in general are conveniently blind to the issues that need to be dealt with, just as they were blind to the need to build resources in preparation for a pandemic. All examples of companies that are developing circular business models represent exceptions from the standard that is set by the majority of companies that do business according to the principles of the linear economy in which supply chains span the globe and resources are used once and then discarded as waste.

The first step in the change that Greta is proposing, and that the EU now has decided to go through with before 2050, will have to be the development of a strategy. Most people must participate and contribute to the transformation, but not in a random way. Change leaders in all developed countries need to create strategies that will have to be communicated and understood by all who want to take a role in the revolution. For the process to work the leaders of change in each country need to coordinate the activities included in their strategies with those of the change leaders in other countries. This will be necessary because similar activities will have to be undertaken in all countries and thus countries need to learn from each other and avoid duplication of development activities. Solutions developed in one country need to be used and improved in other countries as well. In addition to the changes that need to be made to production and distribution systems, the economy needs to be changed as well to become less dependent on economic growth.

All need to participate, but the UN, the EU, and national governments need to take the lead. They need to form the transformation programmes and appoint change leaders on a national level. National governments will also need to finance most of the overall management and many of the activities of the transformation. A few national change leaders in each country will, however, not suffice. There will be a need for change leaders in companies and in regions and municipalities who all understand the logic and overall direction of the change. The present market-based or haphazard approach will never build the critical mass of activity and competence in any sector that will be necessary to succeed with the transformation. At early stages of a development, there are not enough customers that are prepared to pay the high prices of products and services to create the possibility of using the market to fund advancement and make the necessary choices. In these situations, market-based development is a wasteful use of resources, because many innovations are run in parallel and some of these, like the ongoing advancement of hydrogen fuelled transportation (that attracts large sums of financing every year), do not have the potential of ever becoming competitive.[15]

Through most of history, development has been going on in areas where there have not been any existing technologies that people have been used to. Most new technologies have presented solutions to problems that have previously had no solution and they have thus offered new value. The challenge of implementing new technologies and systems in areas where there are already incumbent ones in widespread use is much tougher and more demanding of resources, since the new technologies need to be subsidized or very heavily promoted to become competitive against existing alternatives. This difference between the present challenges and actual implementation of new technologies has not been observed by the blind proponents of market-based change measures.

Why Has Nobody Told Us?

The picture of the future that emerges on these pages is different from the one that is communicated through the media and by experts and politicians. Could this much more challenging picture be realistic and why has it not reached the public earlier?

---

[15] Many large companies and respected research organizations are running projects to develop hydrogen-based transportation, although hydrogen has a number of critical disadvantages (compared to battery electric vehicles) that cannot be surmounted by the improvement of fuel cells or vehicles. The disadvantages are built into the laws of physics and economics, and are related to, for example, the fact that three times as much electricity is required to produce the hydrogen to drive one kilometre as the amount of electricity that is needed to drive an electric car the same distance, and to the fact that we already have the infrastructure in place for the large-scale production and distribution of power, but there is no infrastructure in place for the large-scale production and distribution of hydrogen. The matter will be further discussed later in the text.

For fifteen years I have tried to communicate the picture to experts and decision makers, most of them with technical backgrounds, backgrounds in politics, or with many years' experience in sustainability, and I have often managed to create some interest, but the people I have contacted have seldom come back to learn more, and the dialogues that have been initiated through my first visits or phone calls have been cut short. At the outset I thought that it would be easy to convince people of the relevance of the analysis, build strong support, and start to persuade governments and the EU that the transformation needs to be run in a different fashion compared to how it is done at present. It turned out that it was not that easy, and I started to wonder why this could be. After all, the story I am putting forwards is supported by strong evidence that is publicly available and it requires only common sense to understand its relevance. Something to that effect was expressed by the Swedish MP, Krister Örnfjäder, the energy expert of the Social Democratic Party, to whom I in 2011 presented the ideas and conclusions regarding the need to start a large-scale transformation of transport systems. After my presentation, Mr Örnfjäder responded that the issue was not political, but that it was a matter of common sense to tackle it with determination. At the time, his party was in opposition and it was easy to convince him of the relevance. He offered to join forces and write a motion to the parliament, which we did,[16] and his party, now in office with Prime Minister Stefan Löfvén as head of government, has since then treated the matter as a political issue. Even the green parties who proclaim that society needs to transform to sustainable transportation and production seem unable to grasp the magnitude of the transformation they propose. From a sustainability perspective, it is easy to grasp the relevance of the issue, and the success of Greta Thunberg in promoting her idea that more needs to be done illustrates this, but it becomes a difficult subject once the amount of investment that is needed is considered. It is possible for governments to allocate insignificant amounts of money to the transformation but investing the money that will be required seems impossible. If governments in the nineteenth and early twentieth century had done the same with sewage systems, railways, telephone systems, and power grids we would not have had the society that we have at present.

---

[16] The motion has the number 2012:13 N351 and the title in Swedish is *Storskalig energiomställning*, which in English translates to *Large-scale Energy Transformation*.

Investment in these systems was not dimensioned based on what governments thought they could afford without unduly stretching the budgets of their countries. They first assigned experts to analyse the investment required and then sought for ways to finance the ventures. In these cases, it took decades until the investment started to turn a profit, but it was necessary for the development and national security of countries.

The heads of state who meet with Greta Thunberg may score some extra points with voters, but the leaders who have met her have not yet mentioned how many additional billions of euro their governments will invest in the transformation. Needless to say, it is in the interest of all people on the planet that we succeed with the task of transforming production and distribution to sustainable solutions, but the reasons for this are not only the ones related to environmental sustainability that are put forward by Greta Thunberg. Especially the people who are active in the sustainability sector, of whom I have approached a number, should, presumably, embrace the information that there is an approach that will be more likely to lead to progress and success than the one that is employed at present.

The defences of the blind guardians of ignorance must be broken down. Greta Thunberg and other sustainability experts have started to demolish the barricades against the transformation and build support for the idea that the world can be transformed to sustainability, but they are impervious to the information about the magnitude of the task. Experts who are aware of the enormity of the task need to continue to hammer this message into the fabric of society, because it is possible to do many more things in order to develop solutions other than the ones that spring to mind in a locked-down situation – like a political debate or an analysis. This has been shown by how governments have succeeded to get hold of medical supplies and equipment and how countries have scrambled to build production resources for some types of supplies during the coronavirus pandemic.

Most people are not aware of any need to transform society to sustainability or adapt lifestyles to accommodate a more frugal supply of resources. This silent majority can look to very vocal advocates of a *business-as-usual-approach* to life, the universe, and everything. In his column in *The Sun* of the 27th of September 2019, television presenter Jeremy Clarkson wrote about Greta Thunberg: "WHEN a teenage girl has an angry, tearful strop, most parents just send them to their rooms until they've calmed down." He is not the only celebrity who has reacted negatively to Greta's message, and the derogatory comments illustrate the amount of information that will become necessary in order to convince the doubters of the need to change.

As I have tried to understand why it has been so difficult to achieve results, I have developed explanations as to why it seems almost impossible for decision makers and experts to embrace the ideas related to large-scale change:

- Suggesting that billions, in large countries trillions, of euro should be invested in transforming society to become less dependent on oil and other resources may be necessary, but it will almost certainly alienate many voters short term, because they, like Jeremy Clarkson and many others, have not started to take in the facts related to the transformation. If opposition parties do not support the idea, the party in office may lose in the next election. It will be the task of change leaders to convince increasing numbers of people of the fact that the transformation will be necessary, and that the magnitude of investment will be very large.

- The argument seems simple, but it is quite complex. Greta Thunberg summarizes some of the background and emphasizes the fact that more needs to be done, but she says very little about what activities need to be started and how the transformation needs to be organized and financed. It has taken me fifteen years to build knowledge in these areas so that I can satisfactorily explain the precarious nature of the situation and why it is unlikely that market forces will drive development. To explain this, change leaders need some understanding of innovation and the way new technologies penetrate markets, they need to grasp the power of the market and its limitations as a tool for driving transformation, the status of development of electric and hybrid cars, and the systems contained under the umbrella of the circular economy, the financial consequences of a decline in oil production, and the effects that this is likely to have on affluence and the ability to provide food and other necessities to people in countries where oil is likely to become scarce (this is likely to happen to many countries in Europe over the next decade), not to mention some of the most important consequences. When a person who has access to the necessary information describes the relevant points, most listeners understand most of it, but they do not seem to understand how vulnerable the systems in society are to economic shocks caused by resource shortfalls. Another thing that seems to be difficult to intuitively understand is that all persons in developed countries will be affected by a decline in oil production. This is probably due to the overly simplified visions of the power of the market that have been communicated. It may be hard to accept that the experts could mostly be wrong, but few of them understand the complete picture and resort to projecting the trends of the near past into the future and turn a blind eye to the fact that development in past centuries has seldom followed the same path for very long. Now that the coronavirus pandemic has broken the trends of the past it should become easier for people to understand that other shocks can create similar problems in the future.

- There are few short-term incentives that support the spreading of the overall picture. Even if everybody on the planet, in principle, has an incentive to get the transformation started in the right direction, few can change their lives short term and make a living within the circular economy or by promoting electric mobility. Short term, many people will have to admit that they, in their own minds, publicly, or among friends, have simplified the process of transformation, not just a little. Many will need to admit that they have contributed to spreading information that is largely misleading and that they, perhaps for a decade or more, have assisted in hindering progress by downplaying the complexity and underestimating the amount of resources that will be needed in order to drive transformation at a faster pace. As the correct information starts to spread, more will contribute to leading the change and, in various situations, take on the role of change leader. Many companies also face an uncertain future in a situation of declining oil production and large-scale transformation efforts are likely to present a challenge, rather than an opportunity, even to companies in the automotive industry that are heavily reliant on sales of petrol and diesel vehicles.

- People like to cling to the strands of hope that they can find. It has been very difficult to build political and popular support for the transformation. How difficult will it then be to generate support for investing ten, twenty, or fifty times more in implementing e-mobility and the circular economy? When people receive the information, at first it may sound reasonable to bring it forwards and try to engage more people in the pursuit of a transformation programme that may have a chance of success, but afterwards, when people discuss with their peers, it is likely that many people, at least for the time being, revert to their former beliefs and arguments that they have held and expressed for a long time. This will not only be because it will feel uncomfortable to argue in favour of exorbitant investment, but also because it will be challenging for many to keep the relevant facts in mind. It will be difficult for many at first to describe the challenges to others in a way that does not attract unwarranted criticism or confusion.

In a transformation programme, the experiences from large-scale change programmes in large companies need to be taken seriously, and the principles and methods that are included in the discipline of change management need to be used. More about this later.

Chapter Three

A Naïve Image
of Society

The early twentieth-century painter Henri Rousseau depicted nature, humans, and the built environment using naïve imagery. His paintings lack perspective, they often depict dreamy images and human figures without realistic features.

In a similar manner, present-day media and literature provide images of society and the economy that are naïve and that are not built on an understanding of how the world works. People are given the image of a very simple financial and economic system where successful people are able to lead lives that ordinary people can only aspire to, and the majority of individuals can with awe and envy imagine how they themselves, as generation after generation improve the affluence of modern society, get to share more of the spoils of successful life-styles. Even politicians, who are supposed to work to create the future, subscribe to these naïve and highly simplified descriptions of the world, and so do experts in many fields of technology, who predict existing technical trends to continue into the future. These images do not reflect how society really works, and planning the future based on politically correct, but factually incorrect, assumptions about reality is bound to be disastrous. People may think that the warnings about the future are exaggerated and that everything is bound to work out in the end, but the present situation related to the coronavirus pandemic and the need to transform society to sustainability is not similar to previous ones. Humanity has never been up against challenges of the present size, and this statement is easy to verify using publicly available data.

To the people who view the works of Henri Rousseau, it is immediately obvious that the painter is not attempting to paint a realistic picture of reality. The same, however, does not seem to be true of the majority of people in contemporary society, who take in the images of successful lifestyles that are provided by the media. People do not seem to realize that the development towards increasing affluence cannot continue in a world where everybody will have to cut down on consumption. If the amount of oil produced ten years into the decline in oil production amounts to only 70 to 80 per cent of present volumes, small-scale change will not be sufficient. It is also likely that the downturn is going to continue so that 20 years after the start of the downturn volumes will have reduced even more. The difficulty of grasping these relatively straightforward aspects of the future may be due to the fact that there are few images that balance the pictures provided in the media and literature that depict success as the ability to use increasing amounts of resources—and failure as that of a lifestyle where people have little ability to travel and live lives of less opulence and wealth. It is difficult to see that the visions of the future that are communicated by the media are irrelevant and naïve and that expectations for the future need to be revised.

An example that illustrates how difficult it sometimes is to adjust expectations for the future can be taken from the reactions of some of the tourists that went from Sweden to Rhodes on the first trip when Greece once more opened up to receive visitors from other countries at the beginning of July of 2020.[1] In articles in major newspapers, tourists complained that they were served by personnel with face masks and that the buffets of the hotels that offer all-inclusive packages were gone. Instead they were served their plates by waiters behind plastic shields. The tourists seem to have believed that everything would be the same and that the service at hotels would not be affected by the experiences of the pandemic. Many were appalled when they found that shops outside the hotels were closed and that employees at the hotels were taking precautions to avoid becoming infected. These experiences illustrate how difficult it often is to adjust expectations and understand that everything will not remain the same after a major change. Many tourists argued that the travel companies should have informed them that the service at the destinations would not be exactly the same as they had become used to during previous holidays.

In the same way, citizens are likely to be very surprised after the peak in oil production and wonder why nobody informed them of the fact that a reduction in oil production would affect the affluence of

---

[1]   This example was related in the newspaper *Aftonbladet* on the 4th of July 2020 in an article titled "Kändes som om vi kom till en spökstad". The English translation: it felt as if we came to a ghost town.

countries and the transformation to sustainability would have to involve very large investment that has to be paid by taxpayers, consumers, and investors all over the world.

In modern film and literature, as well as in newspaper articles and television productions, lifestyles of people who live frugal lives and use few resources are seldom depicted, and nowhere in literature or in science are there any fully fledged ideas as to how humanity could organize entire societies that use substantially fewer resources than people do in our present society. Change cannot be confined only to small superficial adaptations of the lifestyles of recent decades. Modern society generates resource consumption through all activities. Even the simple decisions made by many to take a picture using the camera in their mobile phone and save it on a server generates volumes of information that are multiplying at an alarming rate. A simple act like taking an increasing number of digital pictures increases the need for servers and energy to run the increasing number of computer centres that are needed across the world. Walking with a mobile phone in one's pocket constantly generates information about the position of the phone and its bearer that will be stored for a long time in the computers of telecom operators.

Even though many people are aware that society as a whole has to cut down substantially on the use of resources, little attention is paid to how this could be achieved on a large scale. There are numerous small-scale experimental cities, like that of Masdar in Abu Dhabi, and there are theories that are being developed of Stable State Economies, like the ones developed by Professor Herman Daly of University of Maryland,[2] but no attempts can be found to develop a viable way of transforming the entire global economy to a sustainable system. There are at present seven billion people on earth, but nobody seems to have any idea as to how we could create a viable way for the entire global population to move forwards into the future, and few seem to be aware of the need. Instead, most seem to take it for granted that we can continue with our present lifestyles and make current society sustainable within a few decades. In the present climate of unquestioning acceptance of the naïve image of society that is relayed by politicians, researchers, the media, and people in general, it has become impossible to ask questions

---

[2] Professor Daly presents his ideas in the book *Beyond Growth* from 1996. Now, almost a quarter of a century later, the ideas have not been widely discussed in the public debate and have not been tested in large-scale experiments.

about how the image can be sustained in a situation of decreasing oil production. The naïve picture becomes unquestionable as intelligent individuals refuse to see the reality behind the Potemkin village.

One reason behind the blindness to the challenges is likely to be the fact that most people lack even basic knowledge about business and economics, and very few have the knowledge necessary to understand the global economy and identify the risks that are building up as people ignore the landscape of the unobserved territories. The lack of knowledge among most people about business and economics means that few have an intuitive ability to see through the naïve illusion. Most subjects are taught from an early age at school and pupils arrive at a relatively sound understanding of, for example, physics or biology. The relatively high level of knowledge makes it impossible to report naïvely on these subjects in the media. In many areas, knowledge is seen as an important aspect of being well educated and learned. People want to be around persons who can quote Shakespeare, Oscar Wilde, Goethe, or other great playwrights, poets, and authors, and knowledge about politics and human rights issues is appreciated in a similar way. But few have a similar grasp of business and economics, despite the fact that business and economic processes are responsible for creating the wealth that we all enjoy and that will be crucial to taking our society into the future. Television shows about animals or natural phenomena need to build on what people know to be true, and there is no opportunity for physicists or biologists to provide descriptions that are not based on fact. Scientists popularize their subjects and demonstrate their superior knowledge by, in an accessible way, telling the almost unbelievable truths about quantum physics or the human cell that scientists have discovered in past decades, without losing track of the big picture. In the case of the processes related to business and economic growth, the subjects are often vastly simplified, probably for political reasons, and important aspects are forgotten or deliberately omitted. The result is often a greatly distorted picture of reality. The examples of successful business development that many have heard about and can relate to are the success stories of Apple, Microsoft, or Google, and many build an overly simplified understanding on such examples and believe that these stories represent normal instances of business and technology development.

While it would not be conceivable to get people to believe that it may be possible to defy gravity, it is possible to convince people that all countries on the face of the earth can continue to grow their economies to the level of the most affluent countries without causing resource shortfalls. It is also possible to get intelligent people to argue that transport systems consisting of more than one billion cars and 100 million heavy vehicles will be transformed to sustainability as soon as oil prices reach a high enough level. People with no training in business or economics and who have never worked in areas related to these subjects may argue that it is achievable to transform the global economy to circularity and use and reuse resources in never-ending cycles in only one or two decades. Experts without any background in business or economics and people who have no experience from change management or large-scale business transformation may argue that the change towards sustainability is well underway and that it is only a matter of a few years until all production of the most necessary products has become local. Anyone who tries to see through the naïve forecasts of the future is likely to discover that there is little substance behind the projections. A more plausible scenario involves decades of development of new business concepts and technology solutions from the present level, and billions of euro in investment to develop all components and build the new systems. They are also likely to find that there are important risks that threaten progress and the entire edifice of modern society.

Understanding the fundamentals related to the large-scale transformation that must take place is not extremely complicated. People need to take in facts that are seldom collected in one book or on one website.[3] But few people have an incentive to do this, and many even have an incentive to reject attempts to paint a realistic picture of the future. The reason for this is to a large extent political. Political groups and parties have built their platforms of voters on ideologies that make it possible to only take into account some aspects of society and the economy and they thus assign insignificant roles to the areas that do not fit their ideologies.

Ideological Perspectives

When people look at society from an ideological perspective, the picture often becomes naïve. The ideology that, since the fall of the Iron Curtain, is the leading ideology in the world is often called liberalism, or capitalism. This philosophy is based on the idea that the market is

---

[3]   In my previous book, *Redrawing the Map of the Future – Digitisation, Artificial Intelligence, Industry 4.0, E-mobility, and the Circular Economy*, I presented a number of important facts.

the best tool for allocating resources. The market allocates resources to the most competitive offerings, and less competitive offerings are left to perish or they have to be improved so that they become competitive. Companies that offer the most competitive products grow and those with less competitive ones decline in terms of turnover and they will be forced to lay off personnel and ultimately go out of business.

One alternative view is socialism, which says that governments should manage the development of society by planning the economy, deciding how much should be invested in different areas. Few openly support these ideas, as it has arguably been proven through the failure of the Soviet Union and the former Eastern Bloc that the market is the superior tool for allocating resources in an economy. People who support a left-wing agenda may want more equality and they may want to reduce the wealth and influence of the richest and most influential people on the planet, but the argument that this should be achieved through a planned economy is seldom put forward.

When only products and services in mature industries are taken into account, the principle is impossible to contradict. The market is clearly the superior tool for resource allocation in mature industries. Who would like to eat more expensive and less tasty food or buy less comfortable or less fashionable clothes because politicians have decided that the shops should only carry these less competitive items? Similarly, few people would think it would be a good idea if politicians determined how many cars of a certain brand should be manufactured or how many shoes of a certain size should be available. Clearly, the market is a tool that makes it possible to allow the needs of buyers to determine what and how much is produced.

One aspect of the naïve worldview that is communicated in the media is the carefree lifestyles and consumption habits of virtually every character and person that is depicted on TV shows and on film. These images mimic the carefree lifestyles that most of the world's population aspire to, and characters with lifestyles that counterbalance this view are seldom presented. Environmentalists may be depicted as quaint side characters that mirror the success and affluence of the mainstream main characters. The message that is built into almost every show and most films, with very few exceptions, is that a successful lifestyles involve the unrestrained consumption of the world's resources.

It is usually an implicit assumption among politicians and businesspersons that the market will automatically and in no time drive the development of new fuels, transport systems, and new materials as soon as the resources that are used at present start to become scarce and more expensive. The carefree lifestyles of the successful seem to be based on the conviction that the market is not only the most efficient tool for allocating resources, but the market is also by many believed to have the power to create new resources that can be sold at the same price as presently existing alternatives, if only a pressing enough need arises. The pressing need is signalled through increasing price levels that immediately generate a response in the form of the development and rapidly increasing growth of alternatives. I have understood through discussions that many people believe that new transport systems will rapidly grow and replace the present ones, when the oil price increases to high enough levels, but it is never specified what "high enough" means in this context. The speed of the transformation, however, is limited by the capacity to make batteries and this is growing slowly over decades, rather than rapidly over months or quarters. There are visions of electric road systems, but no plans to start their construction, and at least one large-scale venture to build a network for long-distance transportation, that of Better Place, has gone bankrupt and lost 850 million dollars of investment.

The belief that new systems will be automatically developed in no time at all is, however, unfounded, one that is not only wrong, but also very dangerous. It teaches people to relax and remain passive, even as humanity faces the risk that our most important resources are about to become scarce. During the coronavirus crisis people have experienced the risk of leaving preparations for pandemics to the market, and we have seen the consequences when it turns out that the market has not been able to organize any meaningful preparations. It is a very sad experience to find this out in hindsight when it is too late to change anything. More people could have been saved in the coronavirus emergency if governments had prepared and built stocks of the most critical supplies and other resources that are necessary to meet the challenge of a pandemic.

The naïve approach to development is implicit in virtually all communication, primarily through the absence of a sign of an awareness of the challenging times that are approaching, but also through the values that are communicated. The glorification of consumption is probably the most apparent. People are not likely to recognize that consumption has been glorified, as most of us have become so accustomed to our present lifestyles that most are unable to realize that we must change. It may seem more attractive, less problematic, and not entirely unrealistic to aspire towards the lifestyles of the rich and famous, as they are depicted by television shows like Top Gear and other shows that take the values of the twentieth century to an extreme. The fact that many experts argue that to maintain present-day consumption patterns it would require the resource equivalents of four earths does not seem relevant as there are seemingly knowledgeable individuals who argue that change will happen automatically as soon as the prices of resources increase to higher levels. A true description of what the market does is that it only determines a market price and keeps the market in balance. When a resource becomes scarce, the price increases, but the market can never make sure that there will be new inexpensive resources available that can perform the same function, only because humanity has used up one cheap resource in an irresponsible way.

It is not without regret that I write these lines. It would have been so much easier for all individuals if unlimited reserves of resources had been available, and it would have been much easier if the transformation of society to more resource-efficient habits were started earlier, or at least if the increase in resource consumption had stopped at an earlier point altogether. But this would have required insight among large numbers of people, not only into the problem, but also it would have required an understanding of the possible solutions. The development of this insight has been made impossible by the guardians of ignorance. People's adherence to a naïve image of reality has almost turned the belief into a religion that cannot be questioned. It is fair to say that the solutions that will become necessary in order to achieve a reduction in resource consumption have in many cases not been developed yet, and most have not been advanced to the point where they are ready to replace existing fuels and production and distribution systems. The recycling of small amounts of plastics and other materials or the implementation of electric and hybrid vehicles on a small scale has not stopped the growth in the use of oil or in the products that are made from oil, and the time when consumption may start to decrease still cannot be seen on the horizon, despite the fact that the International Energy Agency and other independent forecasters warn that oil production is likely to start to decline as soon as the next few years. The coronavirus situation changes all this as it has become increasingly apparent that people need to change their lifestyles and countries need to reverse aspects of the development that has been going on in recent decades and become more resilient.

A Battle of Ideas and of Knowledge

Covid-19 has also provided the important lesson to mankind that we cannot choose our lifestyles and decide ourselves when we want to change. The development of society can be described as a battle of ideas where parties with different ideologies have fought for power in the parliaments of different countries. Some ideas have been shared by all, but other ideas have been discussed and voted on. Democracy is an idea that is shared by most people and that is seldom the subject of public debate. Everyone seems to agree that democracy is a necessary building block of a modern society. Ideologies like liberalism, socialism, and environmentalism are philosophies that are debated to determine which parties will be allowed to govern countries. The belief in democracy is well-founded. The alternative would be totalitarian regimes where citizens would have little power over their own lives and would not be allowed to express their ideas, and where the opportunity to discuss ideas and vote for the politicians that are favoured by each voter do not exist. The market ideology is on its way to acquire a similar position as democracy, but for less obvious reasons. The market has many advantages, but in a well-functioning and progressive society it must be complemented by collective action. Without long-range and large-scale government investment, adapted to the needs of the situation, the world would not have had access to the multitude of well-developed technologies that it has, that have in their early phases been financed through public investment.

One problem with democracy is that it must be developed on a foundation of knowledgeable individuals who understand the consequences of their choices, as voters, but also as consumers, investors, and in other roles in society. Resigning the power over the development of society to the impersonal forces of the market, with the price mechanism and the drive to reduce cost as the most prominent features, may seem to work for some time, but there will be a point when it becomes apparent that citizens need to make conscious choices and decide which type of society they want. Since the end of the Cold War it has seemed like a good idea to reduce emergency supplies and nothing bad has happened because of this, but then the coronavirus pandemic strikes and it becomes obvious that it was not such a good idea after all. In the same way, people do not see a problem with having only a small fraction of cars, trucks, and buses with electric drive, but when the decline in oil production sets in it will become clear that delaying the transformation has built up an enormous risk. Global and national vehicle fleets cannot be transformed in a few years once oil prices start to increase. People may react with surprise, arguing that they could not have known—petrol and diesel vehicles were the most competitive alternatives—but that will not help. In the same way, nobody could be expected to understand that it may not be such a good idea after all to increase global dependence on production in far-away countries and rely on long-distance transportation in a world where all intelligent individuals know that oil is a finite resource. It is only through the active interest of experts, decision makers, and members of the public that the transformation can be made to take off. Different groups in society need to build knowledge about the new transport systems and elections need to constitute battles between different concrete ideas of how countries can approach the transformation to sustainability. The advantages of liberalism are well known, but the limits of such a system have not been widely discussed. Instead, politicians and experts in various fields have turned people's attention away from discussing the limitations of the market, while at the same time deciding about the initiation of a large-scale change programme to make Europe carbon-neutral by 2050.

From now on, the individuals who possess the knowledge of what the emerging situation with scarce resources will mean for modern society and how it can be dealt with need to convince people with other ideologies that activities to transform society to sustainability and resilience need to be prioritized. The importance to all oil importing countries, and many exporting countries as well, of reducing the dependence on oil is becoming less of an ideological tenet and more of a statement of fact, but the knowledge about oil, energy, and the interest in these areas are not widespread enough to attract the attention of large swathes of the public. The opportunity to continue to increase consumption and investment over the long term is becoming increasingly hypothetical, and the realization that humanity needs to dramatically reduce the consumption of oil for different purposes needs to permeate society to a much higher degree than at present. The change leaders of the future need to discard the naïve images that have become the lore of present society and build knowledge about the actual situation and the actual transformation needs. Reducing resource consumption represents a part of making society more resilient. People need to understand how resilience can be strengthened and how governments can contribute to developing a sustainable society.

As mentioned above, the understanding of how decision makers need to work to reduce the dependence is at present vague. This is probably to a large extent due to the lack of understanding of the magnitude of oil production and the facts that surround the replacement of oil. Some of these facts include:

- Global oil production amounts to 100 million barrels of oil per day,[4] more than 1,000 barrels per second. This translates to more than two litres of oil per person in the world every day. In western countries the usage amounts to some five litres of oil per person and day.
- If all barrels of oil were stacked on top of each other it would take less than five days for the stack to reach the moon. It took slightly more than four days for the crew of Apollo 11 to go to the moon.
- The amount of oil used every year is so vast that electricity is the only new fuel that can replace oil. If all agricultural land on the planet was used in order to produce biofuels, the entire volume produced would only cover 25 per cent of the oil that is used at present, and there would be no grain left to eat.
- There are 1.2 billion cars in the world and at present less than 6 million of those are electric and hybrid vehicles. The number increases by slightly more than 2 million per year, which means that, at the present rate, it would take 500 years to replace the entire global fleet of cars.
- An electric or hybrid car is about 10,000 euro more expensive compared to an equivalent petrol or diesel car.
- There is no competitive system solution for electric heavy transportation that can be implemented in the next few years.

The above points are examples of facts about the transformation of transport systems that are not well known even by decision makers and experts. Most people who work with electric mobility seem to believe that the transformation can happen in only a few years now that there are many models of electric and hybrid cars on the market. This, however, is not realistic, and more individuals need to turn their attention to the transformation of transport systems to electric mobility and companies need to develop cost effective vehicles and transport systems that can take over large volumes of transportation when oil

---

[4] According to www.statista.com the daily global oil demand in 2019 amounted to 100.1 million barrels per day.

production starts to decline. In the case of petrol and diesel cars, automotive companies can rapidly ramp up production when the demand for a model increases, but in the case of electric cars and trucks production is limited by the manufacture of batteries and this increases very slowly, because of the very large investment that is required in battery production plants. The battery plants that are planned will increase the capacity to some seven million cars per year by 2030, but more investment will be necessary to increase capacity above this. Batteries will also be in demand for buses, trucks, and for stationary battery facilities that may be built to store power that is produced through intermittent energy sources, such as wind and solar. The batteries that are used at present are made from lithium, a mineral that is abundant in the earth's crust, but there are few places where the concentration is high enough for mining to be profitable at present and some experts fear that lithium will become a bottle-neck for the expansion of e-mobility.

Some readers are at this point likely to remark that large batteries will not be needed for very long as there are plans to build electric highways, where vehicles are charged inductively by electric rails in road surfaces or via pantographs that take electricity from power lines above vehicles. While these ideas exist, the investment will be very large and the only reasonable way of financing it is likely to be via public–private partnerships or other similar solutions that involve the large-scale and long-term co-financing by governments. If it should be taken on by private investors, the development of electric roads will be a high-risk endeavour requiring billions of euro in investment over coming decades, an effort comparable to the construction of railways in the nineteenth century, when these technologies were new and expensive. As mentioned previously, the American-financed company Better Place declared bankruptcy in 2013 after having attracted investment of 850 million dollars for the development of a global business for the expansion of e-mobility based on building networks of battery switching stations. At the time, the capacity of batteries limited the range of electric cars to about 100 kilometres and there was one model of car, the Renault Fluence, that had a hatch at the bottom that made battery switching possible. Better Place had launched its offering in two pilot markets—Denmark and Israel—and built 19 switching stations in Denmark. Customers of Better Place could, on longer trips, switch batteries at the stations, each switch taking about five minutes.

This is most likely not the last large bankruptcy that will occur as innovative companies experiment with e-mobility technologies and business models. For every successful venture there are normally hundreds of failures of companies that tried approaches that did not work. Under normal circumstances this experimentation is not a problem, because most companies fail at an early stage, before hundreds of millions of euro or dollars have been invested. But, in a situation where the world rapidly needs to transform production and distribution systems to sustainable alternatives, failures need to be minimized in order to lose as little time and as few resources as possible. The only players in an economy that can both invest large amounts of money and at the same time reduce risk are governments, as they have the ability to decide about standards of technology and develop business without the need to turn a profit short term. The investment of 850 million dollars is small compared to the amount that will be necessary to electrify road networks in entire countries. In the case of Sweden, unofficial estimates indicate that the price tag for this development would amount to a similar cost as that of building a new high-speed train network, some 25 billion euro. This, however, would not include investment in expanding power production and distribution, or the investment in the development of the vehicles that will be necessary for the transportation. Financing in other countries would be different, depending on the status and structure of their power grids.

Competition between Technologies

The truth is that the transformation is progressing at some speed in only a few countries and that, in all countries, there are significant obstacles to overcome to rapidly increase the sales of electric cars and light transport vehicles. A general obstacle is the comparatively high price of electric cars, which requires large subsidies for them to become competitive. In the countries that have the highest sales figures for electric vehicles, the government offers significant subsidies to offset the high price. Norway has high taxes on petrol and diesel cars, while electric cars are tax free, and there are a number of further advantages for electric vehicles, for example free parking, free trips on ferries that cross fjords along the coast, and access to bus lanes into Oslo and other big cities. The opportunity to buy electric cars without tax means that even a Tesla may, in some cases, be less expensive to buy than a petrol or diesel car, such as a Golf, and this — in combination with the fact that electric cars have been marketed in Norway since the Olympic Games in Lillehammer in 1994 when the Norwegian electric car Think was launched — has brought the figures for electric cars to half of all car sales. Norway is still a country with substantial oil production and only five million inhabitants. The substantial income from oil, which has increased in the past decade as the price of oil has increased, despite declining production volumes, allows the Norwegian government to invest large amounts of money in the transformation of the nation's transportation to electric mobility. In Sweden, the government in 2018 increased the subsidy for electric cars from 4,000 to 6,000 euro, which caused an increase in the sale of electric cars to 8 per cent of total car sales. In Sweden there are no other advantages of driving an electric car and the range of most electric cars on one charging is lower than 450 kilometres — and for the more affordable models, like the Renault Zoey, the range is lower than 350 kilometres. Sweden does not have the significant income from oil production that Norway has, but the country has a strong tradition as a leader in technology development, the automotive industry is strong and innovative with companies like Volvo Car, Scania, and AB Volvo (trucks, buses, and construction equipment), and there is a large number of people with sustainability focus in Swedish politics and in the public sector, plus a strong demand from green parties that the government invests in reducing Sweden's dependence on oil. At the present pace, Swedish car fleets would be transformed in only 150 years, compared to more than 500 years for global fleets. Few sustainability experts realize that the pace is as slow as this since the guardians of ignorance have made the world blind even to obvious facts about the transformation. In Germany there is also a subsidy of 6,000 euro for electric cars, but this has not had the strong effect that the subsidies have had in Sweden. It seems as if subsidies on their own do not necessarily lead to large increases in sales. Denmark, similar to Norway, is a country with high taxes on cars and with no tax on electric cars, but sales of electric cars are still very low, despite high hopes and great ambitions of the government for more than ten years. Large countries, like the UK, France, and the US, like Germany, also have only reached a slow rate of transformation, that indicates a time for the transformation of car fleets of about 500 years at the present pace.

In some countries, such as Poland, there is a resistance to sub-sidizing electric cars because, in a country that still has many poor families, using tax-payers' money to subsidize the affluent is a sensitive matter. Driving the transformation is problematic in many ways from a political point of view. One of the biggest obstacles, the elephant in the room that few discuss but that is present in the background, is the fact that the automotive industry is dependent on the sales of petrol and diesel cars, and many countries are dependent on the production of

petrol and diesel cars for a large share of employment. Large investment will have to be made in the development of electric vehicles for
them to become profitable. It is impossible to be certain that the manufacturers that are the leaders in the automotive industry at present will
be able to keep their positions in the electric vehicle industries of the
future—and that is a big and legitimate worry, but it does not reduce
the need to go through with the change.

Now that the need to rebuild economies after the coronavirus crisis
has emerged as a new priority, the question of transforming transport
systems to e-mobility becomes even more complicated. Covid-19 will
leave countries with weaker economies, but oil consumption is to a
large extent built into the structures of the global economy and it does
not go down very much during an economic dip, at least not permanently. Through the coronavirus crisis, global oil demand temporarily
decreased by almost 30 per cent,[5] but after the crisis demand has come
back to pre-coronavirus levels. Some effects of coronavirus may linger,
but oil demand will remain close to 100 million barrels per day and the
risk of the decline is as high as it has been in the past few years. When
the Peak Oil alarmists started to warn of the decline, consumption
amounted to slightly more than 80 million barrels per day and it was
worrying even at that level.

A pace of transformation indicating a time frame of up to 500 years
is not meaningful in terms of change. The transformation of most of
transportation needs to be achieved in the next one or two decades, but
this will be a tremendous challenge. The efforts of some small countries
to reduce their dependence on oil more rapidly are not enough to
reduce the global dependence on oil, and even the leading countries,
except Norway, are not expanding their fleets of electric vehicles at a
high enough pace. In order to take effect, there is a need to rapidly
increase global sales to 10 or 20 million electric cars per year and push
sales of vans and light trucks so that this also takes off, but how is this
going to be managed when the purchasing power of companies and
households has decreased through the coronavirus pandemic? There
are no longer the same number of buyers as before that can afford to
buy substantially more expensive cars and trucks and, if it used to be
difficult for governments to set aside large sums of money for large-

---

[5]   According to the April 2020 Oil Market Report by the International Energy
      Agency, oil demand in April was expected to be 29 million barrels lower
      per day compared to the same month in 2019.

scale transformation programmes, this is likely to be even more difficult in the near future. It is time both for governments, experts, and citizens to wake up and realize that the transformation of the global economy to sustainable and resilient production and distribution flows will be so large that it cannot be driven by market forces left on their own, just as preparations for the next pandemic, or any other type of disaster, cannot be left to the market either.

At present the global capacity to manufacture electric vehicles is limited and the ability to expand this production is limited as well, at least short term. A number of factors hamper the ability to produce vehicles. One is the capacity for battery production, which is slowly expanded. The bulk of capacity is located and planned in China, and European and American producers need to speed up expansion to not entirely lose out to the Chinese. Tesla, together with Panasonic, run the Gigawatt battery factory, which is the leading battery manufacturer outside of China, and the battery plant that is about to be built in Sweden by the company Northvolt will have a similar capacity. Still, these factories will only cover a fraction of the battery volumes needed to transform the world's vehicle fleets to electricity and the Northvolt plant is expected to reach its full capacity by 2023. One aspect of the battery factories that has not been widely discussed is that these facilities will use very large amounts of electricity for their production processes. Battery production will increase the demand for power in a way that few have anticipated, and this need has to be placed on top of the amount of energy that will be needed in order to charge the vehicles once they have been built.

Strong Measures Will Still Be Necessary

Electric systems represent the most promising alternative to petroleum-based transport systems, and they represent the only alternative that can realistically be implemented on a large scale. Governments need to hold detailed investigations into the investment that will be necessary to implement these systems and make them grow rapidly. As has been argued above, coronavirus has not reduced the need to analyse the situation and make plans and decisions for investment and decide about the pace of the transformation. Many governments made long-term plans for their future power supply in the 1970s and 1980s, a period when the demand for electricity was much lower than at present. But demand increased substantially and countries had to expand power production to cover the expected requirements. Without the plans and investments in the expansion that were made at that time, present generations would not have experienced the economic growth that we have in recent decades. Some countries focused on nuclear power, while others built coal-fired power plants. Later, wind power and combined heat and power generation have contributed to expanding production, while solar panels in most countries remain a marginal source of generation. Electricity demand has in recent decades remained relatively stable, but with the expansion of the ICT sector — with an increasing demand for data centres and the expansion of e-mobility and industries that consume increasing amounts of power — the curves are starting to point upwards again. Just the transformation of one short-distance ferry line between Helsingør in Denmark and Helsingborg in Sweden to electric drive increased the load on the local grid substantially as the three freight containers of batteries on each ferry are charged in only seven minutes (and this happens four times every hour). Airplane manufacturers and airlines also join the chorus of sectors of society that plan to drive the transformation forwards. According to optimistic forecasts, the first electric flights of small passenger airplanes will start by 2023. It will take many years until large airliners or the majority of small planes will be able to use batteries to power short- or medium-distance routes, but if that should become a reality the power demand would increase as well. There are at present developments other than transportation that contribute to increasing the demand for power, for example the increasing demand for computing capacity, which drives the need to build new data centres. Depending on the choices between technologies, some countries may experience significant increases in power demand in coming decades. In many countries the load on national, regional, and local distribution grids is approaching full capacity at hours of peak use, especially in the coldest days during the winter, or in the hottest days in the summer, when heating and air conditioning are used at their full capacity. Also, nuclear reactors and many power plants are approaching the end of their operational lives. When the transformation to electric mobility takes off, it will be a matter of years to plan significant expansions both of production and distribution capacity. The Danish industry organization Dansk Energi has calculated that it will require investment of 6 billion euro to facilitate the charging of one million electric cars if no smart grid technologies are used, and it will require only 4.1 billion euro with the use of smart grid technologies. The difference is due to the lower transmission and distribution capacity that will be needed if smart grid technologies are implemented. The Danish car fleet amounts to over two million cars, so this investment would facilitate a reduction in the number of petrol and diesel cars by almost 50 per cent. The need to build new capacity for power generation has not been included in those calculations. The need to invest in additional generation capacity is likely to be substantially larger than the investment in the expansion of grids and it is about time that countries start to discuss these requirements as well.

The transformations to e-mobility and the circular economy that will be necessary to reduce dependence on oil cannot remain "black boxes" to decision makers, to which leaders of different parties and groups can assign a random number of years and euro to the ambition of changing to sustainable and resilient systems and production flows. The rough analyses I present in this and my previous books rely on publicly available data, about oil production, the use of petroleum for different purposes, the pace and cost of transformation, and the realistic time frame for the change—and these data indicate unequivocally that countries need to prepare for a reduction in oil production and start large-scale investment into the development of alternatives. The only advancement that at present pushes the beginning of the decline forwards is the increase in the production of unconventional oil. I have put the most important bits and pieces together to get an overview, a picture that few have been able to take in up until now. Many estimates of the time frame have been made for political reasons and dubious conclusions about time and cost have been drawn. For example, the EU has decided that the entire union will be carbon neutral by 2050, in only 30 years, and for the moment the pace of transformation of European car fleets indicates that it would take 500 years at the present speed only to transform car transportation. As mentioned before, there is no competitive alternative about to be implemented for long-distance heavy transportation. Without political decisions and government financing, the transformation of this sector may not start until 2050. Who is going to tell EU politicians about this?

If the matter were analysed in detail, experts and decision makers would quickly realize that the investment that would be necessary to achieve the transformation would be very large and that it would take decades to achieve significant progress on a global scale. Due to the long-term perspective and the short-term threat that oil production will go into decline, other measures will be necessary to reduce dependence on oil. This is where the need for unambiguous communication becomes clear. To communicate a message to people that they can take in and understand, both intellectually and from an emotional per-spective, governments, media companies, and members of the general public need to take responsibility. The message of the transformation can no longer be communicated primarily via non-fiction books with a limited readership and between people that belong to the sustainability sector or to left-wing political groups.

As governments struggle with the need to buy enough supplies of medical equipment and pharmaceuticals to combat Covid-19, it may start to sink in that governments have underestimated the risk of a global pandemic and failed to store enough supplies to meet their needs in an emergency. During the rage of the pandemic, MD Björn Olsen relaunched his book *Pandemic – the Myths, the Facts, the Threats*, originally published in 2010.[6] Olsen has warned of the risk of a pandemic for more than ten years but been met with no response. In a similar way, experts on oil production, such as Professors Kjell Aleklett and Mikael Höök, have warned of the peak in oil production for almost twenty years, without getting decision makers to understand that Peak Oil will pose a serious threat to the global economy. My books are among the only ones that argue that countries need to start systematic programmes of large-scale investment to reduce their dependence on oil and transportation. Peak Oil experts primarily point out the problem, and argue that more needs to be done to mitigate reduced supply. Presumably the present book will be easy to understand once the decline in oil production has started, but the transformation needs to start as soon as possible and hopefully people will be able to take in the message, now that Covid-19 has helped open the minds of individuals to the mistakes that have been made in the past as countries have relied too heavily on the market in their preparations for the future.

A mistake has been made in framing the transformation need as an environmental issue that can be solved through small-scale mitigation activities, while at the same time all other developments in areas such as digitization, artificial intelligence, new materials, and research can continue to be pursued with the same intensity as they are at present. We may note from the activities to fight coronavirus that unexpected costs arise as governments discover a new threat, and that governments, short term, have to save companies and jobs and start procurement activities to secure supplies of different types of equipment and material. In the case of combatting the pandemic, the unexpected costs arise for only a limited period during the pandemic. In the case of

---

6   The book is only available in Swedish with the title *Pandemi – myterna, fakta, hoten*.

mitigating the decrease in oil production, other measures will become necessary, but the investment needs and cost will remain for a long time, as the decline in oil production will be permanent and the need to transform society will not go away until society has been transformed to a reduced dependence on oil—this conversion will take several decades. For this reason, it will be necessary to reduce costs and investment in other areas to be able to allocate more resources to the transformation.

Up until the start of the coronavirus pandemic, development was going in the opposite direction, as the move towards increasingly global supply chains has been going on at least since the Second World War. At present, a very large share of the world's goods is manufactured in Asia and shipped to customers in Europe and North America, and it will take time and involve large investment to move production back closer to customers. Despite the pressing need to build the circular economy, much more money is still invested in the linear economy, the global production system where resources are used once and then become recycled or go to landfill. Virtually everything we buy contributes to the growth of national and global production systems that are mostly linear in nature. It is only when people buy products that have been made in circular business processes that they contribute to the development of the circular economy, and there are not yet many of those. As there are many more products that have been made in the global economy than ones that have been produced by companies that apply circular business models, it is very difficult for people to avoid contributing to the growth of the global economy and many do not seem to realize that the fact that there are projects and other initiatives that promote the circular economy does <u>not</u> necessarily mean that the circular economy is gaining importance at the expense of the global economy. Due to the small number of products that have been made in circular production systems, it is almost impossible, and at the same time cumbersome and expensive, to primarily buy goods that have been produced via circular systems. The image that the transformation to circular production and distribution systems is well under way is another example of the naïve image of society that has been spread by different groups in recent decades.

Change leaders need to become aware of these relationships, raise their voices, and demand that more investment be made in the creation of circular businesses and in e-mobility, so that it becomes possible, less expensive, and less difficult to find and select products that contribute to the development of a sustainable society. The choice to build the new production, distribution, and transport systems on a large scale will have significant consequences. First, we need to understand how the new systems can be expanded, and then we will have to understand the consequences of the resulting transformation and how society can avoid the negative effects, taking as much advantage as possible of the positive.

Chapter Four

Organizing Transformation

Large-scale transformation to a more resilient and sustainable society will not happen by itself. For change to succeed, the cooperation of millions of people will be required and this cooperation will need to be planned and organized. The goals need to be defined and all participants need to find their roles in the big picture, and they need to be provided with the tools and other resources necessary to do their jobs. For this to be possible there will be a need to develop a strategy and a plan for the transformation and, to do this, an overall view of the changes and the building of resources will become necessary. This is not a political statement, no argument in favour of a socialist planned economy, simply a recognition that the market cannot create specific results in a brief space of time. 400,000 Americans were involved in the Apollo Programme, an effort that was organized in steps as NASA procured development and production services from an increasing number of companies and as they organized their own activities throughout the programme. But organized efforts on a large scale have been performed throughout history. We know little about how the construction of the great pyramids at Giza was organized, but there are later examples of efforts that historians have studied and described. As an example, at the beginning of the thirteenth century the Republic of Venice received the assignment from the Pope to build and equip a fleet of some 100 ships for the Fourth Crusade. The republic at the time had only about 100,000 citizens and everybody would have to participate in the immense task, as the entire project had to be performed in only one year. Venice was the leading seafaring state at the time and the Pope, and his aides, knew that only Venice could succeed with the task. They were promised a payment of 94,000 marks upon the delivery of the fleet, including the food and equipment for the 9,000 squires and 4,500 knights that were to go on the crusade.[1] The building of the fleet was meticulously planned, both from the point of view of manpower and space in the city. All over Venice ships were built, ships of different sizes that were built to serve different purposes. There were ships especially constructed to transport the 4,500 horses of the knights and there were cargo ships for food and equipment. Venetians had to bake enough bread and cure enough meat for the two years that the crusade was estimated to last. Grain, flour, meat, and other food products had to be purchased within a radius of more than 100 kilometres of Venice in order to manufacture enough resources for the entire voyage.

Market forces, often referred to as "the invisible hand of the market", could never have been relied on for the preparations. If the inhabitants of Venice had not worked to a well-defined plan for the venture, there would have been too much of some things and too little of others. It would have been impossible to produce exactly the right number of ships of the proper sizes, equipped with the right equipment and the relevant amount of food on board.

The market is the most efficient tool for allocating resources in mature industries where the exact outcome is not critical and when the time frame does not matter. It is not important if some people buy Volkswagens and others buy Toyotas, other than for the companies involved. Over time a certain brand of car will grow, and another may shrink in size. Successful companies may acquire the less successful and the exact structure of the car industry does not matter as long as unemployment is kept in check and large recessions and depressions are avoided. The companies that most effectively satisfy the needs of car buyers will be more successful than the ones that are doing this with less skill.

In the case of the transformation to a sustainable society, advocated by Greta Thunberg and many other sustainability experts, politicians, and celebrities, the transformation will be such a huge endeavour that resources will have to be focused on the most important aspects of transformation and the most cost and resource effective solutions will have to be chosen. When the market guides development a large number of ventures are started that never come to fruition, because customers do not find enough value in the products and services when

---

[1]   Facts about the role of Venice in the preparations for the Fourth Crusade can be found in *City of Fortune* by Roger Crowley.

they are launched or companies fail to develop offerings rapidly enough to earn high enough revenues before they run out of money. If the time frame is of no importance and the exact structure of the resulting industrial landscape does not matter, the improved efficiency of the system as a whole outweighs the cost of the resources that are expended on ventures that fail. This is true in a situation where incremental innovation is needed and where the speed of each improvement is not very important. Economic growth gets measured on a monthly and yearly basis and governments and national banks can adjust their policies slightly to stimulate growth or reduce optimism to keep the economy from overheating.

The change to sustainable production and distribution systems will not be a matter of incremental improvement of the present system. Many people seem to think that the change will primarily involve the task of making existing companies more sustainable, but the problem is related to the structure of the global economy as much as to the unsustainable practices of each company. The production of any product involves the transportation of raw materials, components, and semi-finished products several times around the globe. In addition to this, production relies to a large extent on scarce materials and on energy-intensive production processes. This situation cannot be changed by improvements in the operations of individual companies or through the tools that are available to governments or national banks when they stimulate the business cycle. The problem can only be solved through the development of new structures, almost from scratch, in a way similar to how the Apollo Programme[2] and subsequent space programmes built the space sector in the United States and Europe, and how the investment in the development of the IT industry was driven by the United States government and then merged with the communications industry to become the global Information and Communication (ICT) Industry.[3] The difference of the transformation to sustainability is that there are incumbent companies with different agendas that need to participate in the transformation and become part of the new structures.

---

[2] In *Apollo* Charles Murray and Catherine Bly Cox describe the programme in detail.

[3] The processes of financing the development of computers and the internet is analysed in detail by the late Professor Vernon W Ruttan in *Is War Necessary for Economic Growth?*

Full Attention

At present few people give the matter of the transformation serious attention, and there are few change leaders who see the complete picture of the shift that will become necessary. Even though the change is key to the continuation of our society into the future, the details of the transformation, the magnitude, or the specific activities that need to be undertaken are seldom discussed. The issue that is to some extent discussed is whether countries should go through with the transformation or whether it is not important enough to warrant increased resources. For example, in one of his tweets from the 12th of December 2019, President Donald Trump wrote of Greta Thunberg: "So ridiculous. Greta must work on her Anger Management problem, then go to a good old fashioned movie with a friend! Chill Greta, Chill!" Presumably, believers in the unlimited power of the market economy are bound to think that, if it had been important, the market would already have signalled this importance and companies would have noticed and started to allocate significant resources to the change. The truth is that if nobody sees any significant business opportunity in it, short term, players in the market are not going to finance the transformation, and large-scale business opportunities do not emerge in early phases of the development of a new technology. Companies did not see any business opportunities in the development of space travel in the 1960s. Those opportunities emerged much later when development had been going on for a few decades and Elon Musk can reduce the cost of space travel through his company Space X. Even if it takes twenty years to prepare for a transformation by developing the technologies and systems solutions necessary for the change, the market does not signal until there are business opportunities and money to be made by entrepreneurs with foresight. At the point when enough business opportunities emerge, large investments are made by many investors, without government backing, but this situation still lies many years into the future.

The transformation to sustainable production and distribution systems will have to involve dramatic changes in many different areas. Transport systems is only one example and the primary alternative is to change these, and the vehicle fleets in countries, to electric alternatives. There is also a need to reduce the demand for transportation overall and this can be done in various ways through the implementation of different aspects of the circular economy. An increasing share of local production will, for example, be necessary to reduce the need for transportation. Local production systems are also at an early stage of development and it will take decades to build them to significant proportions so that they can take over an increasing share of production and distribution from the fragile and transport-reliant global economy. This may sound like a politically motivated statement, but it is not very different from the dimensioning of the engines for a rocket that is going into space. To give enough thrust the engines need to have a certain power so that the speed of the rocket becomes high enough to take it out of the earth's gravity. The same is true for the ability of local production to take over large enough chunks of business from the global economy. Local production needs to grow substantially to do this. Since oil is likely to become scarce in the next few years and there are no new transport systems that are ready to become implemented on a large scale, local production systems need to grow very rapidly to take over a significant share of production. This will make production more sustainable as well as resilient, but large investment will be needed in local production to facilitate the change.

Due to the lack of awareness of the need for large-scale transformation programmes, few people and virtually no decision makers give the matter of the change their full attention. In the present day and age substantial energy and focus are needed in order to turn ideas into action—even if the problem threatens the future of our society the attention is far from sufficient to take the issue from something that a few experts discuss to actual large-scale transformation programmes. Greta Thunberg has contributed to raising awareness, but it is nowhere near the point where governments set aside large amounts of funding to create a resilient society. Projects need to be started in all countries with the goal of planning the transformation to rapidly reduce the dependence on transportation and the use of resources that this causes. For this to happen, people who aspire to lead the change need to spread the same message: that countries need to organize and start up large-scale transformation activities and, for this to happen, change leaders need to prepare the strategies and plans of the change programmes.

Structuring a Programme

The space programme of the United States was started by President Eisenhower, by forming the Space Task Group in 1958. The group consisted of 37 engineers assigned with the task of investigating the challenges of manned space flight. Eisenhower was not very optimistic about the opportunities of a space adventure and kept activities at a low level. The Russians took the lead in the space race through the first manned space flight, and President Kennedy, in 1961, set the goal for the United States to send a man to the moon and bring him safely back before the end of the decade. In the 1960s 400,000 Americans became involved in the Apollo Programme, as employees of NASA or any of the companies that bid on the large number of procurements that were issued throughout the programme. The programme was an example of building an entirely new business sector, almost from scratch, in less than ten years, but it required very large investment on the part of the government. It also took back to the United States the initiative in the space race and gave its space industry a global lead, and technology and solutions were developed and enhanced – efforts that have contributed to boosting the United States' economy and global economies ever since.

A programme similar to the Apollo Programme or any of the other development programmes contributes in a number of different ways to advancing the advancement of an area:

- Technical and systems-related problems get solved.
- Decisions get made and standards are set as some technical and business solutions are selected and others are discarded.
- Industry structures are built.
- People are hired for new tasks, receive training, and build experience.
- Business opportunities outside of the programme are identified and pursued, for example opportunities to use new materials for applications that are not space-related, such as to apply new design methods for lightweight and miniaturized constructions in the electronics industry.

Decision making gives direction to development. Decisions are made about which technologies will be selected, which standardized formats will be used, and which alternatives will be discarded. The market does not give this type of direction at early stages. An example can be found in the assortment of biofuels, where all possible biofuels are discussed, despite the fact that none of them are viable for production on a large scale to replace oil. In those situations, many different solutions are developed, and many unpromising opportunities are pursued alongside the more viable ones. The standards for electric plugs and sockets that can be used in each country is a good example. By standardizing the shape and size of plugs and the form and position of the poles, the advancement of all other alternatives come to a halt and all players can focus their development resources on improving the standard plug. This is a simple example and it does not fully illustrate the advantages of making decisions about standards, but consider the fact that in an electrical system there are hundreds or thousands of aspects that are standardized, or the fact that companies focusing development efforts on the selected alternatives speed up development considerably compared to a situation where several alternatives for each solution remain in development for a long time. Having a large variety of alternatives, for example different ways of designing a plug, is usually no advantage and standardization substantially reduces cost and speeds up development. In the case of the packaging of food and other products for sale in supermarkets there are in each country binders of requirements that suppliers need to conform to for their products to be considered for distribution. The rules have been set down to reduce the cost of in-store handling and reduce the cost of customer complaints. Companies need to comply with all requirements to sell their products to supermarkets. Examples are requirements for bar codes, labelling, closures, sizes, and weights. By agreeing on these standards, producers can focus on improving the important things, such as the quality of the products that are packed and sold in the packages.

Compare this situation to the one that at present exists in the field of electric truck transportation. Many people argue that electric roads with continuous charging, either via power lines in the air, above the vehicles, or via electric tracks in the road surface for inductive charging, will be necessary in order to transform a large share of long-distance transportation to e-mobility. Trucks with substantial battery packs for medium distance transportation will also soon be on the market. At present, neither of these solutions is competitive enough to take over a large share of truck transportation and it will take several decades for them to become competitive. Many different technologies and solutions are developed in parallel and there are few initiatives to make decisions and standardize important aspects of the systems.

Investing in ventures to build networks of electric roads will be very risky, as logistics companies will need long stretches of electric roads to be able to convert their truck fleets to electric trucks. In this situation there is a chicken-or-egg problem. For logistics companies to buy electric trucks there is a need for long stretches of electric roads, but these are not likely to be built until investors know that logistics companies will rapidly buy electric trucks once systems are in place. Otherwise there is a large risk that ventures turn out the way Better Place did—going bankrupt. In the case of Better Place, investors lost 850 million dollars trying to create a game-changing standard solution for electric car transportation that would reduce the need for cars to be equipped with large batteries. The sales of battery-equipped trucks are not likely to drive development to large-scale transformation, as it will take decades for these trucks to become competitive against diesel trucks. They may take some market share, but in the absence of large subsidies they are not likely to take any substantial share of truck transportation. The situation is likely to develop to a static situation where little happens in terms of change and where decision makers and experts continue to wonder why so little is being done to transform the truck transportation sector. To break up the status quo governments need to step in and finance the most promising alternative, like they have done so many times through the history of technology development. For example, in the case of the Apollo Programme, most technical solutions had been selected by the end of 1962, only 18 months after the speech of President Kennedy on the 25th of May 1961. The experts at NASA had to decide on the best alternatives and it was important to make rapid decisions to have as much time as possible available for the development of the solutions. Even though this situation is not identical to the decisions that need to be made in order to pull the plug on the development of e-mobility, it illustrates that government bodies have in recent centuries made thousands of decisions in matters of technology, and decisions open up the opportunity for market-based advancement as development projects are procured and the technologies that are developed arrive in the market. The situation is similar today. If governments wait twenty years for market forces to decide before they start to make decisions about standards and other important topics, the necessary technologies are not likely to become competitive against petrol- and diesel-based transport technologies during that time. When Greta argues that governments have not done enough to drive the transformation to sustainability rapidly enough, some of the things that need to be done—but ones that she and other sustainability experts fail to mention—include selecting the most promising technologies, standardizing many aspects of the systems, and financing the development of the selected alternatives. Change leaders need to identify the most important decisions that need to be made and point them out, together with the consequences of the failure of governments to make the decisions and set the necessary development programmes and projects in motion. Without the decisions that have been made by NASA officials and companies appointed and financed by NASA for different development projects in the past sixty years, Elon Musk would not have been able to create the amazing innovations and improvements that he is now developing at Space-X.

Governments, however, can hardly set standards without running large-scale test installations. Without such installations, the determination of standards is likely to rely on random selections of one alternative over another. Test projects, like the Apollo Programme, or the construction of the first railways or power grids in different countries, force governments and investors to choose which technologies and solutions they prefer, and often such choices become standard. In the case of the implementation of e-mobility, this will be important as it will reduce the dependence on imported oil. But with a time frame for the implementation in excess of a hundred years, oil is likely to run out entirely before electric transportation grows to take over a significant share of all road transportation. There is also the risk that a large share of batteries and other components for electric cars will be imported from China. It is important to rapidly replace oil as the most important fuel, but at the same time this should not be done in such a way that other significant risks to supply systems and European economies arise.

Coming back to the implementation and expansion of electric road networks and the delays that are caused by having a number of different alternatives and no market that can drive the development of any of the solutions forwards, in order for logistics companies to be able to invest in electric trucks on a large scale there must be long stretches of electric road networks between major cities across continents, like Europe or the United States, in place. Electric trucks are significantly more expensive than diesel trucks, and without extensive road networks where they can be used electric trucks cannot be efficiently utilized. Systems solutions need to be developed and checked in test projects, such as the Apollo Programme, or through the building of a regional electric road system. Test systems need to be extensive enough to put the competitive potential of the new technologies to the test. The trials need to be large and complex enough for the experimenters to identify all the relevant weaknesses in a system. For example, the use of a few million electric cars in all countries of the world does not help companies, governments, and users identify all the challenges related to the expansion of electric mobility. It is not until many vehicles are used in the same area, charged at the same time, and using the same local electricity grids that the challenges of charging many electric cars become apparent. It is not until many utilities companies and providers of charging infrastructure have built charging resources for a number of years and found that it is very difficult for these investments to turn a profit that governments will understand the implications of this for the operation and expansion of systems. The low profitability of investment in charging infrastructure that is made by otherwise profitable utilities companies is not likely to be treated as an important hurdle until it becomes clear that this may at some point in the future become a major blockage for the further expansion of e-mobility systems. At present, small-scale tests of the technologies involved are run in different places in Europe. These tests need to be rapidly expanded to regional test networks that build entire systems and analyse them in realistic environments. For the tests to become realistic, however, there is a need to run many electric vehicles in each analysis, so that the systems create a significant load on power grids that can be balanced using smart grid technologies.

Small test installations of electric road networks will not be enough to identify the main challenges or develop systems that will be ready for large-scale implementation. The issue of planning the necessary large-scale test projects, finding the financing, and completing the pro-jects should be high on the agenda of any politician who is serious about sustainability, and arguing in favour of large test projects as a means to remove obstacles should be high on the agenda of change leaders. The overall goals for the next decades cannot be achieved without large-scale test installations and those require substantial planning and preparation. They cannot be initiated based on the cries of Greta Thunberg or on the experiences from the Covid-19 pandemic. They need to involve the building of a long-term vision of the roll-out of the new systems and the ambition to find the most cost effective and least risky way of organizing and financing the roll-out.

In a similar way, now that countries have experienced that the dependence on China for imports of all kinds of products represents a significant risk to society, governments need to take measures to reduce the dependence on imports from far-away countries. To achieve this, European governments will need to cooperate and focus on producing different products in different countries, because all countries cannot build production resources for everything inside their own borders. For production to become efficient, advantages of scale need to be pursued, but many products will have to be produced in several locations to reduce transport distances. In the case of both sustainability and resilience there is a need to develop a strategy, and the most important changes need to be prioritized and receive significant financing in the next few years. This process of strategy development and prioritization needs to be led by people with industrial experience and knowledge about industrial transformation, rather than by sustainability experts, pharmacists, or nutritionists.

The decisions that must be made as preparations for large change programmes are probably the most important aspects of the programme. Deciding about the overall structures of production will be key to building an efficient basis. This must be done through a combination of market-driven development and planned decision making. The expansion of European and American production resources must in many areas be stimulated. This can be done through limitations on imports of certain products and in some cases through government orders of products to domestic or European manufacturers and loans with beneficial interest rates for investments in the expansion of production or distribution. It is likely that European laws for public procurement will have to be changed to make it possible for countries to stimulate production inside their borders.

In the present situation, European countries will need to reduce their dependence on foreign supplies and at the same time reduce dependence on long-distance transportation, also within Europe. The need to do this represents a challenge that no country will be able to take on by itself, but the question remains if governments have drawn conclusions from the coronavirus experience that enable them to start up collaboration on a large scale. In the emerging situation it will be important to keep in mind that all countries participate in a global economy and that no country can choose its own solutions independent of others. The needs in each country and region need to be balanced by the limited resources that are available and the need to build new production systems that are resilient and resource efficient, but that are also competitive.

Centralized decisions about standards do not preclude market-driven development, it enhances the opportunity of the market to perform its magic. The Apollo Programme combined the centralized development of solutions by NASA engineers with a dialogue with companies, which ultimately led to the procurement of development services and the development and purchasing of systems and subsystems, based on market principles. All decisions cannot be exactly right, but the fact that decisions are made is much better than development stalling for decades with little progress.

From Large-Scale Tests to Full-Scale Roll-Out

One of the key aspects of the roll-out of technologies is to make sure that there will be sufficient financing behind the solutions that are selected. The alternatives that are selected for the large-scale tests need to be selected with the goal in mind that these technologies will also be used for the future roll-out of full-scale systems. Technology providers need to be strong enough financially to supply the products to customers on a national or continental scale. If companies are not strong enough from the beginning, governments need to create the circumstances where the selected technologies can be used without risk and allow small or financially weak companies to grow and strengthen through the process, alternatively governments will need to help small players acquire the capital needed for the journey forwards. It depends on the strength of the national finances of any country how much money its government can afford to invest in these efforts. Financially weak governments may need to adopt solutions that have been developed in other countries or allow foreign companies to make the necessary investment to build production, distribution, and service resources, while strong governments are likely to be able to participate and co-finance development. Weaker countries may have to take part in a few development projects that are of critical importance, while more affluent ones may be able to drive development in a broader range of areas.

In the case of the Apollo Programme, the experimental trials consisted of doing a number of test journeys of Apollo craft, each of the tests well planned and prepared for in order to push the envelope further towards the ultimate goal of sending a man to the moon and bringing him safely back to earth.

The series of test installations and the exact path from the first large test to the full-scale roll-out needs to be determined based on the maturity of the technologies, solutions, and expectations of users. In the case of mobile telephony, the roll-out of the first-generation systems, the NMT (or Nordic Mobile Telephony) systems, were launched towards a small initial market that grew to become the global mass market that is now served by Apple, Samsung, and a few other suppliers of smart phones. The first launch was a full-scale implementation, but with a very small market in mind. It was believed by the Nordic telecom operators and Ericsson when they launched the first systems in 1981 that the global market by the year 2000 would amount to perhaps one million users. As mobile phone services had never been offered before, people did not have any expectations and the technologies and products had not by that time been developed to the present level of user-friendliness or cost effectiveness. In that sense the launches in the pioneering countries were large-scale tests. As we all know, the development since the launch has far surpassed expectations and the number of users increased to more than one billion users worldwide by 2000.

In the case of e-mobility the situation is very different. Existing systems for car and truck transportation (i.e. petrol and diesel) are very reliable and user-friendly. They are also very cost effective, a situation that makes it more challenging to achieve rapid growth of electric mobility systems. The fact that the new systems need to rapidly become competitive against very attractive and highly efficient petrol- and diesel-based transport systems makes it difficult to get many customers to buy electric cars and trucks. The need to replace existing systems is unusual compared to the penetration of other technologies, because in most previous cases technologies have created new value for customers and with e-mobility this is not the case. The use of electric vehicles does not make transportation more efficient. It does not help drivers get more rapidly to their destinations and it does not reduce the cost of car transportation or free up resources to be used for other purposes. On the contrary, more money needs to be spent on electric vehicles and charging infrastructures, which reduces the money available for other purposes, the exact opposite of what has happened in the past when new technologies have contributed to increasing the efficiency of the economy. People have become accustomed to getting more value at a lower cost in area upon area. The fact that development has been driven by relatively mature, user-friendly, and cost effective technologies has made it possible to drive the development using the market mechanism. As there have not been any incumbent technologies there to defend the market that the new technologies could grow without subsidies. In the present situation the transformation will have to be driven using technologies that are at early stages of development from the perspectives of cost and user-friendliness, and there are hundreds of different industries and sectors of society that will have to be transformed to sustainability in order to increase resilience, reduce the dependence on oil, and reduce the use of other resources as well. The European Union has decided that the goal for 2050 is to make the union carbon neutral and this development must start by creating a strategy and by prioritizing the most important areas to start with.

Simply put, there is no other way of achieving the change that the EU, Greta Thunberg, and many others ask for than by driving the transformation as an organized programme. Substantial financing and support for the changes that need to be made will have to be provided by governments and a large share of the programme management will also have to be financed by national governments. The EU, UN, and other supranational organizations need to facilitate collaboration between countries to minimize duplication of effort and optimize the value created by the transformation and development activities in each country. In each country, region, and business sector, change leaders need to become active who are well informed about the need for change and the means whereby it will have to be achieved. This is a new situation, one that neither governments nor experts or business leaders have expected and, due to the blindness of everybody to the existence of the vast territories where little constructive action has been taken in three decades, people have lost the concepts and language necessary to discuss the activities that need to be initiated to reclaim them.

Chapter Five

Creating Awareness

The most urgent challenge for society is the reconstruction of the economies of countries after the Covid-19 pandemic, but at the same time there is the need to prepare countries for the highly probable decline in oil production that experts have been warning of for almost two decades. The pandemic has severely broken down the economies of countries, but at the same time the need to build a more resilient and sustainable society has become apparent to many. The International Energy Agency has warned that the decline in oil production is likely to start already in the next few years. Another challenge, that there are at present no means of mitigating, is the declining room for improvement in the economy.[1] Nothing can be done in less than no time or at a cost lower than zero and, in many areas, development is approaching the limits of what is possible to achieve and the remaining room for improvement is rapidly declining. This may not appear a big problem, because there is no need to do anything in less than no time and a cost close to zero may seem low enough, but the affluence of our present society cannot be maintained by keeping the present level of efficiency. Each year the economy needs to become increasingly efficient, for present generations to maintain their current level of affluence. As mentioned before, the economic system forces us to collectively run faster all the time to stay in the same place, from the perspective of the world's financial well-being. It is the prospect of future growth that creates and maintains optimism in the economy and that makes people willing to consume and invest. The fact that the economy is gradually running out of room for improvement—as the efficiency of the economy increases and companies and organizations gradually eliminate the waste of time and other resources that still remain in the economy—will present a very tangible challenge for governments and

---

[1]   I launched the concept of declining room for improvement in *The Limits of Business Development and Economic Growth*, published in 2005.

for the global financial system—and there is a need for change leaders to take on the roles that will be necessary to drive the development in the right direction. If the economy fifty years ago could be described as a large number of relatively disorganized regional and national production systems with a very large number of small companies with a low degree of specialization, the present economy is more like a number of rather well-organized trains where the wagons consist of highly specialized suppliers with well-defined roles in their supply chains. Taking the economies of the world from the earlier situation to the present represents a dramatic improvement in efficiency, but when the trains are already in good order and the slack in and between wagons has been reduced to a minimum, the opportunity to further improve efficiency is much lower than it was at first, before the start of the global organization process.

In the present situation a large share of the population needs to understand the challenges that lie ahead and contribute to large-scale change. For this to happen, communication needs to be unambiguous and invite less misunderstanding. Television shows, such as Top Gear, that glorify twentieth-century values and provide an image of successful people who consume the world's resources at an alarming rate, need to be replaced by shows that show the way to a sustainable future. This is, of course, only a valid goal if we believe that it is important and possible to transform modern society to sustainability, which some of the most prominent guardians of ignorance do not. In their world it is better the fewer questions that are asked, and the less people learn about issues related to any form of transformation, except the continuous expansion of the global economy. If that view is shared by most people, trying to promote change is likely to be a futile task. A large-scale transformation effort cannot be financed in a society where most voters and politicians do not understand the challenges of the future. Although perhaps necessary, how could a change in the media offering be brought about in a society with freedom of speech that is based entirely on the principles of the market? Only with the help of many change leaders who understand the challenges and can lead the way forwards can the transformation be achieved.

The present situation is in a sense like an emergency when it is important that the claxon is heard by all and that everybody heeds the message. People may have different political views that make them think differently about the role of the market and what exactly the role of governments should be, but citizens need to pay attention and understand the seriousness of the situation. When scientists build a space shuttle or a particle accelerator, like the one at CERN, all scientists share an understanding of how these technical marvels need to be designed in order to work, and when politicians and the military make decisions about investment in an army, navy, and air force they are in agreement about the type of weaponry to procure and the number of tanks, aircraft, and ships that can be financed with a given budget. In those situations, there are no idealists who argue that countries can be defended by a small number of people with handguns or that a particle accelerator can be constructed and built for a few million euro in two or three years. In the present situation there is a similar need for an agreement on the analysis and a sense of urgency to develop solutions to the challenges of the near future. An agreement on the way forwards cannot be achieved in a world where most of the information both people and decision makers receive indicates that the present level of development will continue and that large-scale trans-formations can be achieved using minimal amounts of resources.

People need to realize that the position seen as politically correct, that of not asking difficult questions regarding the way forwards to sustainability, does not contribute to solving the problem. Further, there is no solution available to politicians. Solutions need to be devel-oped and change needs to be driven by many individuals who under-stand that doing nothing or very little will not lead to a solution.

The strong belief in market-driven technology and product develop-ment does not rest on an understanding of how development really works in the early phases. The first customer categories that are often referred to as 'innovators' and 'early adopters' are too small to finance the development of the new systems. Initially, there are simply too few customers to finance the development of technologies and solutions and create user-friendly products and system solutions that will be able to compete with the existing production and distribution systems that are highly efficient and that have been in development for decades. For large-scale change to take place, a large share of the risk needs to be removed for entrepreneurs and innovators, so that many new com-panies can be started and grow rapidly. The goal of transforming society to resilient and sustainable production and distribution systems can never be reached if circular businesses need to compete against the present systems on equal terms, because terms that may be equal in principle very heavily favour existing producers. Customers are used to existing products and solutions and new products and services are sold in small volumes — and the necessary development will need to be financed through very small sales volumes, while the competitiveness of incumbent offerings is upheld by very large volumes and strong financial positions.

As we have seen during the coronavirus situation, climate change is not the most pressing threat. In addition to the most apparent and discussed challenges, and as mentioned previously, the International Energy Agency warns that the decline in oil production is likely to start in the next few years and that oil producing countries may produce 30 per cent less oil ten years into the decline. Reducing society's dependence on oil to adapt to such a steep decline in oil production will be a tremendous challenge. Even if climate change had been the biggest threat, this would not change anything regarding the challenge. Similar activities will be needed in order to reduce emissions of carbon dioxide as the ones that will be needed to transform production and distribution systems to meet reduced oil production. And the investment that will be needed to build new transport and production systems that will be less dependent on oil will be very large in any case. A rough calculation indicates that, in order to drive all the world's cars on electricity, the power equivalent of some 500 nuclear power reactors will be necessary, a substantial part of which can be covered by power savings and by making use of electricity that at present is lost, as it is produced at off-peak hours. But the investment in smart grid technologies and new power generation will still be very high. In addition to new facilities for power generation, there is the need to expand power distribution through investment in power grids and the installation of millions of charging posts across cities and along motorways. Germany, a country that at present has less than one per cent electric cars — or about one hundred thousand vehicles — is planning to install one million charging posts in the next ten years.

Above all, people need to learn about the emerging situation and the resource-efficient lifestyles that will have to be developed, not only by sustainability-conscious individuals, but by everyone, which creates a need for change leaders in all areas of society. This challenge to communicate a new and largely unexpected situation to almost all individuals and get them to change their behaviours in a very short space of time represents a tremendous difficulty. Top Gear and other television shows must give way to programming that introduces new values. The signal that the lifestyles of prosperous people could include the thoughtless use of large amounts of fuel and other resources legitimizes a type of behaviour among millions of people that clearly belongs in the past. Unfortunately, this is not a political statement. I would very much have liked to continue with my present lifestyle, but this is as untenable as continuing to drive when the petrol gauge is in the red. An increasing number of people need to slow down, start to take in the information about resources, and realize that it is time to step on the brakes and start to lead development down a new path. Once the situation becomes apparent, the mistakes that have been made will become clear to everybody, but it is difficult at present to discern the relevant information about the real situation from the short-term priorities of governments and experts in different fields.

The idea that programming on television should be directed by other factors than the desire of people to be entertained or informed seems outdated and reminiscent of a type of society where govern-ments sought to indoctrinate citizens to adopt lifestyles that were in line with party policy. This is not a type of society that countries should revert to, unless it is necessary, but it is unlikely that the ideas related to the transformation will be accepted by people that all the time get immersed in the values and practices that the world most likely will be forced, reluctantly, to leave behind. When the former presenter of Top Gear, Jeremy Clarkson, scolded Greta Thunberg for being a spoiled child, he illustrated the difficulty of accepting the fact that humanity will have to face a new situation. One of the most pressing problems of the future is likely to be the shortage of petrol and diesel that is imminent, but nobody knows exactly when the supply of oil will go into decline. All can, however, agree about the facts related to the transformation. We use two litres of oil every day for every human being on the planet. Less than 0.5 per cent of cars are electric or hybrid and the share of trucks and buses that can be driven using electricity is even smaller. Car fleets are replaced every 16 or 17 years, on a rotating basis, and electric vehicles are substantially more expensive and the price, availability of vehicles, charging infrastructure, and other factors are not likely to make it possible for all car owners to buy electric vehicles when oil production starts to go down. People are also likely to have to accept that companies will not be able to transport as many goods as before and that people cannot travel as much as they have become used to, whether we like it or not. Both Jeremy Clarkson and Greta Thunberg will have to adopt a new view on life, but Mr Clarkson is likely to be more surprised at what the future has in store for him than Greta. It is, however, very likely that Greta Thunberg will also be surprised by the complexity of the transformation and the fact that the scientists, to whom she so often refers, cannot offer any ready-made solutions that can be implemented at short notice.

A Change for All

One example of a discussion about the need for transformation can be taken from a meeting I had with the businessman and author Rune Westergård, who in 2016 had written a book with the title *One Planet is Enough*. I met him at the book exhibition in Gothenburg where he presented the Swedish edition of the book that was published in conjunction with the exhibition. In the book Mr Westergård argues that technical development makes products smaller and less demanding of resources and that the present overuse of resources will be remedied by the fact that gadgets get smaller and smaller. According to him, nobody will have to bother about reducing consumption, because the problem will take care of itself. At the time, my two Swedish novels had been published by the same Swedish publisher that published Westergård's book, so we inhabited the same stand at the exhibition and had ample time to discuss.

My novels are set in a not too distant future when the reduction of oil production has started and the world experiences a strong recession. The stories start before the peak in oil production in the years leading up to the reduction and the two main characters explore the type of behaviour that has led up to the calamitous situation. I explained to Mr Westergård that, according to forecasts by a number of independent researchers, oil production will go into decline in the next few years. Apart from that, resource and energy consumption increase despite the fact that products decline in size and weight, primarily because increasing affluence makes more consumers buy increasing numbers of products and use increasing amounts of services that also contribute to increasing resource consumption. A further factor is that more products are launched in the market every year and increasing affluence makes people able to buy more products, something that contributes to increasing use of resources. These developments that contribute to increasing resource consumption by far outweigh the reduction in weight and size that is only relevant for some products. When I had explained that oil production would start to decrease, and the other aspects mentioned here, Mr Westergård replied that, in that case, if there is a fixed time in the near future when oil production will start to decline, it is obvious that the argument that one planet is enough is invalid. I thought perhaps then that Mr Westergård would retreat from his position, become less active in promoting his book that we had agreed expounds an irrelevant analysis and point of view and did not think more about this until I, upon writing these lines, googled Rune Westergård and found that he one year later went on and had the book, that he himself had admitted was based on inaccurate assumptions and that included irrelevant reasoning, published in English.

The example illustrates the difficulty of informing people about the need to adopt new views and lifestyles. People tend to continue to live their lives in the way that they have done up until now until it becomes impossible to continue. Westergård, a successful businessman in his native country, Finland, was not likely to go back to his supporters and tell them that he had been wrong, simply because I had told him so. Instead, it would add to his self-esteem and add to his recognition among peers to have his book published in English as well, so why not do this? In the same way, we cannot expect Jeremy Clarkson to change his mind about his lifestyle and openly declare that he would join Greta's movement. That would be seen by his followers as a betrayal and it would under the circumstances be completely inexplicable, as any risks of carbon dioxide emissions or depletion of resources are obviously exaggerated.

In the case of the transformation and the reasons behind it, the financial aspects of an economy are not different from physics. People cannot argue with gravity and get nature to send rocks or footballs that are stationary on the ground up into the air. In the same way it is not possible to change the facts of the transformation to a sustainable future and pretend that the change requires only small investment when large ones will be needed. The amount of investment that a country or the global economy can muster is also limited at a certain point in time, but it can be extended through wise economic policies. The ability to invest in the transformation is limited by the amount of money that can be set aside for the purpose each year, but as we have seen during the coronavirus crisis, in the case of an emergency other expenses can be cut and the amounts for the most highly prioritized activities can increase.

There are earlier examples of great development and construction programmes of later dates than the previously mentioned effort of Venice to build the fleet for the Fourth Crusade. From 1942 to 1969 the US government mobilized financial resources for three extraordinary ventures that have greatly contributed to shaping the world as we know it. The presidents, their cabinets, and Congress found the endeavours so important that they mobilized the financial resources, despite the very high cost. In hindsight, it is clear that the huge endeavours were necessary in order to develop the society we experience today, but this must have been less obvious to the politicians who financed the programmes back in the day. The programmes were, first, entering the Second World War in order to help European allies to win the war against Nazi Germany and transforming US industry to war production, becoming "the Arsenal of Democracy", second, investing in the Marshall Plan to help with the reconstruction of Europe after the war, and third, financing the Apollo Programme by which the United States sent three men to the moon and started its space adventure. A recent example from Europe is the reunification of Germany and the decision by the German government to invest the substantial amounts necessary to build up the parts of the country that had belonged to the German Democratic Republic. There are many examples through history of efforts that have been successful, despite the fact that they have required great financial and other types of sacrifices short term. The transformation to e-mobility and the building of a circular economy is likely to require more resources than all the mentioned efforts combined, which is the reason why a strategy will become necessary.

The new circular economy that will be built on resource-efficient practices will have to be built in steps, the entire economy cannot be changed in one go, because society consists of individuals who work in their present jobs and the new supply chains and companies need to be started before people can get new jobs in the circular economy. The existing economic system could be likened to a tightly knit net of relationships between people and companies. In order to rebuild the economy, the present net needs to be carefully unravelled and the new net of the circular economy needs to be built step by step. It is important that the process does not go too fast, because new job opportunities in the new resource-efficient system need to be created that can offer job opportunities to people. To change all aspects of human activity to resilient and sustainable practices, large investment and substantial effort will be needed and the transformation needs to be performed over many years. The funding of such an endeavour will either have to be generated through the present economy in the forms of profits and economic growth or by loans, in the way that the large-scale programmes mentioned above were financed by the United States and Germany via their existing economies, or via some new type of economic system that has not yet been invented. The challenge facing anyone who wants to attempt to develop a new economic system will be to create one that will be able to generate enough leverage to sustain investment, while at the same time not replicating the weaknesses of the present system that have caused the present dependence on suppliers in far-away countries and overuse of resources.

In a world where oil is likely to become scarce and where the decline in oil production is likely to continue forever, without a new fuel or transport system in the pipeline to replace it, people will not, a few years into the decline, be able to drink beer that has been produced on another continent or travel to the other side of the globe in order to dip their bodies in the ocean. People need to realize that they cannot continue to buy lamb produced in New Zealand or fruit and vegetables, or fruit juices for that matter, grown on the other side of the planet. There are more important products that will be more difficult to replace by locally produced goods and the remaining oil reserves will have to be used to transport those. Depending on how this change gets handled by decision makers and on how the burdens of saving fuel and energy are distributed between countries and groups of people, the change could either lead to a significant programme to alter global and national economies or cause the entire global economy and international collaboration to break down. If governments handle the transformation in a constructive manner, the global economy will be put under pressure, but the consequences may be contained and the decline in oil production may be the start of a new development based on a discretionary use of resources.

Despite efforts to convince people of the need to change, some readers may still think that we can continue to live our lives in the way we are used to, because some new technology will appear, fully developed, and make fossil-free transport possible across the world over night. As has been argued above, this is very unlikely to happen as it takes decades to develop new technologies and create competitive systems, and the replacement of 1.2 billion cars and 100 million heavy vehicles will inevitably take decades. The rapid and seemingly unexpected emergence of a new technology, such as mobile telephony, on the global scene is deceptive. The technology that mobile telephony was based on, called radio telephony, had been developed for many decades out of sight of consumers and employees at companies, as the technology was used for communication in emergency systems, between alarm centres and fire engines and police cars, and after the launch of mobile telephony it took decades until the technology became inexpensive enough to be used by almost everybody. The speed of penetration was also increased by the fact that each phone only costs a few hundred euro.

Technologies are developed in a sequence of steps where they become more affordable and user-friendly for each new step. As there is no new transport technology that has already come a few steps on the way to becoming a general-purpose technology able to compete against petroleum-based transportation, the technology is primarily used in high-end cars aimed at the most affluent consumers. It is not very likely or, in fact, completely impossible, that a competitive technology will emerge that will become cost effective enough to replace petroleum driven vessels and vehicles for a broad range of purposes over the next ten or twenty years. For electric cars and trucks to take over a large share of road transportation, governments will have to start large-scale programmes with the goal of driving the transformation to completion and invest large amounts of money in the change.

Change leaders will have to communicate the facts related to the transformation in a way that cannot be misinterpreted. The methods of the transformation need to be communicated forcefully in several ways to get through to individuals across society. The current way of communicating is confusing, because it gives people the impression that we will be able to continue to live like in the twentieth century, despite the fact that an increasing number of experts try to inform people that oil will soon start to become scarce. Facing the need for a dramatic transformation, the global community cannot afford ambiguous communication.

As television companies all over the world compete for the attention of viewers, they develop shows that attract as many as possible. The way to attract many viewers is to appeal to values that are held by most people — and most people get thrilled by fast cars, travelling to distant sunny or snowy locations, and participating in adventurous leisure activities. The concept of Top Gear fits this bill ideally. The show communicates an ideal of fast cars, adventurous journeys to far-off countries with dramatic road trips along scenic routes. A situation where everybody needs to contribute to a reduction of resource consumption, with a particular need to reduce the use of oil in all its various forms and uses, shows that building the picture of successful people as entitled to use inordinate amounts of resources for pure pleasure strongly contributes to preserving ideals that we, in the near future, need to leave behind. And people will need guidance in developing their new lifestyles. The presenters of Top Gear are role models for viewers, many of them aspiring to lead exciting lives. In several ways the lifestyles of the future need to become less opulent with regard to the use of resources, and television companies need to contribute to helping people adopt lifestyles that are in line with the more frugal conditions that we will be forced to accept. Maybe some readers would argue that it is not at all given that we will have to accept harsher conditions, simply because oil is getting scarce. There is still the possibility that someone will invent glorious new technologies that can offer increasing affluence even in the face of some resources becoming scarce. This is exactly the point I'm trying to make! Efforts to develop new technologies that help conserve energy and contribute to resource efficiency and build new transportation and production systems based on those have been going on at least since the oil embargo in the 1970s. Due to the lack of insight that the new and resource-efficient systems will soon have to be applied everywhere, little money has been invested in the testing and implementation of new transport technologies on a large scale. We already have access to more new technologies than we need, but we have not started to tackle the knotty issues related to applying the most promising solutions on a large scale, or inventing new breakthrough technologies that can take human life into the future. Few experts have started to consider if the new technologies can become competitive, or which of the alternatives are most promising when all different aspects of development and growth are weighed into the equation. Developing prototype technologies is inexpensive and can be done in a few years. Integrating technologies into well-functioning and competitive systems takes decades and requires very large investment. For the most promising technologies to be developed to the point where they become competitive, resources need to be focused and development of less promising technologies needs to cease.

Developing a strategy involves selecting the technologies that show the biggest promise, establish missing technologies that will be needed to build complete systems, and implement the new systems on a large scale. We should not let ourselves be fooled into believing that the task of developing systems and investing in their growth can be done over the course of a few years, as oil starts to become scarce.

Television and film strongly influence the ideals and lifestyles of viewers. Over the past decades the way that women have been portrayed in the media has been under scrutiny and debate and measures have been taken to contribute to a more balanced portrayal of both genders. The #MeToo movement has contributed to highlighting the inexcusable way that women are sometimes treated by men and some men have been taken to court because of this. The fact that more people have turned their attention to these things has helped turning the minds of people towards issues that have otherwise been neglected. Attention from the media and from people in general has contributed to changing our culture and the way men view and treat women, and also to changing the way that women are depicted on screen. Now it is time to realize that gender and racial equality are not the only issues that have to be kept in mind by producers, directors, and programming planners at media and film companies as they make productions. Transformations to e-mobility and a circular economy are challenges that present generations will need to face in the next few years and people will need guidance from role models in the media to make better decisions. This will be a challenge for media companies, but one that probably can be mastered, as the industry has mastered other challenges in the past.

In several ways it will become apparent that people cannot continue to use resources in the way we have done in the past. Politicians and business leaders will face the challenge of leading the transformation through a period that is likely to be turbulent and that will require unprecedented changes to the way we live and consume in the developed world. During the coronavirus pandemic, people have experienced some of the issues that arise when products cannot be produced and delivered because of problems in the supply chain. As the crisis continues an increasing number of people argue that similar things will happen in the future as well, which seems likely, but it does not seem to occur to decision makers at the moment that disease is not the only problem. It is about time for everybody to realize that they need to contribute to a more resource-efficient and less vulnerable future. Unfortunately, up until now the sustainability debate has focused on climate change and the need to reduce emissions of carbon dioxide. Emissions will be dramatically reduced as oil production starts to decline. The most pressing issue will be for our oil dependent society and the global economy to continue to function in a time when countries will have access to less oil.

This will be a very difficult challenge as all developed countries are entirely dependent on oil for transportation, and on products that are made using oil as a raw material. Oil is necessary for food production, as diesel is used to fuel tractors and combine harvesters, and it is used to make fertilizer and nutritional components for animal feed.[2] It is also necessary for the transportation of food and all other products from manufacturers to users. In the global economy many products travel several times around the earth on their way from raw material

---

[2]   In *Eating Fossil Fuels* Dale Allen Pfeiffer describes ways in which and to what extent the world is dependent on oil for food production.

production, via manufacturing of component parts, to the user of the final product. Thus, without enough oil people will experience shortages of all kinds of products and it will become increasingly difficult for companies to continue to run their businesses at full capacity. Reduced oil production will even have an impact on the functioning of society's critical infrastructure, as maintenance of systems depends on a constant supply of spare parts. This is also true for manufacturing companies. They are constantly in need of spare parts for production equipment, as few companies keep parts in stock. Instead they rely on the just-in-time supply of parts, as needs arise. Over the past three decades companies have reduced their stock of both spare parts and components and raw materials for production. This has been driven by the implementation of Lean Production, the operations concept pioneered by Toyota, which relies on the principle of zero stock. This practice dramatically reduces the cost of operation and the application of all aspects of the Lean Production package has become necessary to remain competitive. As beneficial as this has been for profits, it has also made society vulnerable in the event of reduced oil production, because there are virtually no buffers in the supply chains, something that has also been demonstrated through the Covid-19 pandemic. By closing entire regions, the Chinese government effectively stopped exports of all kinds of products to foreign markets, thereby showing the world the risks that China's economic wonder has created for companies all over the planet. Without buffer stocks of even the most important components and equipment, shortages emerged almost immediately and many companies had to close production while waiting for manufacturing once more to start.

From the perspective of a reduced oil supply, present generations have adopted unfortunate habits and principles that need to become reversed in order to reduce vulnerability to an oil shortage. As oil production is likely to go down by one to two per cent per year in the first few years of decline, countries will struggle to keep up with the pace of reduction. Later, experts predict that the annual decline will be larger, amounting to two, three, and after some years four or five per cent per year, a decline that is likely to be irreversible. Only very large new discoveries of conventional oil can then bring production back on the growth track and it is not very likely that this will occur. New discoveries have been in steady decline since the 1960s and they are now down to only a few per cent of annual production. The largest oil field in the world, Ghawar in Saudi Arabia, has been producing since the 1960s and it has since then delivered three to four million barrels of oil per day, more than one billion barrels per year for more than forty years. At present, a discovery amounting to 300 million barrels of recoverable oil is labelled *large,* even though the volume amounts to less than four days of global production. Decision makers and ordinary people alike do not understand how dependent the world, and each country, is on oil and they do not have a picture of the magnitude of the transformation that will be necessary to reduce dependence. The dependence is especially unfortunate in Europe, as the continent has very small oil reserves and is to a large extent dependent on Russia and the Middle East for its supplies. The United Kingdom and Norway used to be large producers and Norway once ranked as the third largest oil exporter in the world, but the production of both countries has halved over the past decade. Only a very small number of countries, primarily the United States and Russia, can still increase production slightly. Saudi Arabia, the country that was once the largest producer in the world, is approaching its production peak. OPEC estimates for the period from 2020 to 2024 that production will decrease from 35 million barrels per day to 32.8 million.[3] This is unfortunate, to say the least, as OPEC has increased its production from 2002 to 2019 from 28 to 35 million and thereby helped compensate for the reduced production of a large number of countries like Norway and the UK that have had to reduce their production due to the depletion of reserves.

In the face of this type of information it becomes increasingly difficult to avoid thinking that there is a high probability that the declining oil supply will pose a significant threat to the global economy in the next few years. It becomes increasingly obvious that the transformation is extremely urgent. The next thought is likely to be what needs to be done and there is no comfort in the fact that the global economy needs to substantially reduce its dependence on oil in the next few years, but there are no new transport systems ready to rapidly replace oil as the world's most important fuel. There are also no local production systems in place that can make it possible to turn the economy into a new mode after Covid-19.

As mentioned above, only 0.5 per cent of the cars in global vehicle fleets can be driven on electricity and most of the existing cars are hybrids that can only drive up to fifty kilometres on electricity. The rest, some two million vehicles, are fully electric cars with a battery

---

[3]   CNBC, 5 November 2019, "OPEC lowers forecast for oil demand growth, says its own market share is dwindling".

capacity of between ten and five hundred kilometres and a time of charging of between one hour and twenty hours, depending on the capacity of the charging equipment, in order to fully charge the battery. Existing electric car fleets are hardly ready to take over a large portion of the transportation work of the world's car transport systems.

Admittedly, it does make sense to maintain a sense of optimism in the face of adverse events, but it is not a good idea to act as a blind guardian of ignorance and not allow facts about humanity's challenging future to reach decision makers and voters, because the ability of countries to take constructive action depends on the existence of informed citizens with relevant knowledge. There is obviously a big gap between the realistic future that we can intellectually conclude as the most probable and the rhetoric that people are fed on a daily basis. The present situation is nothing less than an exceptionally tragic case of the blind leading the blind and there are few people who can break the circuit of misinformation and auto-suggestion that blinds people to important facts and information. If most citizens after the coronavirus pandemic want to continue to lead their lives as if it was still 1990 and there were no serious structural threats to economic growth, the world will meet the decline in oil production and the ensuing economic decline entirely unprepared. If, on the other hand, a substantial share of the global population were to start to become accustomed to the idea that the future is not what it used to be, we may at least hit the ground walking and it will be possible to increase the pace of transformation so that present generations find a way to move with dignity into the future.

To do this, a few hundred million people need to start to change their lifestyles and consumption habits on a large scale, in ways that not even the most dedicated sustainability experts seem to have anticipated. The norm for most people at present is to adapt some aspects of their lives to sustainable practices, but few people seem to have considered reducing their resource consumption to levels that are sustainable for the longer term and there is no clear picture of what would constitute such a lifestyle. If a small share of the population changes some aspects of their lifestyles, towards sustainability, in the way that is done at present, the change is not likely to be significant enough to bring about a transformation to any part of society.

Part 2:
Driving the Change

Chapter Six

Re-engineering the Economy to Resilience and Circularity

Large-scale change cannot be achieved through small-scale and random activities. There is a need for systematic transformation by applying the most powerful change tools that are known and ones that have been tried and tested for decades in other circumstances. The principles that are known as re-engineering have been applied by large companies and the experiences from re-engineering and other change methods have been collected to create the discipline of change management. Re-engineering and change management can become cornerstones of the projects that need to be initiated to transform society to sustainability.

What Does Re-engineering Mean?

The concept of re-engineering was developed and introduced in 1993 by Michael Hammer and James Champy in their book *Reengineering the Corporation*. At the time, digitization had made it possible to completely reorganize business processes inside organizations. Re-engineering means that managers started to reorganize activities based on modern flows of information, doing away with the inefficiencies of the pre-digital economy. Now this development has been in progress for more than two decades and it has significantly improved the efficiency of the economy. Based on re-engineering efforts and the application of other methods of change, the discipline of change management has been developed. Practitioners in this field build knowledge of how large-scale change projects need to be managed to succeed. A similar approach needs to be taken with the implementation of e-mobility and the circular economy. Experiences that have been had by companies need to be translated to the contexts of countries and the global economy at large. The Covid-19 pandemic has created a new and entirely unexpected situation and there is suddenly a realization that western countries need to become more resilient and their supply systems also need to become sustainable. Countries need to rapidly reduce their vulnerability to shocks, their dependence on oil, and invest significant amounts of money and other resources in the creation of a sustainable future. To achieve this, they need to collaborate to develop strategies that achieve the most important changes in the shortest time possible and at the lowest possible expense. Cost effectiveness has become a critical priority as the economic circumstances have become worse through the coronavirus pandemic.

One early example of re-engineering is the production of a passport, which used to involve a number of steps, such as (in Sweden) going to a photographer to take a photograph, bringing the photograph to the police or, depending on the country, some other national authority responsible for passports, who sent the material consisting of a photograph, the necessary personal information about the applicant, and a signature in the mail to the authority responsible for producing the passport, who then went through the steps of production and sent the final product back to the police station where the application was filed. This used to be a costly and time-consuming process, requiring several weeks. The new process, after re-engineering, involved taking an electronic photograph at the police station and writing the signature, that is digitally stored, at the same time. The personal information of every citizen is already available in the database. The photograph, the personal information, and the signature are integrated in an electronic document that gets printed and made in a continuous process and the finished passport is then sent back to the police station where the application was filed. After re-engineering the process only takes a few days and the cost is substantially reduced. At the same time, passports become more difficult to forge, as the old process of pasting a photograph into a pre-printed passport has been replaced by the production of a high-tech passport with a number of security features.

In the case of internal administration at companies, documents were manually shuffled between departments. A customer was visited by a salesperson, who ordered a product. The salesperson took down the order on a form and put it in the order tray at the sales department, where it had to wait for a week to be picked up by a clerk, who kept one copy of the order to be archived, and sent the remaining copies to the stores for delivery of off-the-shelf products. At the stores, the products were dispatched, one copy of the sales order was kept at the stores where the delivery was entered into the system for keeping track of stock, and one copy was sent to the accounting department for invoicing. The remaining copy was sent back to the sales department with a scribbled note confirming the delivery. When stock reached a certain level—called an order point—a production order was manually created, which was sent to production and, when components reached an order point, purchasing orders were created, also manually, and sent to suppliers. The entire process, including waiting times in the in-trays at each department and lead times for the preparation and fulfilment of orders in many companies took between four and six weeks. Customers were used to the long lead times and had to plan accordingly. As a consequence, companies with a seasonal demand often had only one opportunity to guess the demand for a product in the coming season, because it took too long to go through the process again and order a second batch, which would have arrived after the end of the season.

After re-engineering, a sales order was entered by a salesperson and this automatically generated all the other transactions, including accounting transactions and invoicing. In the 1990s examples were reported of companies, like Benetton and Toys'R'Us, that used so-called point-of-sales systems to monitor sales in shops. Sales of the most popular items immediately triggered production orders at plants, where new products were made and sent to stores within a few days. At Benetton, undyed garments were held in stock waiting for sales figures to trigger the dying process. Many automotive companies copied the practices developed by Toyota to allow a customer order to trigger the production of a car. When a customer placed the order the production order was planned into the flow at the assembly plant and only hours before the car body went up on the assembly line the parts were sent from suppliers that were all located close to the plant. This practice was called *kan-ban* or just-in-time deliveries and it was implemented to minimize the amount of capital tied up in stock. The complete set of improvements have in a number of companies been made in many steps during recent decades. The implementation of the new practices has required investment and changes to shop lay-out and employee routines, and each improvement has reduced the remaining waste of time, money, and other resources at companies that have adopted the methods. This management process is known as change management. The method described here was developed at Toyota and has become known as the Toyota Production System, or Lean Production.

Now this development has been in progress for more than 25 years and it has significantly improved the efficiency of the economy and contributed to economic growth. Step-by-step and through the investment of billions of euro in equipment, software, and consulting services to help manage the process, companies have improved their operations using digital and manual tools. Change management builds knowledge about how large-scale change projects need to be organized and run to succeed. Another important aspect is the amount of resources that are needed to succeed with a change and the tendency of organizations to gravitate towards existing routines. Most change projects fail, because not enough attention is paid to the details of the change and because too few resources are allocated to support transformation. While there are often individuals and groups of employees that embrace change, the majority prefer to keep things as they are and continue to do business as usual. This tendency to resist change can be overcome through determination and well-structured change programmes. To succeed, change must be supported by managers at all levels, and areas where quick wins can be achieved need to be targeted to get examples that show that the transformation will be possible. This builds morale and creates examples for others to follow. Success stories need to be communicated together with the approaches that formed the bases for success. A similar approach needs to be taken to the implementation of e-mobility and the circular economy and to other change projects where many individuals need to contribute to large-scale change. Experiences that have been had by companies need to be translated to the contexts of countries and the global economy at large. Development projects in different areas will need to be run in parallel in different countries and the results must be shared and multiplied generously between nations.

Large-scale change requires large-scale training and information activities, investment in expansion of facilities and the closing down of others to optimize production structures, and the adoption of new tools in all parts of the business, for example developing e-business systems that can extend the reach of new offerings and organize local markets across the world.

The new trend of re-engineering became a lucrative business proposal for consultants all over the world who helped companies to substantially reduce the time and cost of production and distribution and introduce entirely new ways of doing business. For many years, the word re-engineering carried the meaning of change measures aimed at achieving radical improvement goals, many times made possible by modern technology that offered new possibilities. In later years, Lean Production and Lean Management with their well-defined tools of change have taken prominence over re-engineering. Lean Management, however, implies a reduction in resources, while re-engineering means that routines are changed. The concept of Lean Management can hardly be applied to the creation of sustainable and resilient production and distribution systems, since the new systems are for a long time likely to be less lean than the systems they are going to replace. The concept of re-engineering can, on the other hand, be applied to any type of change, which makes it more suitable in the present context. The principles that need to be applied throughout the transformation to sustainable production and distribution systems, and sustainable administrative principles, must borrow aspects from all change philosophies. The process will have to start almost with a blank sheet of paper and the new systems have to be based on the needs that will be determined by access to resources and the speed at which oil production will go into decline.

Decision makers and change managers will need to apply a similar mind-set as the one applied in re-engineering projects. The measures that will be needed to reduce global dependence on oil will have to involve very large investment and transformation activities that dramatically change supply chains in entire industries. Every effort will have to be made to succeed with the transformation, as the opposite can hardly even be contemplated, and all citizens need to get involved in transformation activities of various kinds. One of the most pressing needs will be to increase the demand for local products and services as these require less transportation than ones produced in global supply chains on the other side of the globe. But in general, the demand needs to increase for products that can be made and distributed using fewer resources.

Resource Demand Will Increase

It is important to realize that large-scale change will not be achieved in a short period of time and that the initial phases of the transformation will not lead to a reduction in resource consumption. Overall, the transformation to e-mobility and the circular economy will require that countries have many decades of generous resource supply ahead of them that can be used throughout the transformation. These types of large-scale changes require decades of investment when sustainable systems gradually take over from the present ones. This will inevitably involve large-scale public financing for many years until the new systems become competitive against the present—and the new systems that will exist in parallel with present ones will inevitably be inefficient from a resource perspective and add to resource consumption, before they start to contribute to a reduction. Any other expectation would be wishful thinking. Even if the ultimate goal is to make the new systems more resource efficient than the ones they are intended to replace, they will initially cater to only a small share of consumers or industrial customers and they will be relatively inefficient compared to the systems they will be replacing. Present systems will for a long time remain more resource efficient overall than the new systems and they are likely to offer products and services at lower prices, unless governments put a tax on the systems they want to replace. The problem with present systems is, of course, the fact that they rely on a large amount of transportation and this reliance represents a gigantic risk to society and to the companies that depend on it. This we can observe as the world goes through the Covid-19 crisis, but the risk will become even bigger as the world approaches the peak in oil production.

Transportation will become more expensive as the price of oil increases, but the cost of oil represents a small share of the total cost of a product or service, which means that even a very large increase in the price of oil will only raise the cost of products by a small amount. In the case of the implementation of new production and distribution systems, these will be significantly more labour intensive at the early stages, as companies that will apply circular business models will need to build up their businesses from scratch. The opportunity to automate production will be limited, since turnover will remain small until large numbers of consumers become aware of the need to buy local products. In the absence of a large change it is likely that demand for these products will remain small for a long time. Most start-up companies never reach the stage of growth where they become large volume businesses, and this is not likely to change because the transformation is necessary. This is one of the reasons why there is a need to adapt communication and transformation measures to the needs of the issue at hand. If the forecasts of the decline in oil production turn out to be correct and the decline starts in the next few years, there is simply no time available to correct mistakes. Everything must, from now on, be done right, and the first steps of a large-scale transformation need to be taken. This is an unfortunate situation, as humanity has never had to deal with anything similar before. Previous generations have implemented new technologies to replace existing ones, but never driven change of the presently required scale.

Doing things right, however, will be difficult because very few persons see the magnitude of the transformation and understand what will need to be done to transform society to a reduced dependence on oil. Society needs to leave many of the behaviours and habits of the twentieth century behind and develop new principles and lifestyles in most areas, principles and lifestyles that make countries less dependent on oil and other resources.

One of the most important things to start with is to find ways to reinforce understanding of the change and the activities that need to be initiated to achieve this and reduce the number of conflicting messages, even if messages are sent as entertainment. It will require forceful politics and information campaigns to deal with the strong forces that act against change and convince opponents of the need. I enjoy watching Top Gear myself, once in a while, but this does not invalidate the argument. Our appreciation of the show prevents us from under-standing what needs to be done to create a sustainable future.

In his chronicle in *The Sun* of the 27th of September 2019, former Top Gear presenter Jeremy Clarkson makes it clear that he in private holds the same worldview that he embodies in the show, saying that Greta Thunberg is a spoilt child who should be grateful for what former generations have done for the children of today. Using the perspective of the twentieth century, Clarkson is definitely right. The hard work of the generations that in the nineteenth and twentieth centuries laid the foundation of today's society deserves our admiration and gratitude. If there is a chance that teenagers like Greta really will inherit a society that will provide opportunities to lead affluent and comfortable lives — in a world where environmental and resource problems that we are discussing at present will be solved one by one through investment that will be financed by the market without interference from governments — Greta and I need to rest our cases and admit that Jeremy Clarkson was right and we were wrong. If, on the other hand, it turns out that Greta in fact underestimated the transformation that society will have to go through within the next few years — and that oil production starts to go down in 2022, 2023, or 2024 and that this causes a dramatic downturn for the global economy — Clarkson and a large number of other public figures, politicians, and experts will have to admit that they were wrong when they downplayed the need for change. Regard-less of what will happen, Jeremy Clarkson is to a large extent right. We should be grateful for the efforts that were made by people in the nineteenth and twentieth centuries to build the comfortable society that we experience today. What we need to be more critical of is the inability of the more recent generations that, after the oil embargoes of the 1970s and 1980s, did not continue to develop a sustainable society. It has always been known and accepted that oil is a finite resource, but it has been taken for granted by decision makers that countries can move to another fuel when it becomes necessary, and that this move will not have to be prepared or planned for. Decision makers have never seen a risk in increasing the dependence on oil, and the cost of transforming transport systems and the time frame for making the change to a new fuel has never been discussed, despite the fact that both of these facts are very important.

Gradually, but still very slowly, the world is discovering that the cost and time frame will be substantial. After several decades of debate of the choice of fuels and several false starts in different countries, where governments have decided to implement transport systems based on ethanol, biogas, or electric cars, the global share of electric cars now amounts to about 0.5 per cent, and the number of electric and hybrid cars sold amounts to slightly more than 2 million per year, out of global car fleets of 1.2 billion cars. In order to fuel 1 million cars the equivalent of half the production of a nuclear power plant will be needed, but a share of the power needed for the first million cars in any large country can be covered by utilizing electricity that at present is lost during periods during the day of low demand when power production is running at a higher level, and through savings in energy use in other areas. For the second million cars and further on through the transformation in any country, surplus energy will run out and investment in new production capacity will have to be made. When the need to expand power production arises, the cost of expanding e-mobility will be high, and it will become obvious that every transport need will have to be scrutinized. Still, despite this, electricity is the only realistic alternative to petroleum-based fuels.

A Brief Evaluation of Fuel Types

Biofuels represent seemingly competitive alternatives to fossil fuels and the idea of humanity being able to locally grow the fuels that are used for transportation is beautiful and perhaps more logical intuitively than the idea of pumping oil or natural gas from the ground and transporting it around the world to use it for transportation. The problem with biofuels is that oil volumes are so large that countries cannot replace oil by fuels that are produced in agriculture. If all agricultural land on the planet were to be used to produce biofuels, the volume produced would only amount to 25 per cent of all the oil that is used on the planet and no grain would be left to eat or use as feed for animals.[1] When seen from the overall perspective of transforming the world's entire transport fleets, biofuels seem to be an impossible alternative and it seems like a bad idea also on a small scale. There are several reasons for this, one of them being the fact that efforts to implement alternatives that do not have large-scale potential detract attention and resources from alternatives that have the potential to replace oil and that deserve full focus. Exchanging oil for similar amounts of biofuels is not a viable idea and is one that needs to be discarded.

Electricity production for e-mobility can be expanded almost infinitely, through the application of wind, solar, and nuclear power plants. Contrary to the situation with regard to biofuels, there is already large-scale production of electricity — a large amount of electricity is lost on a daily basis that can be used to charge electric vehicles and there are transmission and distribution systems in place in all countries, and regional and national grids are connected into larger systems covering Europe, North America, and other parts of the globe. The availability of electricity and the infrastructure in place represent great advantages, as countries can start to build fleets of electric and hybrid vehicles without spending time and money investing in building new production and distribution systems for fuels. Expansion of the present systems for power generation will have to take place as fleets of electric vehicles grow, but initially the power supply will be unproblematic. The availability of systems is a risk, because decision makers and people in general get the impression that electric vehicle fleets can be rolled out on a large scale without major investment, which is not the case. To implement electric transportation on a large scale very large investment will be needed in:

- the expansion of battery production;
- the development of increasingly competitive models of electric vehicles;
- the transformation of the automotive industry to the sales, production, and maintenance of the new vehicles;
- the timely expansion of power production and distribution in combination with the development of smart power grids;
- the development and installation of charging equipment and digital services;
- other investment that will become obvious as the transformation process progresses.

Electric transportation is the most competitive and promising alternative for the large-scale transformation of transportation to new and sustainable systems, but the change will require tremendous investment and large resources for the development of technologies and system solutions and management of the large-scale implementation projects.

---

[1]   Therese Uddenfelt, *Gratislunchen*.

Hydrogen fuel cells is a technology that is at an even earlier stage of development than e-mobility and there are no resources yet in place that can facilitate the expansion of such systems. Fuelling cars with hydrogen would require hydrogen production on an extensive scale and large-scale distribution systems for the gas—both aspects that need to be built from scratch. Hydrogen is at present primarily produced from oil and on a small scale, for industrial purposes, but other feedstocks are researched as well, such as ammonia and water. The production process is based on the technology of electrolysis, which requires large amounts of electricity. The amount of electricity that is needed to produce hydrogen to drive one kilometre is more than twice that needed to drive an electric car the same distance (approximately 3 kWh for the fuel cell vehicle compared to 1.5 kWh for the electric car). This means that the volume of power production that needs to be built to produce hydrogen for fuel cell vehicles will be two times as large as that which will be needed to produce electricity for electric ones. The equivalent electricity production of some 500 nuclear power plants will be needed worldwide for electric cars and 1,000 would be needed for hydrogen powered cars, and the same number would be needed to power heavy vehicles. But many experts doubt that hydrogen can ever become relevant for heavy transportation, due to the low energy density of the gas. The tanks necessary to store the fuel needed to run a truck 500 kilometres will take up too much space and thus too little space will be left for goods.

As it is difficult to mobilize the financing and resources for the transformation to electric cars, the idea to invest in hydrogen fuel cell transportation seems impossible. The systems that countries start to build need to be able to cope with large-scale transformation. Research is done into hydrogen transportation and a small number of cars have been sold. Hydrogen fuel cells seem a dangerous side-track. The naïve idea that hydrogen may be the fuel of the future—which is put forward by some technical experts and politicians—takes attention and decision-making power away from the expansion of electric mobility. One of the reasons why the expansion of the world's stock of fuel cell vehicles goes slowly is that the purchasing price is higher than 50,000 euro. It is likely to forever remain well above that of the more affordable electric vehicles, because the volumes of electric vehicles sold, now over one million per year, drives the price down faster than the pace of the price reduction of fuel cell cars. It begs the question if it will ever become relevant for large numbers of car buyers to choose a fuel cell vehicle when there are less expensive electric cars that offer better performance and better access to charging. The small volumes of hydrogen fuel cell vehicles that are sold contribute very little towards development costs and the thus advancement is bound to continue to go slowly (i.e. the expansion of production and distribution infrastructure for hydrogen is likely to be slow and the investments necessary in the electricity grid will be twice as large as the ones required to facilitate e-mobility). The argument that lithium will become a scarce metal and that fuel cells represent a way to circumvent this does not seem to be valid. The production of fuel cells requires rare minerals and advanced materials that are likely to become scarce as well. The invention of a battery technology that does not involve lithium seems to be a more viable proposition than the use of hydrogen fuel cells on a large scale.

Developing e-mobility is not likely to be a walk in the park. There are very serious and difficult problems that need to be dealt with. But electricity is the only fuel that seems realistic for large-scale expansion from the standpoint of the opportunity to produce large volumes of fuel, financing the transformation, and driving the development at speed. The speed of progress is a critical factor that should guide decision making and it is at present much too slow. Countries need to find ways to speed up the expansion of vehicle fleets, expand power distribution, and make power grids more flexible.

Most likely we will all find that decision makers today are making the same mistake as the members of the British government led by Prime Minister Neville Chamberlain at the beginning of the Second World War. The prime minister and the members of his cabinet argued that Britain should negotiate with Adolf Hitler to get a favourable peace agreement and thus avoid invasion. Many politicians in the late 1930s and early 1940s did not understand that Hitler's goal was to dominate the whole world and that he would not honour a peace agreement for long. This became apparent later when the extent of his plans for global domination were revealed.

In a similar way, a decline in oil production is not likely to be modest and slow and allow ample time for countries to build up new transport systems. The speed of the decline in oil production will not provide time for countries to organize and finance their transformation projects to keep pace with the decline. The speed of the decline will be determined by geological and technical factors related to the depletion of wells and to the cost of the new transport technologies that are available. The coming decline in oil production will be rapid and the realization that oil production will go into permanent decline will turn the present favourable economic progress into a recession that is soon likely to become a depression, and the consequences will go beyond anything that has been experienced by humanity. As always, it will be easy to spot the mistakes in hindsight, like we can now see the political genius of Churchill, compared to the narrower understanding of his contemporaries.

The Covid-19 crisis has opened the eyes of many to some of the risks of being dependent on long-distance transportation and production in far-away countries. But it is still likely to be difficult for people who doubt the relevance of warnings—or who believe that decision makers can simply press the "go" button and set in motion a series of activities that have been planned for a long time, but never turned into action — to motivate themselves to spend the time and effort and think through the process of transformation to realize that the change process will be complex and that there are no ready-made plans. The present situation has shown countries that a pandemic is possible and many believe that more will come in the future, but at the same time the price of oil has gone down to the lowest levels seen in recent decades. If people do not realize that this is a temporary development and that the world is heading for the peak in oil production once consumption goes back to pre-coronavirus levels it will be increasingly difficult to persuade decision makers that a reduction in oil production may be the next big problem.

Greta Thunberg, who is 17 years old and who has not yet gone to university or built experience from industry, can read up on the literature about climate change and impress listeners with her knowledge of carbon dioxide levels and emissions, but understanding the transformation process is a completely different task. The same is true for idealists like Jeremy Clarkson, who fight for people's freedom to live their lives as they see fit and allow market forces to determine the boundaries of what each person can do. Experienced people like Mr Clarkson are not likely to appreciate the complexity of the global economy and the risks that are connected to relying on the market to drive the changes that will be necessary to create the future. After all, it has worked in the past and the market economy has proven far superior to planned economic systems in terms of driving growth and improving the affluence of citizens. It requires significant determination for an individual to reason their way to the conclusion that the situation now is very different from previous decades and that humanity is now facing challenges that have previously not been experienced.

Even people who have worked in leading roles in industry all their lives do not immediately see the complexity of the transformation process. Most jobs in management and development have a relatively narrow focus and people mainly learn about their field of focus. It is not until people understand the magnitude of oil production and the time and investment that are needed in order to develop new technologies, almost from scratch, that many realize that it will be a tremendous transformation challenge. Most people have the development of mobile phones and portable computers in mind when they discuss technology advancement and the prospects of e-mobility, but these technologies have in recent decades become mature and the price of a phone is only in the area of 500 euro. It is easy to forget the decades of development that preceded the growth phase and assume that all technology development starts from a relatively high level of maturity. In addition to this, a smart phone provides users with substantial utility and it would be difficult to navigate modern life without one. E-mobility is at a very early stage of development and each vehicle comes with a price tag of more than 30,000 euro. The dynamics of car purchases is, for this and other reasons, different from the dynamics of the purchases of mobile phones, fax machines, and other technologies that have rapidly penetrated markets in the past. Each car has a lifetime of more than 15 years, and when only a few per cent of cars that are sold are electric or hybrid it will take a very long time to transform global vehicle fleets to electricity.

What Clarkson and his compatriots need to do is to take a long hard look at the figures related to oil production, the forecasts of decline, and the time it will take to build new transport systems. After this they can come back with their verdict. Or is the task of understanding the logic of oil production and the time frame and cost of large-scale trans-formation too complicated for most people on the planet, including Jeremy Clarkson? I do not think so, but the number of facts that need to be considered and the job of verifying whether information and calcu-lations are correct, or at least relevant or not, is substantial and few take the time to go through this process without being forced to do it. It is not very complicated, but it requires that people are willing to lead their thoughts into uncharted territories and face facts and aspects of development that they are not familiar with.

Up until 2004, before I realized how bad a situation humanity has created for itself, I would have been inclined to share Jeremy Clarkson's position and to some extent I can still relate to his outburst about Greta Thunberg. If the arguments that have been communicated to support the need for a reduction in the use of oil have not been made clearly and convincingly enough to get through to the majority of people, it is hardly the fault of those who have been on the receiving end of communication. The party that can correct a communication error and the one who has the task of making a message understandable to the receiver is the sender. The tearful approach of Greta Thunberg or the mild encouragement of Sir David Attenborough and other researchers to take these issues seriously are not likely to get through to hard-line proponents of the market ideology, such as Jeremy Clarkson. If there is a need to reduce resource consumption and in particular reduce the use of oil it must be very confusing for Jeremy Clarkson that the television show that he has been part of continues to go on air year after year and that car and fuel sales continue to hit new records all the time. After all, if there is a real problem, somebody should be able to explain it in such a way that decision makers, television presenters, and the public become able to understand the seriousness. Despite claims about its scientific foundations, it seems completely incomprehensible that a society that is supposed to be the most advanced of all societies through history could fail to make up its collective mind regarding the direction of development. Surely, Greta Thunberg must be at fault when she scolds world leaders, saying that they have stolen the future of the young generation? Jeremy Clarkson is certainly not the only person who is confused.

Present society is really an extraordinary and complex organization. The level of specialization is amazing and the technologies and organization principles that previous generations have developed are astonishing. The fact that this complex organization can be run on a day-to-day basis with very small stocks of products is impressive. Instead of having large stores at home and in shops, society depends on the flawless functioning of transport systems that deliver everything we need to shops and production facilities, and we have a tremendous choice of products and services that contribute to people's feelings of strength and invincibility. The problem is that this system is strongly dependent on transportation on a daily and hourly basis, even to supply people with the bare necessities of life, and for this reason it is very vulnerable. What Jeremy Clarkson and most other people are not aware of is that oil, the very fuel of the cars he loves to drive and of the whole economy, is about to become scarce and that production may start to decline by one or two per cent already in the next few years — and that production volumes, according to the International Energy Agency and other independent experts, may decline by as much as 30 per cent by 2030 or soon thereafter. This is really bad news, both for Jeremy Clarkson and the rest of the world, and all countries and their citizens need to start to adapt to this information or prove that it is wrong. There is no other way.

Specialization

The problem with communication that seems to have confused Clarkson and surely many more than him to a large extent goes back to specialization. At work and in their spare time individuals specialize in a small number of increasingly narrow areas and there is no person or function in society that has the task of keeping track of the overall direction of development. Most people are likely to, without thinking about it in detail, assume that all the most important tasks in society are taken care of by someone with the responsibility to make sure that there are no unexpected pitfalls for society that have not been identified and prepared for. Surely, there must be some expert at a government agency, central bank, or at a ministry that has a clear vision of the future and who has approved the route of development that European governments and those of other countries around the world have embarked on? I thought so too when I, fifteen years ago, started to investigate how society needs to transform to prepare for a future with less oil. I thought that it would be easy to find people interested in the overall picture of development and would welcome the information that governments rapidly need to lead development down a new path towards a reduced dependence on oil. I did not find anyone with this type of task or with systemic insight who was able to take in my message, understand the point of view, and identify a handful of people we could go and talk to in order to spread the word.

Instead I have concluded that in an increasingly complex society each person becomes more specialized, but the web of knowledge that develops, built on the knowledge of highly specialized experts, contains an increasing number of loopholes, areas in between competencies where there is no expertise, issues that nobody, or very few, have looked into. The risk is especially high when the competencies that need to be developed are cross-disciplinary. In the case of the transformation of society, Greta Thunberg and many other sustainability experts argue that governments need to invest more in the transformation to sustainability, but these experts do not have any training or experience from the areas of society that need to change—several global industries—and their lack of knowledge is illustrated by the fact that their arguments never include advice for the transformation or any reliable estimate of the resources that will be needed for the change. On the other hand, there are people like Jeremy Clarkson, Donald Trump, and conservative and liberal politicians and business leaders all over the world who firmly believe that the problems are exaggerated and that the market or innovative inventions will take care of any serious problem—and that no human being will have to bother intervening. Between these groups there is a chasm filled with un-knowledge that has not been observed by any of their members, most of whom are facing inwards, discussing with their peers, sometimes shouting over the shoulder to their opponents in the other group, arguing that they have not even begun to understand how the world really works. The members of neither group have bothered to step out of their comfort zones and started to chart the territories between the descriptions of the environmental and resource issues and the ability of the market to take care of complex transformation challenges. It is these territories, and the knowledge that needs to fill the chasm, that are described in this book and that few sustainability alarmists and television presenters dare to admit even exist.

No government agency in any country has been assigned the task of monitoring all relevant aspects of development to produce realistic forecasts based on the big picture. There has never been a government agency with this task and throughout history people have found out the hard way that there are unknown stumbling blocks that pose challenges for governments, economists, policy strategists, and people in general. When I first wrote those lines in the last quarter of 2019, there was no recent example of a crisis where the actions of governments had been in focus, but as I now edit the text during the coronavirus crisis it has once more become clear that governments have failed to foresee and prepare for even highly probable events that cause deep crises—and it is once more apparent to most that Covid-19 is not the last big event to change the lives and the future of people on the planet. As events unfold it becomes increasingly obvious that governments may not be able to prevent them from happening, but they can lead the preparations necessary to reduce the effects of future disasters.

Through the Big Depression, governments discovered that weak demand and strict financial policies can cause lengthy depressions. In the 1930s Europe found that placing too much power in the hands of ruthless politicians can lead to dictatorship and a world war, and in the 1970s and 1980s the world experienced an unexpected period, often referred to as "stagflation", with stagnating economic growth and high levels of inflation, caused by the fact that new technologies that would later come to drive growth had not been developed to the point where they were able to do this. In later years we have experienced how one person's irresponsible and risky investment could bring down the venerable Baring's Bank, and how irresponsible trade by investment bankers with sub-prime loans could bring the investment bank Morgan Stanley to bankruptcy—and at the same time bring the entire global economy into a recession that lasted for several years. As late as in the early months of 2020 the world experienced the coronavirus crisis which brought the economies of several countries to a temporary standstill, and nobody really knows the exact consequences. It has become clearer than ever before that governments have a role in preparing for the future and that it must be them, with the support of organizations at all levels in their respective countries, and transnational organizations, all in collaboration with companies of different sizes, that take the lead in the efforts to prepare and make sure that future disasters do not threaten to wipe out a large share of what present and previous generations have built.

Currently many experts warn that climate change poses a threat to mankind and urge that countries need to increase their mitigation activities. Greta Thunberg has in recent years been one of the most vocal proponents supporting the need to invest more in the preparations to prevent climate change. Few experts discuss the consequences of the transformation for economic growth, both of doing too little and of doing more. All alternatives will have dramatic consequences and there is no way for any country to avoid taking action. Large-scale investment in new technologies that have not yet reached maturity will inevitably have consequences for growth.

It will not be possible to create a more resilient and sustainable world without making many changes to the way people live and to how society works. It is time for people to find out what these changes will mean and how countries can tackle them and get through the processes. Many are likely to by now realize that it is a bad approach to not develop strategies or prepare plans for the changes that need to be made. But, do people want to take in the complexity of the landscape of the territories of ignorance that has built up as decision makers and people in general have been looking the other way? Will Greta Thunberg and Al Gore admit that there are no plans ready to be implemented that will drive forwards the development that they both think the world so badly needs? And will Donald Trump and Jeremy Clarkson admit that continuing to move forwards in the present direction will soon become impossible due to a number of different issues that they so far have been blind to? Or will new leaders emerge that take the challenges that appear in neglected areas seriously and lead humanity in a pragmatic quest to develop a resilient and sustainable society for the future? Will the media find ways to describe the complex challenges and attract the attention of people across the world to the substantial needs for change and investment, and will researchers and experts abandon stark simplifications of how development works and acknowledge that the most important technologies of the future are in early phases and need to be developed to become cost effective alternatives to existing ones? And can this be achieved within an economic system that creates a basis for affluence in the absence of economic growth?

Chapter Seven

What Have They Been Doing?

People have been given the impression that the transformation to sustainability is well under way and that the solutions to the environmental problems have been developed and are about to be implemented. There are already electric cars, and experts on the circular economy speak as if the transformation to sustainable transport and distribution systems has come a long way towards completion. This is, however, far from the truth. Decisive steps towards sustainability would have contributed to making countries more resilient in the face of Covid-19, because the development of local production systems would reduce the need for transportation and would represent an important feature of a sustainable society.

A more reasonable description of the situation is that the transformation to sustainability has almost not started and that the progress of the technologies of artificial intelligence and the production solutions of Industry 4.0 are at early stages of development as well. Pilot projects have been implemented, but the bulk of development and activities, as well as investment, remain to be started. Activities have been run in a few areas, but the focus has not been on a dramatic reduction of the dependence on scarce resources or on the complete transformation of all of society to sustainable practices. This may to a substantial extent be due to the confusing communication of the goal of sustainability activities. Adding to the confusion, the issue of the peak in oil production has arrived as a more pressing and serious threat to the future of mankind, which has not been incorporated in any way into the debate on climate change, and now Covid-19 and the threat of future pandemics have been added to the complex set of challenges that mankind is facing. Amid this confusion, further developments of digitization have been routinely projected into the future. Why should they not simply continue, for example by providing everybody with autonomous car services or an increasing number of digital services based on artificial intelligence, and other amenities that have already been written into the story of the future that is accepted as fact by many people?

After all, previous technology developments and implementations have resulted in changes that few experts could foresee. The first mobile phone systems were launched in the 1980s and now, almost forty years later, everyone not only has a mobile phone, but they have smart phones that are as powerful as laptop computers. To many citizens it does not seem to be a too far-fetched idea that the same could happen in the cases of the technologies that are discussed in this book. The fact that the implementation of mobile computing has been limited to the application of a few new technologies, while the transformation to a circular economy includes the transformation of all activities in society, is only part of the explanation. Why could the trend of buying some locally produced foodstuffs and some drivers sharing cars not lead to the large-scale transformation to a sustainable society where everything is made according to the principles of the circular economy and where no waste is created and left behind for future generations to take care of?

The answer is that, in order to understand the difficulties that lie ahead, change leaders need to consider the entire array of challenges that present society will have to face in the next few years, and realize that the solutions remain to be developed. In the case of the mobile phone the first generation, Nordic Mobile Telephony, or NMT, was launched in 1981 in the Nordic countries, but the basic technologies had been developed for decades as radio telephony. In the case of the concepts needed to create a circular economy, such systems have been the norm throughout history in agrarian and pre-industrial societies and they dominated well into the twentieth century in Western Europe and the United States. It was not until the past fifty years that politicians and business leaders dismantled sustainable systems and replaced them with the global and national supply systems that form the basis of modern society. The challenge humanity is now facing is to once more reverse this development and build new sustainable systems, possibly backed with modern technologies — but this represents a tremendous challenge. Up until now politicians of all camps have made sweeping references to transformation activities and assumed that the change can be achieved within a decade or two, but the fact is that the growth of global systems is still going on. Much more money is invested every year in the expansion of the global economy than the small sums that are invested in the development of circular systems. Anyone can observe the progress of the global economy by reading pink newspapers like *The Financial Times* and *Wall Street Journal*, or the business pages of any other newspaper. These newspapers are not filled with news about profitable investments in the circular economy, but with the news about the expansion plans and investments made by global companies, most of which have nothing to do with circularity. The appearance of Greta Thunberg on the global scene has added some urgency and may have forced governments and the EU to make decisions and start mitigation activities to speed up the transformation to sustainability, but still few have thought about mapping the need and the magnitude of investment and project activities.

Environmentalism in the Early Twenty-First Century

Instead of discussing the magnitude of the transformation, sustainability experts have done their best to maintain a profile of political correctness. No leader has presented the truth about the future or started to discuss how humanity needs to organize mitigation activities to successfully tackle the challenges connected to large-scale change. Instead, I have heard professors in various environmental disciplines argue that the technologies exist, and it is only a matter of implementing them. While this may be true in a sense, early versions of the technologies, products, and systems exist, but they are expensive, due to their novelty, and they have not been integrated into user-friendly products and system solutions. Electric vehicles and the concepts of the circular economy may have been developed to the level of readiness of computers in the 1960s or 1970s. Their use is not widespread, and the solutions are expensive. Electric cars amount to 0.5 per cent of the total of 1.2 billion cars in the world and the number is growing very slowly by slightly more than 2 million new electric cars every year, out of approximately 65 million that are sold. The pace of replacement will increase, but no more rapidly than the expansion of battery production, which is growing relatively slowly due to the heavy investment that is necessary, and it is uncertain how much and how fast the increase in production capacity can proceed. In the case of the different concepts that are included under the umbrella of the circular economy, none of them contribute at present to the resilience of modern society in the face of a permanent decline in oil production. All systems require large amounts of resources during their implementation and it is not until they mature and become cost effective that they will contribute to resource savings. When the decline starts, the need will immediately arise to secure the supply of food, clothes, and spare parts of critical infrastructure and production machinery. The discussion of the circular economy has focused on examples such as the efforts by small fashion companies to offer in-store repair services and the opportunity to rent or buy clothes second hand. Other examples are the offering by light bulb manufacturer Philips and other companies to buy light instead of light bulbs (i.e. the customer pays for the number of hours that rooms are lit, not for the light bulbs) and efforts by multinationals like Nike, IKEA, and Tetra Pak to reduce the use of virgin fossil-based plastics. In the case of Nike, this company makes trainers from plastics retrieved from the sea, and IKEA and Tetra Pak use biological plastics for packaging and the production of caps of beverage packages respectively. The growth of sharing services has been hailed as a means to reduce resource consumption and a key aspect of the lifestyles of the future, since several customers can use the same car or power tool, and the taxi service Uber is often described as a way of utilizing private cars as taxis and thereby reducing resource needs. But sharing has probably up until now increased the demand for resources rather than reduced it. It has not been established that sharing has started to reduce the number of new cars sold in a year. Instead, sharing services offer people who do not want to buy a car the ability to use one when needed and some then realize that they need to buy one instead of sharing. Sharing services represent a slightly new twist on rental and other business models that have been in use for decades, but they do not seem to represent a large-scale solution to the problem of over-utilization of resources.

It may be a tempting goal to maintain present consumption patterns and only change production and distribution to sustainable alternatives, but the process of transforming all of production to circular flows and increasing the share of local production should probably not start with taxi services and the selling of light instead of light bulbs. It has been demonstrated that circular concepts are possible and we have known this all the time, since entire society and all supplies of food, clothes, and other necessities were based on circular flows one hundred years ago, and for a long time into the twentieth century most necessary raw materials were sourced locally and most production was done for local markets as well. The difficulty lies not in proving that such systems are possible, the challenge is to transform modern society to circular flows on a large scale and get circular business models to grow significantly and rapidly gain volume from companies that work in a traditional fashion. A further challenge will be to achieve this transformation and keep national economies healthy, in spite of the fact that the new systems are likely to be less efficient and that it will be difficult to maintain economic growth throughout the change.

Instead of focusing on the areas of society that are most critical to transform in the face of a resource crisis, environmentalists and experts on the circular economy have chosen to randomly promote all kinds of business concepts and small-scale changes that can be included under the umbrella of the circular economy. They also fail to recognize that the implementation of new production and distribution systems that are labelled as circular will for a long time increase resource consumption instead of reducing it. It is not until the circular concepts and technologies have significantly grown in volume on the global market that they become competitive against existing concepts and start to render resource savings. The build-up period will last for decades until savings are achieved and it is important to develop strategies for the implementation and growth that as far as possible reduces the time frame of the transformation so that the most powerful concepts for resource reduction are implemented and they start to render savings as soon as possible. Modern society seems like too complex an organization for most people to understand, but it is important to start to unravel this complexity, by explaining the functionality in an accessible way, and making it possible for more individuals to grasp how the complex system works. Without a widespread understanding of the mechanisms in the system, the transformation is not likely to succeed. Trying to change the global economy without decision makers and experts who understand the system would be like trying to repair a car without having a competent mechanic present.

Production and distribution cannot be transformed on a large scale based on knowledge about sustainability and nature. It takes knowledge about business, economics, and the principles of change management to transform the operations of all, or at least most, companies to circular flows — and the change cannot succeed without a strategy. In the past, products and service concepts have gained volume because most offerings have become cheaper and new technologies have made it possible for everyone to use their time in a more productive fashion, for example by using computers to write books while travelling — as I am doing when writing the present book — or doing the weekly shopping using a smart phone between meetings. Changing consumption habits to get people to buy products that are significantly more expensive — without offering any significant additional value — or give up the convenience of having access to most necessary gadgets and garments at home that are immediately accessible when people need them, or having to renounce the large selection of products from all over the world in supermarkets and instead only choose from smaller ranges of products that have been made locally, will require very strong change efforts.

Complex Society

Over centuries society has developed towards increasing complexity. Two hundred years ago most people were farmers, all performing almost the same tasks season after season. Since then the specialization of society has increased to the present level where a large share of the workforce consists of specialists that perform highly focused tasks.

One of the definitions that archaeologists and anthropologists use to determine the complexity of a society is the number of different tools that are used. In primitive societies only a handful of tools were utilized, that were made of bone, wood, or stone. In a modern society many tools are used for increasingly specialized purposes. New tools are created all the time as materials development creates a demand for new tools to cut and form the new materials that are developed or to improve ones that already exist. In ICT, each new app represents a new tool that helps users do things that they could not do before or helps them do similar things, but in more user-friendly or resource-efficient ways. By using Excel and other generalized programs users can create their own tools, customized to each specific set of tasks.

This development towards increasing complexity improves productivity and helps the economy grow, because each person becomes more productive at work and at home, making it possible both to produce and consume more. The downside of specialization is that tasks that used to be performed by one person are divided between different members of a team or different suppliers that are specialized in different steps of production. As specialization increases, the cost of administration increases as more people need to be involved with coordinating activities and an increasing share of resources must be spent on administration and control. In a system consisting of highly specialized individuals, more people need to become involved when something needs to change and it becomes increasingly difficult to get everybody who needs to be involved in a change programme to understand their role in the new organization and see what they need to do in order to contribute to the change. The archaeologist Joseph Tainter developed the theory that increasing complexity was the cause of the collapse of societies throughout history, such as the Roman Empire, the

Maya, the Inca, and all the other societies that have collapsed until now. According to Tainter, when complexity increased, these societies fell apart and could not handle challenges of the kind that they had successfully dealt with earlier in their development.[1]

To illustrate how the ability to transform production has changed since the Second World War, we can take the transformation of American industry to military production in 1942. President Roosevelt managed to convince congress to make the United States "the Arsenal of Democracy" and produce large volumes of military equipment instead of the civilian products that companies made up until then. The goal was to help its European allies win the war both by producing military equipment and by supporting with troops.

To manufacture all the products and resources that were needed, a new government agency was created. The manager, Donald Nelson, was recruited from Sears Roebuck, the leading catalogue retailing company, where he had been Vice President responsible for purchasing. As a purchasing manager he knew the country's manufacturing industry inside out and knew which companies were best placed to make certain items. To start supplying material, companies had to immediately change their lines of production to military equipment.[2] Changing production from one day to the next was possible in the 1940s because manufacturing was to a large extent manual, and it was not as complex as at present. A large part of a product and its components were made in one and the same plant and the production methods were basic, primarily turning, milling, welding, painting, and other relatively straightforward methods, such as pressing of plates, riveting, or screwing. The degree of specialization was low, and a mechanical engineering company could in virtually no time, or as soon as they received the drawings, change production, and make airplanes or tanks instead of cars. The agency that placed the orders could make sure that the drawings and the right raw materials were sent to plants and they could produce most of the products in-house.

The situation at present is completely different. Supply chains are in most cases global and a large share of components production and assembly are done in Asia or in low-cost countries in other parts of the world. This means that the production resources in Europe and the

---

[1] Joseph Tainter, *The Collapse of Complex Societies*.

[2] In *An Empire of Wealth*, John Steele Gordon, on pages 353 to 359, describes the change to military production.

United States are only sufficient to make a small fraction of everything that is used, and most labour-intensive tasks are performed in low-wage countries. Compared to the situation in the 1940s, operators of machinery in production plants are highly trained. Most machines are computer controlled and operators need weeks of training and experience to run equipment, and modern automated machines need to be programmed for a certain sequence of production. To change the manufacturing process, they need to be reprogrammed and large-scale change will require reprogramming of machinery in tens of thousands of machining companies around the globe. In many cases, components and the finished product travel several times around the globe before they arrive in a shop to be sold to the final customer. Throughout the chain no single person has knowledge of all the parts, materials, or production steps that are included, because the manufacturer of the final product specifies to their suppliers, called first-tier suppliers, the requirements for the components they purchase. The first-tier suppliers specify their needs to the second-tier suppliers, and so on, back to the raw material producer, and no participant in the chain has full knowledge of all the activities or by whom they are performed.

No researcher or expert at a government agency or in a company has analysed the entire supply chain of every product to find out how it needs to be changed to make production and distribution sustainable, or circular. How could present-day supply chains be rebuilt to local production? In the 1940s, a small number of people had to be informed to stop the production of cars or civilian clothes and instead, the day after, start to produce airplanes, tanks, or military uniforms. In 1942, the transformation was performed very rapidly. From that point and to the end of the war in 1945, American car companies made fewer than ten civilian cars and the situation was the same in many other industries. People still had to be able to buy clothes and other necessities, but civilian production was kept to a minimum and production for the military was maximized.

If consumers decided that they wanted to primarily buy products with circular characteristics, most of which must be produced locally to reduce resource consumption, this would be a challenge for manufacturers. Modern supply chains have not been developed with this objective in mind and for many mass-produced products that are sold at low prices it would not be possible to find any competitive manufacturers locally and the volumes of locally produced products are small. The changes that would be necessary are extraordinary and must be built on activities that are almost the exact opposite of the development that has been going on in recent decades. In the past companies have used advantages of scale and scope to reduce production cost and consequently offer better products at lower and more competitive prices. Through this development, products have been made smaller, lighter, and often less durable. Many households can afford to buy inexpensive power tools, sewing machines, computers, washing machines, dishwashers, mobile phones, motorboats, and cars. This development has driven economic growth, because it has contributed to increasing productivity in all areas of society and consumers have enjoyed the improved affluence and the access to a plethora of products that have made life more comfortable. The development has caused excessive consumption of resources and raw materials and we are facing the limits of what it is possible to achieve in terms of productivity, so the opposite development will be necessary to create a society with sustainable production and distribution systems. Products need to become increasingly durable and people need to take less interest in short-term fashion trends and develop an understanding of the value of timeless and robust design in combination with the use of renewable materials. Advantages of scale through centralized production in a small number of production plants located in low-cost regions of the world must give way to local production of most necessities. Cost will increase and prices will be higher, but customers will value the knowledge of where products have been made and that sustainable methods have been used.

All this sounds very good. The only problem is that the transformation will require significant amounts of resources for many different activities. It has not been difficult to persuade citizens to spend several years training for challenging positions in large companies or working at small companies and selling niche products to customers across the world or taking on other increasingly challenging tasks that involve travel, but it will require a large amount of information and training to teach people to develop behaviours and lifestyles that are completely opposite to the ones people have become accustomed to. Many change leaders need to become active and inform their peers about the ways that production, distribution, and lifestyles need to change.

Needless to say, very large investment needs to be made in the transformation. When EU politicians decided that the EU will become climate neutral by 2050, they have only taken the aspect of climate change into account and assumed that climate neutrality can be achieved through a small number of relatively simple measures and that society can continue to function largely in the same way as at present. But in 2050 the supply of oil is likely to be negligible, and long before 2050 new production and distribution systems will have to be implemented on a large scale. Significant progress needs to be made as soon as the next few years. That this will happen seems highly unlikely, but an increasing share of citizens needs to accept this as a fact. Many people will need to work with the production and distribution of necessities in the local systems that remain to be developed, and fewer will have the opportunity to work as consultants or as managers or experts in global companies. These seem to be relevant and unavoidable conclusions, and in any other area it would not have been seen as a sensitive matter to discuss these aspects, but for many reasons common sense is sensitive in the areas of sustainability and market-driven development. This is because blind guardians of ignorance have designated some lines of reasoning as politically correct and others as less so.

Consequences of Complexity

In a highly complex society productivity can be high, but it becomes increasingly difficult to drive radical change. A high level of complexity was the reason for the demise of the Maya and Inca societies and of the Roman Empire. Tainter relates many examples, most of which are not as well-known as the ones that everybody is familiar with. In the case of the Roman Empire it is well-known that it was the intrusion of peoples from Asia into Europe, of which the Huns are the best known, that brought down the empire. The decline of the empire had, however, been going on for several centuries and, for example, forced emperors to debase the currency by blending gold and silver with increasing amounts of base metals. The need to debase coins was created by the reduced productivity that was caused by increasing complexity and the lack of new wealthy neighbouring countries that could be conquered and subjugated.[3]

Invasions had been successfully carried out earlier by the empire and it was because of the higher complexity, the resulting slow decision making and slow military response, and the consequence of a complex administration that the empire failed to fight back and collapsed to never recover. Tainter argues that complexity increases in all societies as they develop. In our society we employ systematic processes designed to increase complexity. Science and technology development are such processes, where the efforts to continually identify new

---

3   Joseph Tainter, *The Collapse of Complex Societies*, pages 54–59.

phenomena and research new layers and levels of reality, and develop new technologies and tools, categorize and make it possible for researchers to develop expertise in each new and narrowly defined discipline, contribute to increasing complexity. Niches in research and technology development become increasingly narrow and it is getting more and more challenging to keep up with developments in any field of expertise. In business, new areas of expertise are developed through technical development, but also through problem solving, where new methods for improving organizations and making the operations of companies more efficient are developed on a regular basis. Each new improvement creates a need for a new group of specialists. The development of mobile technologies has given rise to new areas of expertise, such as the development of devices, touchscreens, and system solutions. In terms of management tools, Lean Production represents an example and Six Sigma another. Since Lean Production was first introduced in 1990 tens of thousands of people have become experts in Lean Production and Lean Management and within this area of competence there are many specialities. People specialize in the use of specific tools, in measuring time and resources used for a process, or in working with different types of organizations or parts of an organization. Overall, there are many different sub-specialities among consultants and practitioners, in Lean Production alone.

The arguments in the present book illustrate how increasing specialization makes change more difficult. In order to drive change, different groups in society need to agree on a definition of the problem and they also need to agree on the solutions, but due to the present high level of specialization people with different types of expertise rarely speak to one another, different groups develop different ways of viewing and understanding society, and they believe in different solutions to the problems they have described. Through the preceding pages I have discussed how sustainability experts and proponents of the market economy have become blind guardians of ignorance, and experts in other disciplines like Peak Oil and different technology areas have been mentioned. One of the challenges is to get these different experts to agree about the situation and find a common understanding they can use as a basis for moving forwards.

Complexity Makes Change Costly and Difficult

As an increasing number of people realize that we need to change present society on a large scale, complexity makes it difficult to agree on the analysis of the issue and the development of solutions. People belong to different groups and subgroups, possess different types of expertise, and are interested in different subjects. Members of different groups seldom go to the same events or take part in the same discussions. As a consequence, different groups tend to describe issues in different ways and advocate different solutions. What experts in sustainability may see as the self-evident cause of many problems in society may be something that other groups, for example the majority of business managers or economists, see as an important pillar of society, one that cannot be changed. As the members of the groups seldom meet to iron out each other's differences and try to arrive at a shared understanding, different conclusions and opinions that are based on different sets of knowledge and experiences prevail for longer than people assume.

As long as the members of each group can continue to do their jobs and earn a living, the differences in opinion between groups are not likely to be resolved. In a situation where the future of present society is at stake, the failure to discuss the differences and find a way to mobilize society's resources to drive the change forwards represents a great danger. Sustainability experts, such as Greta Thunberg, focus on climate change and reducing emissions of carbon dioxide, suggest small scale activities to be implemented, and fail to see the big picture of change. Business leaders and economists focus on business development, the restructuring of industries, increasing productivity, and economic growth, and are happy that the measures demanded by environmentalists do not interfere with economic growth. Instead of making growth more difficult, the development of sustainable technologies has so far been driven on a small scale and contributed new development opportunities and demand for products that have led to new demand and new economic activity, such as the implementation of district heating and energy efficient heat pumps as new heating technologies. In recent months, the coronavirus pandemic has caused an awakening, and many have realized that many practices of recent decades must change. For large-scale transformation to start there is a need for both sustainability experts and market advocates to shed their blindfolds and take in the size of the global economy and the challenges involved in transforming it.

In order for new offerings to be developed in the new fields of e-mobility and the circular economy, and for those to grow, become competitive, and take over large shares of global markets for products and services, there is a need for a rapidly growing demand for sustainable offerings from a large section of the world's customers. This is not likely to happen on its own, without large-scale transformation programmes. There is a need for publicly financed transformation programmes that prioritize the transformation of the most critical sectors of industry to resource-efficient systems. Both these things can only become possible if most citizens understand the need and agree that a rapid transformation is necessary. The communication of new values and lifestyles need to be unequivocal and it will not be possible to achieve this in an environment where communication is inconsistent. Even if few people realize this at present, the situation can be compared to conditions during a war. In such a situation everybody needs to make sacrifices and all citizens need to contribute to the war effort. During the Second World War, young people were drafted to serve in the military and older persons served in the home guard. All experienced rationing and windows had to be blacked out at night. In the UK and other countries, the government collected goods made from aluminium to use as raw material for airplanes. People contributed to the war effort in many ways and they had to make sacrifices for their countries. The threat of a decline in oil production or the emergence of a shortage of some other resource is still for most people a theoretical possibility, something that is highly unlikely to happen or that may become reality in the very distant future, but in reality present generations certainly need to transform society and we cannot continue to put off starting this task.

To anyone who takes the information and warnings from the International Energy Agency and other independent experts seriously and digs into the data related to the peak in oil production to really understand it, the issue becomes less abstract. It becomes clear that even if the decline in oil production does not start next year and that production volumes continue to increase for ten more years humanity would still be in a very tough position. The decline is likely to start in the next few years and it is likely to be difficult for countries to drive their transformation to keep pace with the decline once it has begun. This is like the Covid-19 situation. Even in the face of a pandemic, countries have not been able to rapidly build production of all the necessary products within their borders in order to reduce their reliance on imports. The most optimistic projections of the growth of electric car systems indicate that the share of electric cars by 2030 could amount to between five and ten per cent of global car fleets, and many large countries at present have less than one per cent. The growth to ten per cent electric cars would require very large investment in battery production and in the adoption of electric cars by consumers — and it is not likely to be achieved in ten years. Even an increase to five per cent seems unrealistic. It would also require investment in electric grids to implement smart grid technologies in preparation for the volume growth about to come. In order for e-mobility to grow at this rate, either more governments would have to heavily subsidize electric cars or the cost of batteries and the cars themselves would have to decrease very rapidly, faster than has been the case in the past decade. As has been mentioned above, there is not yet any system for heavy transportation ready to be implemented. Heavy trucks equipped with batteries will be launched in the next few years by Tesla and other manufacturers, but the logistics industry is a low-margin business where companies need to keep cost low in every part of their operations. There is little room for most companies to buy trucks that cost twice as much as diesel trucks and that can carry less cargo, due to the size and weight of batteries.

Even if many buyers of transportation value the opportunity to use fossil free transportation, most companies cannot afford to pay significantly higher prices for freight. There is also the fact that trucks will require very large battery packs and that the charging equipment needs to be powerful to fully charge a truck battery at stops during the day when charging needs to be rapid. To facilitate this, large investment in power grids will become necessary. The examples from e-mobility are used here because politicians, people in the power industry, communications, and the general public in countries like Norway and Sweden, where the development of e-mobility has progressed the furthest, are starting to see the need to expand the capacity of power grids and implement smart grid technologies.

The transformation to the technologies and systems of a circular economy has not proceeded as far and it is impossible to draw a similar picture of this transformation as the one that can be drawn for e-mobility. Similarly, the development of resilient countries and regions is such a recent addition to the transformation challenge that it is not yet possible to discuss this in a structured way. In the case of the expansion of electric mobility, some of the challenges start to emerge and the contours of these aspects of the territories of ignorance can be seen by people who are involved in it. And it becomes apparent that the challenges will not be solved by market forces left on their own. Political decisions in combination with company investment, and collaborative action will be needed.

A Need to Expand Grid Capacity

In Norway, the share of car sales commanded by electric cars had in the first quarter of 2020 increased to more than fifty per cent. The same figure for Sweden in 2019 was 18 per cent. Due to the size of car fleets, the share of electric cars in these countries is still much lower. In Norway in 2019, more than 7 per cent of all cars were electric and in Sweden the share was almost 3 per cent. In neighbouring Denmark, the share was much lower, but in that country the share of electricity generated by wind had in 2018 reached 44 per cent, and this share of an intermittent source of power meant that a storage facility for electricity is needed in order to continue to increase the proportion of wind power. A large fleet of electric cars with their batteries could in the future make up this storage facility. In the UK, Germany, France, and the USA, the share was only slightly higher than 1 per cent. In Scandinavia, governments both at the national and regional levels started to notice the imminent increase in demand for electricity and together with utilities companies they have started to analyse how the capacity of the grids could be increased with the lowest possible investment.

In Denmark, the industry organization for utilities companies, Dansk Energi, calculated that expansion of the grid to charge one million electric and hybrid cars would demand an investment of 4.3 billion EUR if smart grid technologies were used and 6.4 billion without the use of such technologies.[4] Smart grid technologies make it possible to control the utilization of electricity in a flexible way so that cars can be charged when there is a surplus of power available in the grid, and to control the operations of other appliances as well so that un-prioritized power use can be automatically turned off as the price of electricity increases during a day and be turned on again as prices decrease.

In Sweden, the demand for power during hours of peak load in some regions approach the capacity of local power grids. This situation has been caused by different increases in demand in the regions in question – the increase of power demand for data centres, the construction of large research facilities, such as particle accelerators, the charging of electric ferries, and the installation of a relatively small number of fast-charging posts for electric cars are some of the examples of needs that have increased or will increase demand in the next few years. At the same time, companies want to reduce their use of natural gas and instead use electricity to fuel their production processes. At present about 18 per cent of all cars sold are electric, but so far only 100,000 out of a car fleet of 4.3 million cars are electric or hybrid, and the demand for electricity will increase substantially as the increase in electric and hybrid cars continues. This will increase the need for flexibility in the use of electricity, which will require large investment in power grids.

---

4   Tilman Weckesser, *The EV's Are Coming, Dansk Energi 2019.*

Complexity increases the cost and time it will take to move forwards to electric vehicle systems. The fact that groups in society favour ideas that are impossible to turn into reality is one of the consequences of complexity. As has already been mentioned, different discussions go on in different parts of society at the same time, without the participants being confronted with expertise in the areas discussed. People in the sustainability sector discuss change as if it were easy to achieve. Some industrialists argue among themselves that there is no need to change and that any necessary adjustments will be taken care of by market forces as soon as oil prices increase to a high enough level. The stories of the two groups may share some aspects that they learn from each other, such as about change that will start when oil prices increase, but the two groups seldom engage in conversation together and, if they do, they are not likely to discuss the details of the transformation.

The lack of analysis and discussion of details may cause people to believe that some ideas that seem perfectly logical and work well on a small scale or in theory, as in the case of hydrogen fuel cells, face a low probability of ever becoming competitive on a large scale. Parallel discussions go on among different groups in society and some aspects turn up in the media now and then, but key issues related to each system are never penetrated in detail or followed to their logical conclusion. Then, when an expert belonging to one of the groups receives an assignment from the government to investigate the cost and time frame of implementing fossil-free transport systems, as happened in Sweden in 2011, when this task was given to Professor Thomas B. Johansson with a background in sustainability, the resulting analysis excluded a number of relevant facts. For example, the professor and his team did not include the investment necessary to build up entirely new production systems for fuels or the cost of developing, making, and selling new types of vehicles on a large scale.

The resulting analysis that was published in the report from 2013 did not reflect the actual cost or complexity of the transformation.[5] Still, no other group in society had the incentive to discuss the method and conclusions of the report and scrutinize the vastly incorrect result. The professor and the industry minister who had given him the assignment, Annie Lööf, let the Swedish people down, probably without understanding it and without understanding the negative consequences of a

---

5   The report, with a summary in English, is called *Fossilfrihet på väg* (*Fossil Freedom on the Way*), SOU 2013:84.

report that underestimated the efforts needed to transform transportation. The report concluded that the change to fossil-free transportation systems could be achieved by 2030 at almost no cost to society. It did not say anything about the need to mobilize large amounts of resources for the transformation or that the participation of the automotive and fuel industries would be needed. Instead of interviewing automotive companies and energy companies about the areas of industrial transformation required, the professor took the prices of biofuels and compared them to the prices of petrol and diesel and calculated the tax swaps that would be necessary in order for the biofuels to become neutral in terms of price compared to fossil fuels. In the media, the only journalists with an interest in the report were those writing about sustainability, people who shared the conviction of the Industry Minister and Professor Johansson that society ought to start the transformation, because it would not involve any significant cost or require any sacrifices for citizens, anyway.

The fact that the report did not provide any guidelines for decision makers on how to set the transformation in motion, together with the lack of relevance of the method and the lack of realism of the conclusions, has probably contributed to the inertia among politicians to start change activities. For people in general it becomes difficult to understand why so little is being done to drive change forwards when there seems to be strong support for robust measures and the cost of the transformation is negligible. Instead of questioning the situation, most people seem to believe that progress is rapid enough. And why would it otherwise be that there is so little discussion about actual progress? The fact that the experts who advocate stronger mitigation measures do not describe the types of measures that will be needed tends to be overlooked, and so is the lack of documentation that describes the change. I have had the opportunity to listen to several researchers who in similar ways have made unrealistic arguments about the simplicity and effortlessness of change without seeming to understand the consequences of what they have been saying. In one case a leading researcher into the circular economy in Sweden argued that the conversion of society to a circular economy could be achieved by increasing the average customer utility of products five times over the course of two decades without significant cost to society. His argument is based on the fact that cars are designed to last ten to twenty years, but trucks are built to last for fifty years. In the case where cars were redesigned so that they lasted for fifty years, instead of ten, customer utility would increase five times.

The researcher did not mention the investment necessary to redesign the cars of all the manufacturers in the world, or the need for large amounts of financing and the difficulty in getting customers to pay the higher price of the longer lasting cars. In all probability the argument was based on the assumption that, instead of buying cars, all people could participate in car sharing programmes, but the analysis did not include any allowance for the time frame or cost of changing the business models of the entire car industry to one that at present commands less than one per cent of car ownership. Both times when I listened to the researcher, he presented to audiences consisting of individuals with sustainability backgrounds who were interested in the circular economy and did not notice the outrageousness of the claims or the missing calculations.

When I discussed it with some of the participants after the presentation, they thought that these daring ideas are needed to speed up the transformation. They did not seem to realize that increasing the productivity and customer utility created in the way suggested by the researcher is what companies, public organizations, and the government are trying to do all the time, and that their concerted efforts render increases of one or two per cent per year in terms of GDP growth and customer utility. The idea that it would be possible to increase utility by 15 to 20 per cent per year by building more expensive cars and improving other products in a similar way, in combination with getting people to participate in sharing schemes, or change to biological materials, is improbable. I sent the researcher my previous book *Redrawing the Map of the Future: Digitisation, Artificial Intelligence, Industry 4.0, E-Mobility, and the Circular Economy,* but I do not suppose that he has had the time to read it. What the researcher did not seem to realize is that change requires very large amounts of resources and large-scale change will require enormous amounts. Not even China during its years of the highest economic growth experienced the increase in customer utility or economic growth of 15 to 20 per cent, and that this could happen in mature economies of western countries at the present time is very unlikely. If it were possible, it would certainly be an idea of tremendous interest to governments and central banks, as they struggle to maintain a level of growth of a few per cent. Therefore, the method of presenting ambitious figures without pointing out the difficulties in achieving them could be described as a way of deceiving the audiences that consisted of persons without enough understanding of the subject to question the conclusions. It would have been more honest if the researcher had said that it will be a challenge to increase customer utility by one or two per cent and that well-devised strategies and plans will be needed even to achieve that level of progress.

People will have to make sacrifices to facilitate the development of a sustainable economy, they just do not know this yet, because nobody has told them. Some sustainability-oriented people have realized this, but the arguments of experts like Professor Johansson and the researcher mentioned above cloud their understanding and make it difficult for anyone to assess how many resources will be needed to go through with the transformation. When oil production goes into permanent decline, if not earlier, this will become clear and the news will come as a surprise to almost everybody. The magnitude of the transformation, the shocks to society that will be caused by insufficient oil supply that will continue to go down year by year, and the sacrifices that will have to be made will cause alarm and anger and it will be impossible to understand how decision makers, despite repeated warnings, could have failed to plan for such important changes.

There will be a need to let go of many antiquated values and patterns of behaviour that people repeat without thinking, and in order to start this process Top Gear and a host of other television programmes will need to be replaced by programming that is more adapted to the times and that reflect the challenges that our society will be facing in the coming years. How this is going to be achieved is still unknown but change leaders will have an important role in showing the way towards unequivocal methods of communicating the values and lifestyles that will become necessary to drive change. For most people it is probably easy to see that the lack of clarity in the communication about the future is confusing and that confusing messages make it more difficult for people to see the urgency of the situation and understand that they need to contribute. Even though it is not possible to demand changes to the programming under present circumstances, it is necessary for people who want to keep up with developments in society to consider the fact that people, in only a few years, may look back at the present period as one where democratic societies failed to prepare for a challenge that could easily be foreseen, simply by putting together data from a number of publicly available sources—and that the majority of people seemed to be in agreement that there was no need for any major change. In this process experts, journalists, and the media in general are expected to take on the role of scrutinizing information, driving debate through intelligent and incisive articles and television programmes, and helping the public understand and evaluate what is going on in different parts of society. None of this is being done at present. A small number of books and films are being written and made that expose the insufficient measures and the faulty reasoning, but they are few and attract very little attention. Members of the sector of society that is supposed to drive debate and change seem blind to the challenges and become guardians of ignorance through their lack of a critical approach.

The transformation to resource-efficient production and distribution systems is not a trivial matter, the situation is likely to be similar to a war, or the fight against a pandemic, in terms of its severity. The magnitude of the change that will be necessary will be larger than anything countries have so far experienced. At the point when the decline in oil production is experienced as severe disturbances to production processes across society, few other things are likely to be seen as important and news channels and talk shows will have few other things to report, like during the early weeks of the Covid-19 pandemic. The change is a matter of the future of present society and an opportunity to drive global development in a direction that will open new possibilities. The alternative to a successful transformation is too harsh to even be contemplated. Clearly, it would be much easier to continue to rebuild society in the way it was before the pandemic, but Covid-19 has offered important insights into the vulnerability of our present society and it would be a waste to not use them to make society more resilient to future shocks and unexpected developments.

When oil production starts to decline, and the consequences of the decline become obvious to people, they are likely to adapt consumption and investment behaviours to the new situation in the same way that the British people reduced their booking of travel in 2019 ahead of Brexit, a development that brought the travel company Thomas Cook to bankruptcy. When people in the near future realize that the production of oil has gone into permanent decline, many are likely to reduce spending and investment and shockwaves will go through the global economy. This will be a very difficult situation to handle for the world's governments, but the development is unavoidable. It is only difficult to determine exactly when the decline is going to start. The aspect of this development that can still be influenced is the level of preparation that could be achieved before the event. At present the only governments that have started to prepare on a large scale are China and Norway. These countries have invested heavily in the development and implementation of electric mobility in the past decade and they are the undisputed leaders in the field. China is the leader in terms of technology development and broad efforts to implement electric transport systems, and Norway is the leader in the adoption of electric cars, a narrower approach. In other countries, governments have failed to understand the seriousness of the situation, probably because of the inconsistent messages that come from experts in different fields—who highlight issues that are relevant from their perspectives—but scattered pieces of information from different experts make a balanced analysis of the challenges impossible. In order to really understand, decision makers would need to do the same type of work that I have done over the past fifteen years, investigating the different challenges and possible mitigation activities to develop a way forwards that I can believe in and communicate. The idea shared by most people seems to be that development in most areas will continue in the present way for the foreseeable future. The warnings of the independent experts on oil production are likely to be drowned by the cacophony of messages of other groups. With the Covid-19 development epidemiologists with national responsibilities to reduce the spreading of the disease have become spokespersons, but in the case of oil and economic development these are highly politicized subjects and there is a risk that the spokespersons will not be independent experts, but politically motivated lobbyists that argue on behalf of oil companies—and they are likely to be opposed by sustainability experts. It will be important that the spokespersons are the most neutral and knowledgeable experts available, but these are not the individuals that are most prominent in the public debate at the moment.

If present generations continue on the current path, future generations are likely to see this as an act of treason to the generations that will have to deal with the results of our inability to make relevant decisions. When people eventually have access to the outcome it will not only be Greta Thunberg who will be disappointed at the failure of present generations to prepare. Greta and her supporters want decisive change measures, something that will be needed if countries want to prepare. Change leaders need to develop a clear vision regarding the nature of such measures and a strategy and a plan for their implementation.

Who Stole Our Future?

Despite the fact that Greta Thunberg does not see all the challenges that mankind will be facing, her argument that current political and business leaders have stolen the future from future generations seems reasonable. Governments have failed to prepare for Covid-19 and the same is true for the coming peak in oil production and for the challenges related to the diminishing room for improvement, which will make it difficult to drive economic growth in the near future.

Arguably, however, complexity is one of the forces that has stolen the future of present generations, more than the conscious intervention of individuals or groups of people. Complexity makes it difficult for decision makers to see the complete picture and weigh different development needs against each other, and it increases the cost of change because more people need to be involved in transformation efforts in order to understand the challenges and develop solutions. It becomes increasingly difficult to talk to and understand people with competencies that differ from our own and get people with different types of specialization to work together towards a common goal. Complexity also makes it more difficult to continue a productive dialogue in society, because people with different educations and experiences move in very different circles, often quite isolated groups where people confirm each other's views and convince each other that they are right and that others are wrong. Each group selects their heroes that promote their ideas in the best possible ways, as in the cases of Professor Johansson and other leading researchers of sustainability. Complexity creates a situation where truth becomes relative. Anything can be right, provided you are talking to friends who share your worldview. As Joseph Tainter argued in his book *The Collapse of Complex Societies*, complexity has destroyed societies in the past and it will do so in the future. There is no known cure for complexity. Complexity kills common sense by embedding experts and people in general in a false security that their views are right and that they cannot be contested.

People make friends with others who share their beliefs. Groups meet in various constellations, some individuals may join a political party that supports their worldview, others work in the public sector or in companies with tasks suited to their expertise. Even if individuals in these networks could change their minds it is difficult to openly admit this, as people feel that their colleagues and friends may turn against them, fire them, or discredit them. This is sometimes admitted or hinted at in discussions. I have managed to get several individuals to admit that it is common sense that more drastic measures need to be taken to transform transport systems to electric mobility and that large amounts of money need to be invested to reduce our society's dependence on oil. Despite this realization it has been difficult to get them to act and support drastic measures over and above financing another analysis or organizing a seminar on e-mobility. People's views to a large extent define who they are, and a large proportion of people belong to established political groups. When groups face resistance, their views are often strengthened, and their argumentation becomes more aggressive. Instead of listening and learning from each other, groups tend to become stronger against their perceived enemies. Many are not open to ideas that threaten the cohesion of their group and many argue correctly that they have scientific support for their beliefs. Science and experience support both environmental ideas and the view that free market ideologies have been more successful in creating wealth than socialist principles. Scientists work within discourses and often do not start by taking in the full view of the transformation. Instead each scientist often builds on the work done by their predecessors, which creates the feeling for some that they are standing on the shoulders of giants. This, however, does not necessarily mean that the market will be able to drive forwards the implementation of the production and transport systems that will be necessary to create the sustainable society of the future. In the political debate many "details" get lost, such as the fact that large-scale and long-term government investment, in combination with decisions regarding system integration and standards, has been necessary to drive technologies through the early stages of development.

Individual Responsibility

But where does the responsible individual come into the discussion? Is it reasonable to say that specialization, an impersonal force that contributes to shaping society, can be responsible, and does that then mean that individuals are not responsible for their choices? No, of course not. In all developments throughout history where groups of individuals have acted together and driven development in society in directions that have in hindsight been discredited, individuals have been found guilty of the transgressions or oversights that have been made. In such situations, individuals who act under the influence of group pressure are ultimately responsible for their failures to make choices that stand up to scrutiny. It is often tempting to go with the flow and avoid arguments with peers and supporters, but it is this type of behaviour that has repeatedly led to some of the biggest disasters experienced by mankind. The cohesion of political bodies and peer groups reduces the need for individuals to take risks and start discussions about values and choices, but these discussions are critical for the development of society, for finding solutions to problems that have no ready-made solutions, and for building coalitions across sectors of society and between groups with different aims and worldviews. The ability in society to solve difficult problems that threaten to overthrow the prevailing structures in civilization has always been fragile and difficult to maintain, and with ongoing specialization this ability comes increasingly under threat. It then becomes even more important for individuals to be vigilant of signs that routine decisions can no longer be relied upon to solve important problems and be prepared to take up discussions with superiors and friends when they find that development is going in the wrong direction. Needless to say, it is the responsibility of each and every one of us on this planet to make sure that both our individual and collective actions can be made into a rule of conduct that is unconditional or absolute for everyone, in the sense of the categorical imperative of philosopher Immanuel Kant.

Chapter Eight

All Depend on the Global Economy

Globalization, its benefits, and its disadvantages have been greatly debated. Environmentalists are often very critical of the global economy and how global companies exploit nature and use up finite resources. Without globalization society, however, would never have reached the present level of affluence and it seems impossible to only reap the benefits of development and avoid unwanted results. The improved efficiency of the economy that has been created through globalization has contributed to economic growth, and growth has been key to the ability of countries to set aside resources for development and large-scale implementation of the new technologies that form the cornerstones of modern life. There are many unwanted consequences of globalization and economic growth, but it is important that the improvements of modern life, even the development of more challenging and less physically demanding jobs, have become possible through its advancement. The development of new systems that do not involve unwanted aspects of growth needs to be based on an understanding of the systemic aspects of the economy. One example of the consequences of globalization is the increasing need for transportation and the increasing need to travel. The primary measure that sustainability advocates have come up with to reduce the negative effects of travel is the opportunity to compensate for the emissions of carbon dioxide, a measure that may calm the conscience of travellers and slightly increase the cost of travel, but that has little effect on emissions or on the growth of travel and transportation. Instead, the ability to compensate for carbon dioxide emissions is like the offerings of letters of indulgence by the Catholic Church before the Reformation. Now, through the coronavirus pandemic, many people have started to use electronic meeting services like Teams or Zoom, which is likely to reduce travelling, but it has not led to an improved understanding of the role of the economic system and consumption behaviour in forming the future of our society and of the planet.

Affluence has been created through economic growth, and economic growth is necessary within the present global economy, not only to achieve new levels of economic well-being, but also to maintain the affluence that people enjoy at present. The metaphor that is sometimes used is that we, as a society, need to run faster all the time to remain in the same spot from a financial perspective. The need to constantly increase productivity and keep economic growth at a high level exists because the world's collective income depends on the value of real estate and the stock market valuations of companies, and the valuation of currencies and other assets in financial markets. For these assets to keep their value and appreciate, both investors and people in general, as they buy and sell financial assets, homes, and offices and factory buildings, need to have an optimistic outlook on the future. Otherwise they would not continue to invest or increase consumption. In the absence of optimism, assets will not maintain their present value and the economy is likely to slump. In the event of widespread pessimism the value of assets may plunge, and if assets plunge investments and consumption would go down as well and this would lead to an adverse series of events that could be turned around only through increased optimism — and it will be difficult to rekindle optimism in a situation where the challenges on the horizon become known to be permanent, as in the case of declining oil production.

As I have already mentioned, I would much rather go on with my life as it used to be before I started to take an interest in these things, and to stop arguing that we need to drive change on a large scale, but that would be self-defeating. Based on facts, I have concluded that humanity needs to cut down on consumption and investment and accept that we need to develop an economic system that can function without economic growth. I am writing these lines to highlight some little-known facts about the necessary transformation and to convince others to take on the roles of change leaders and lead development down new paths that can create a sustainable society.

I am perfectly willing to do my fair share of the work, but I cannot change the global economy on my own. The transformation will be a very tough challenge, but inevitable to take on. Other analysts have failed to understand the magnitude of the transformation and failed to see how different aspects of development fit together into the complex web of the global economy. The global economy is arguably the most complex structure created by man and no architect or engineer is responsible for its design. It has been developed by the invisible hand of the market in combination with a multitude of political decisions of varying significance, made by decision makers across recent centuries. The invisible hand of the market refers to the collective action of all humans, primarily those in developed countries, through our purchasing decisions in interaction with the development of offerings by companies. To be clear, political decisions are also part of the market, as public investments, purchasing, and initiatives to finance research also form aspects of market activity, and decisions made by governments and public organizations are often critical to the formation and development of well-functioning markets. To develop the necessary technologies and systems to build a sustainable society and create an economy that does not depend on growth, new mechanisms need to be implemented in the economic system, mechanisms that have not yet been invented or tested on a national or global scale.

Increasing consumption causes the use of resources to increase. The idea has been put forward that, instead of increasing consumption of goods, people could demand more services. But it turns out that most services are connected to the utilization of different types of hardware or real estate. It probably is not possible to increase the demand for services without an increase in resource consumption. Concerts, sports tournaments, and other large-scale spectator events need stadiums and sports arenas, concert halls, and other facilities where events can be held. As spectators travel to large events there is a need for airports, airplanes, hotels, trains, buses, restaurants, and other facilities. For yoga and language classes, fitness activities, and cultural activities there is a need for schools and universities, classrooms, gyms, and studios, and for people to get to these activities they need cars, parking, and local transportation. For vacations there is a need for resorts, theme parks, water parks, and transportation by air, train, or boat to and at the destination. To buy insurance, people need something to insure. The list can go on and on, but there is little opportunity to create economic growth without involving the use of increasing amounts of resources. It is even possible that the growth of the service economy increases resource consumption more than the increasing demand for goods in the present economy.

In the face of declining resources there is a need to restructure the global economy to create a system that does not depend on an increasing use of resources. If oil production cannot continue to increase, economic growth cannot be maintained, and there is no other alternative than to rapidly reform the global economy into one that does not depend on growth. It is a necessity and we all need to take in the realities of the present situation and realize that the global economy cannot continue to grow in the way it has done in the past, and that this is a statement describing the physical boundaries of growth rather than a politically motivated one.

A Naïve Image of Transformation

Many have pointed out that it is impossible for economic growth to continue forever in a finite system. It is clearly naïve to imagine that several billion people on earth can use increasing amounts of resources without causing something to run out. When something runs out a need arises to replace it, and if the thing that threatens to run out is used to the amount of 100 million barrels per day it does make sense to consider how a similar amount of something else can be produced at a competitive cost. Upon scrutiny, it emerges as a naïve idea that economic growth can continue infinitely. Growth will at some point in the near future be hampered either by resource depletion or by the fact that the room for improvement runs out as nothing can be done in less than no time or at a cost lower than zero.

However, it must also be described as a naïve idea that the transformation to renewable fuels and a reduced dependence on oil and other resources can be accomplished by market forces left on their own and almost immediately when the price of oil increases to a high enough level. Present production and distribution systems are very complex, and the same is true for society at large. The idea that such complex systems could be transformed without any form of project management or conscious investment decisions by governments or government agencies is clearly naïve. Proponents of the idea that market forces will take care of the transformation have never specified at what oil price the large-scale activities will be set in motion by the market. The scale of the transformation is massive, and the competitive advantage of petroleum-based production and transport systems is so large that the change can never be accomplished without large-scale investment and project management by governments. Furthermore, the idea that affluence and economic growth are given features of the future of our society are naïve notions perpetuated by the media and by experts in many areas. In a society with access to fewer resources, economic growth is clearly at risk and so is widespread affluence. The idea that present and future generations can continue with the present lifestyles in a global economy while at the same time the transformation to a circular economy can go on at leisure in the background is naïve as well.

The present method for change cannot achieve the type of transformation that will be necessary.

The Present Change Method

What is going on at present? Why is it that only insignificant results have been achieved, despite the fact that change efforts have been going on for decades? In some countries, oil heating has been replaced by district heating, heat pumps, or other forms of heating, and the development of electric and hybrid cars has been going on with the goal of replacing petrol and diesel cars. But no experts have noticed that the transformation that will be necessary will be a rebuilding of most production and distribution systems in all countries. Electric cars are already available, but these are only produced and bought in small quantities. More competitive models need to be developed and the same is true in areas of the circular economy. Local production and manufacturing using renewable materials and other circular principles is going on at a small scale, but these products are not about to replace products and services that are created with the global market in mind. Why is it that no researchers or experts have described the magnitude of the change or indicated the fact that the measures that have been taken or that will be made in the future will not lead to the large-scale conversion of the global economy that will be necessary?

Financing of Technology Development

The technical development that present generations have experienced over the past century has been the engine behind economic growth, the development that has made each person increasingly productive and that has enabled more people to work with increasingly challenging management, expert, and productive tasks. Economic growth has, in its turn, made it possible to finance further technology development and growth has also financed the investment that has been made in the development of clean technologies. This virtuous circle of technology development, economic growth, and more technology development has been going on since the industrial revolution, interrupted by temporary setbacks in the form of recessions and depressions when economic growth has slowed down. Now, it is likely that the development will take a new turn.

The development of technologies, and the manufacturing of products and the construction of infrastructure, has been going on since the nineteenth century and thousands of billions of euro have been invested in the creation of the technologies, infrastructures and the real estate and business processes that are now responsible for the affluence of present society.

Local and national governments, or companies owned by them, have in many cases been the ones that have built infrastructure and operated it in initial years. A modern way of organizing and financing infrastructure development is through projects that are run jointly between public and private partners, as Public–Private Partnerships, that can be structured and organized in different ways depending on the requirements of the project, its size, complexity, and expected pay-back time. Governments are in the position to finance endeavours without expecting them to become profitable short term. This is because they are financed by taxes, and taxpayers do not demand a short-term payback. Privately owned companies, on the other hand, cannot invest in high-risk projects with uncertain payback. They need to turn a profit every year and are not able to make large investment in projects that aim primarily at contributing to the development of society, other than on a small scale.

The country that has made the largest investment in large-scale development projects has been the United States, the world's largest economy. This country has contributed the most to the development of new technologies and in several cases financed large shares of the development of major new technologies by itself and financed investment in the first large-scale systems. The late professor Vernon W. Ruttan of University of Minnesota in *Is War Necessary for Economic Growth?* concluded that large-scale and long-term financing is necessary for economic growth, because very large investment is necessary throughout the initial phases of development. For technologies and products to become inexpensive and user-friendly examples of "general-purpose technologies", products that can be used in many different applications, there is a need for very large investment over decades. He analysed the development of six different technologies — the American Production System where standardized components are used, airplane and space technologies, and the development of computers, the internet, and nuclear power. All these developments have been financed on a large scale and for the long term by the United States government with the purpose of winning military and strategic advantages and at the same time developing business opportunities for companies. The development of computers and information technology was financed through a series of projects from the end of the Second

World War. At the forefront of this development was the company IBM, first a major player in punch card technology, which had been in use since the late nineteenth century. The government invested heavily in computers and became the customer that through its purchases financed a large share of the progress in ICT. In the case of the internet, the Advanced Research Projects Agency financed a series of large-scale projects to develop the ARPANET, which initially connected twelve universities and research centres in the United States. Ruttan concludes that without the financing from the United States government the economic growth that has been created by the computer development would not have occurred until the twenty-first century.[1] It would have taken several decades more to develop computer technologies and people today would not have had access to smart phones or the internet. They may still have been developed later, but they would not have been developed to the present point by the year 2020. If the slower course of development had become reality, many things would have been different.

Yet, in the early 1990s the economist and Nobel Prize winner Robert Solow noted that computers could be seen everywhere in society, except in the productivity statistics. Up until that time companies and public organizations invested more in the development and implementation of computers and software than what was saved in total by their use. It was not until the early twenty-first century, after five decades of large-scale investment in the development of computers, mobile phone technologies, and the internet, that computers and IT services went down enough in price that information and communication technologies became so inexpensive to purchase and use that they started to contribute to economic growth. This was more than 50 years after development had started and more than a century after the start of the creation of punch card machines, the predecessors of computers. Ruttan argued in his book, published in 2005, that at that time there were no emerging technologies that were on their way to becoming general-purpose technologies. He related this observation to the end of the Cold War. In the 1990s, after the fall of the Soviet Union, the United States no longer perceived a threat from Russia against its global dominance and there was no longer a motivation for the government to

---

[1] Professor Ruttan relates the involvement of the United States government in the development of computers and the internet on pages 91 to 129 of *Is War Necessary for Economic Growth?* and the conclusion regarding economic growth can be found on page 110.

invest in the types of large-scale and long-term technology development projects that had turned some of the most important fledgling products into mature general-purpose technologies.

Many of the infrastructures that people now take for granted have been developed and implemented for purposes other than military, but they have strong importance for national security and for the development of society, and government organizations have taken a large role in their development. Sewage and freshwater systems were developed for sanitary purposes and public transit systems have been expanded to make transport available at reasonable cost to the public so that more people can afford to go to work where good wages and salaries are paid. Telephony was developed to facilitate communication across countries and these networks later advanced into the backbones of ICT systems that were enhanced by optical fibre. In many countries these investments were made by local and national governments and in some countries public organizations became the first users and thus to a large extent financed the development of the private companies that invested in the construction of the systems.

In different ways it has been public investment that has made these advancements possible and that for decades have made the large-scale investment that has been necessary to build both the infrastructures themselves and promote the widespread use of them. When we are now contemplating the improvement of e-mobility and the circular economy, some wonder why these developments do not progress more rapidly. The answer is that the different players have not found their roles or identified the level of investment that will become necessary for different parties to drive the process forwards.

The main reason behind this is that technologies and business models in both these fields are at early stages of development and neither electric vehicles nor the different concepts that are included under the umbrella of the circular economy are, by a long chalk, competitive against incumbent technologies and concepts in the present global economy. Many of the companies that are involved in the development of the circular economy lack the financial resources to invest the large amounts of money that will be needed to build strong companies and supply chains and, while many people think that large companies would have the financial strength to do this, global firms are risk averse and are not likely to invest heavily in building circular businesses that cannibalize their core interests until customers clearly favour circular offerings and existing products go into decline.

Four hundred thousand Americans were involved in the Apollo Programme and it lasted for almost ten years. The only player with enough resources to invest the necessary amount of money in the advancement of space travel was the American government, and it must then be kept in mind that the country had in the preceding decades financed the supply of material for and the engagement of troops in the Second World War and the Marshall Plan after the war, both large investments that must have burdened the economy. In parallel with the investment in the Apollo Programme the government also financed the arms race against the Soviet Union, with all the development efforts that were included in this, and it financed the expansion of computers, nuclear power, and airplane technologies, only to mention some of the most important technology developments that the country was involved in at the time. Yet, the goal of the pro-gramme was to send only three men to the moon and bring them safely back to earth. The investment in the Apollo Programme amounted to 25.4 billion dollars in one decade, which in today's currency translates to 152 billion dollars.[2] The idea that countries could not muster the investment that will be necessary to build a sustainable and resilient future is likely to turn out to be wrong. Governments can finance large development projects if they have the political will.

In the case of e-mobility and the circular economy, the global challenge is to convert 1.2 billion cars and more than 100 million heavy vehicles to electric mobility and to transform most of the supply chains within the global economy to circular principles, involving the use of biological materials and recycling, sharing services, constructing products so that they can easily and inexpensively be disassembled and then recycled, and a number of other advancements that will be necessary in order to develop the circular economy that many sustaina-bility experts believe will emerge out of the present small-scale projects that are financed by governments, companies, the EU, and other financing bodies. This involves convincing almost 1.2 billion car owners and their families of the advantages of driving electric cars and convincing the managers and boards of the logistics companies, governments, and industrial firms that own the 100 million heavy vehicles that they need to buy electric vehicles in large numbers in the next few years. The difficulty is, however, not only to convince them of

---

[2]   Forbes.com, 20 July 2019, https://www.forbes.com/sites/alexknapp/2019/07/20/apollo-11-facts-figures-business/.

the advantages of e-mobility, but also to create the financial circumstances for the owners of these vehicles to buy electric alternatives next time and convince governments and automotive firms, utilities companies, and service providers that they need to invest the very large sums of money that are needed to build the vehicles, the charging infrastructures, and the service offerings that will be necessary to accommodate hundreds of millions of electric vehicles on the world's roads.

As previously discussed, one bottleneck is the power supply. Large amounts of power will be needed both for the regular charging of electric vehicles and for the manufacture of lithium ion batteries. To drive all the world's cars and trucks on electricity there would be a need for some 1,000 new nuclear reactors or the equivalent power produced by wind or solar. The number of nuclear reactors that are in operation in the world at present is 440, and nuclear power accounts for ten per cent of global electricity production.[3] The charging of electric vehicles is likely to require electricity amounting to some 20 per cent of present global power production. This is 2.5 times the amount of power that is produced by wind turbines and solar panels.[4] The expansion of power production and the increase in the capacity of transmission and distribution grids will be so large that it requires a stretch of the imagination to consider how it could be achieved. A large amount of electricity will also be needed for the production of batteries for electric vehicles. The exact volume cannot be determined at present, but if calculated in terms of nuclear reactors the number is likely to amount to more than one hundred reactors, or the equivalent production from other sources, only for this purpose. Clearly, the transformation of production and distribution to sustainable systems will require very large investment and the establishment of new systems in many industries. Few politicians and business leaders are aware of these numbers and the debate on sustainability is unrealistic, to say the least.

---

[3] www.world-nuclear.org, the website of the World Nuclear Association, which was updated in March of 2020.

[4] Production from wind turbines and solar panels contributed in 2018 to 7.5 per cent of global electricity production, according to the Global Energy Statistical Yearbook, www.yearbook.enerdata.net.

Part 3:
Starting the
Transformation

Chapter Nine

Is Large-Scale Transformation Possible?

The current economic system, the foundation of the global economy, is dependent on economic growth. Economic growth creates the virtuous circles in the economy that have created the present state of affairs with global trade and challenging job opportunities that people enjoy. Economic growth has also freed up resources for development and created the opportunity to invest in new technologies, sustainable development, and new materials with many new properties that make it possible to make products smaller, lighter, and less expensive than before. This advancement is the consequence of more than a century of growth that has been fuelled by inexpensive oil, electricity, human brainpower, and manual work. The global system that has been built is increasingly adapted to performing only one task, driving the present development forwards towards a global economy with increasing levels of specialization. Unfortunately, the system needs to change, and countries need to embark on a new journey towards increased resilience and sustainability.

As has been argued above, economic growth is needed, among other things, to invest in new development. All assets that investors and people in general have invested in are valued at their current levels because of the expectation among people that growth will continue far into the future. A large share of the current value of assets has been created through the appreciation that has been ongoing and does not represent real money in investor's pockets or bank accounts and if many investors tried to sell their assets to realize profits all at once, prices would plunge and a large share of the wealth of our present society would vanish.

As long as investors expect the economy to continue to grow, they are prepared to pay more, and the prices of assets will continue to increase. Without this expectation the value of resources would dramatically decrease and a recession, and probably a long-term depression, would ensue. With declining oil production, increased consumption will become impossible and the most probable outcome will be a long-term economic decline. In theory there may be alternative scenarios that could buy time for the transformation, but in practice all changes that could make a difference require large-scale and long-term investment to become reality. Experts on the circular economy argue, for example, that people need to buy more expensive and durable products and that a larger share of all products need to be remanufactured and reused—and that these developments are going to substantially reduce resource consumption—but such a change will require very large investment in a number of areas, of which most are never discussed in the debate on sustainability. In order to go from the present small-scale efforts that promote growth among a small number of people who are active in the sustainability and circular economy movement to widespread transformation in society overall there will be a need for large-scale information and communication campaigns where the reasons behind this transformation will be explained to people who have not been exposed to these ideas to the extent necessary to adopt new behaviours and turn them into habits. There will also be a need for production facilities for a lot of products closer to markets than at present, which means that large numbers of workers need to be trained to produce the goods or the manufacturing plants need to be highly automated, which requires even larger investment.

It may not be easy at present to build the political support for a large-scale transformation to a resource-efficient economy, but the prospect of a permanent decline in oil production that almost no country has started to prepare for is daunting, and politicians need to bring these issues into the political debate. Unfortunately, countries have put off the transformation for too long and not taken the warnings seriously. Authors on subjects related to sustainability, technology development, and economics have continued to project present trends forwards into the future, without asking necessary questions regarding whether this will at all be possible. The optimistic books and reports have been in high demand, because they have helped maintain the positive outlook necessary for economic growth to continue, but this has had the consequence that preparations for the most probable future

— involving reduced amounts of resources — have not been started.[1] For those not inclined to think about the issues that need to be tackled to build the future, the books and reports that have downplayed the magnitude of the transformation have provided an excuse to continue as before. Environmentalists and people who have been conscious of the volumes of resources that have been used for production and distribution have approached the issues from the perspectives of emissions and pollution, or as a vague need to reduce resource consumption in general on a small-scale or voluntary basis. These ways of viewing the problem do not generate large-scale solutions. A more productive way of viewing the problem is as a large-scale industrial transformation.

There is a need to prioritize activities and identify those that provide the largest possible result for the smallest investment. One key activity will have to be a mapping of available resources in each region that can be used as building blocks for the establishment of local supply chains for the most important goods and services, because a large-scale transformation is likely to be possible, despite the seemingly weak odds. In the past, dramatic changes have been achieved when there has been an urgent need or when there has been a strong enough motivation. Large investment in the development of resilient and sustainable systems for production and distribution will create demand for many products and services in the way that the Apollo Programme and other large-scale development programmes have done in the past, which will maintain a high level of economic activity during the changeover. There is a need to mobilize the necessary resources and develop a strategy for the transformation and a method that combines market-driven change with large-scale change measures financed by governments. Governments and the EU already spend small amounts of money financing technology development and projects that promote the development of the circular economy and e-mobility. These investments amount to billions of euro each year, but they are dwarfed when compared to the

---

[1] There is no shortage of optimistic books about the future. Authors with different backgrounds describe various aspects of a future that seems similar to the present, only that some aspects are enhanced, such as increased affluence and ongoing digitization in *The Inevitable* by Kevin Kelly, *21 Lessons for the 21st Century* by Youval Noah Harari, *The Rise of the Robots* by Martin Ford, *The Second Machine Age* by Erik Brynjolfsson and Andrew McAfee, and *Future Politics* by Jamie Susskind. In *Cradle to Cradle* and *The Upcycle* William McDonough and Michael Braungart expound their theory of how the present economy can be transformed to a circular economy.

investments that are made in the expansion of the global economy. Developing a strategy involves putting in place a framework that makes it possible to prioritize the most promising and necessary efforts.

The strategy needs as a minimum to include the following aspects:

- Speeding up the transformation of transportation to electric mobility to be able to maintain distribution in the face of reduced oil production.
- Rapidly increasing the share of local and regional production of food, clothes, pharmaceuticals, and other prioritized goods and services to reduce the need for transportation.
- Building manufacturing systems for important consumer goods and key industrial replacement parts and raw materials close to major customers, to reduce the need for transportation and make supply chains more resilient.
- Making products more durable and reducing the influence of fashion trends in many industries.
- Focus on the development of technologies and system solutions that will be needed to drive the above-mentioned advancements forwards.

For the above to be possible there will be a need to pool the financial and programme management resources of governments and large companies and to develop large-scale plans that can make the transformation programme successful.

Is there Intelligent Life on the Planet?

Interpreting technology and business development in the light of what has happened in recent decades, with the rapid adoption of many new technologies by households and companies that has driven economic growth and improved affluence, gives an incorrect picture of development. At the moment there seem to be no new technologies that are on the verge of becoming inexpensive general-purpose technologies that can contribute to economic growth when the power of present drivers of growth wanes. The failure of our society to appreciate that the present situation is very different from the one in the 1980s or 1990s becomes the story of how intelligent people avoid important insights that may sway them into applying relevant strategies and tactics for change.

It is easy to advocate changes in principle and talk about subjects that people are familiar with, such as carbon dioxide and the need to reduce emissions. It is an entirely different matter to realize that the transformation cannot be achieved through theoretical arguments — actual change activities are needed and for these to get started governments need not only tearful speeches, they need detailed analyses of alternatives that can form the basis for financing decisions. Sustainability experts need to discuss matters they are not familiar with and admit that the arguments up until now have been overly naïve and, strangely enough, optimistic. It has been naïve and optimistic in the sense that Greta Thunberg and other would-be change leaders have underestimated the complexity of change and they have underestimated the resources that will be required to drive the transition. At the very least they have not discussed the resources that need to be put into a change programme, something that seems natural, considering the amount that will be needed.

When I put forward arguments related to the transformation and the magnitude of change to leaders at different levels and in different roles, they usually listen politely and show an interest, but they avoid discussing their new insights with their peers. Leading society through the transformation would seem like the next logical step for sustainability experts who argue that the revolution is necessary and overdue, but discussing the details of change does not seem like an attractive proposition. It would require sustainability experts to hand over the initiative to change experts, people who have worked for decades with business development and transformation. Change leaders seem to only want more ideas of small-scale change activities that they can promote, instead of the large-scale ones that will be necessary to start a shift at the level of society. Encouraging people to buy trainers made from plastics that have been retrieved from the sea is easier than arguing in favour of a large-scale transformation of production and distribution systems to sustainability and resilience. Most intelligent people can develop business or sustainability initiatives on a small scale, developing prototypes that prove that a new technology can do the job from a technical perspective. It requires business experience to drive change on a large scale, or at least change leaders need to be willing to tackle issues related to large-scale investment, marketing of new concepts and products, and understand how the competitiveness of new technologies and companies develop throughout the growth cycle.

If the transformation were widely discussed it would also mean that the general public would realize that the shift will be more complex and demanding of resources than sustainability experts and politicians have indicated, which may cause a backlash in the support of the movement.

Local Production is Not Local

Local production systems need to form the basis of a resource-efficient economy. Needless to say, local production is present almost everywhere. Across the world there are people who work with production of different necessities and speciality items. The problem is that most companies do not sell directly to local markets. It is much more efficient and competitive in the present economy to distribute goods through national or global distribution systems or sell through sales representatives or resellers to customers around the world, depending on the type of products. In most cases the products that have been made locally are transported hundreds of kilometres to be sold in supermarkets to the people who made them and to their neighbours. New production and distribution systems need to be developed by which locally produced goods are sold to local customers. This, however, will require large investment and entrepreneurship by the people who drive the change, and it will also require support from governments to make the new systems competitive. In some towns there are local food markets, but the volumes sold in such markets are small compared to the total volume of groceries that are distributed through supermarkets.

It makes sense to once more remind readers that the need to reduce global sales does not come from a political conviction that globalization is bad, it comes from the realization that the global community needs to cut down on resource consumption and in particular the use of oil. A reduction in transportation reduces the use of different resources and there is no better or more cost effective way to start a reduction of resource consumption than to focus on expanding local production and distribution.

Goods are sent from manufacturers to warehouses and they are from there distributed nationally or internationally through distributors and wholesalers. In most industries there is no way for a company to send goods directly from their production facility to local supermarkets or speciality outlets. Normally, everything needs to pass through the large-scale distribution systems that all of the rest of the products go through, because this reduces cost and it is likely that local distribution, due to the need to handle smaller volumes, would lead to higher cost and increased resource consumption, instead of the opposite, as long as only a small number of companies did this. Local production and distribution systems need to be built one step at a time. Local systems will be small at first, but they need to rapidly expand to become more competitive and efficient. Local systems are likely to require more manpower per unit of goods sold compared to existing systems, but they will require less fuel for transportation, as the need for long-distance transportation will be reduced. It will, however, take time for this effect to emerge. When only small volumes of goods are distributed in the new systems, the resource use of local systems is likely to be higher than that of the global ones.

Signalling

To start the process of change, customers need to demand more locally produced goods. Shelves with products that have been manufactured in the local area could be marked in stores so that customers easily find the ones that have been transported the shortest distances. For this change to become possible there will also be a need for wholesalers who trade regional products, because it would be very inefficient to distribute all goods directly from producers to shops. This has been the case for the entrepreneur Anders Lareke, founder of the company En God Granne (A Good Neighbour). This company creates systems of local food producers that deliver their products to local supermarkets. En God Granne organizes joint distribution. Before they joined the collaboration, the entrepreneurs often spent a large part of their working time transporting products to retailers, a poor use of time for people who need to concentrate their efforts on developing their businesses.

In existing supply chains, wholesalers also market the products to retailers, reducing the need for producers to engage in sales and marketing to each and every chain or shop. This interaction is very time consuming and costly for retailers as well. Shops need to be able to order products in the most efficient way possible and receive them in containers that are easy to handle and display. Each supermarket receives products made by hundreds of manufacturers and it would not be possible to order products directly from each one. Wholesalers have a number of important roles in facilitating efficient trade, and without wholesalers that carry assortments of local and regional products it is unlikely that local production and distribution will take off.

It is critical to develop local distribution systems, but it is likely to take a long time until these systems start to reduce resource consumption. As mentioned above, systems that are in the process of development and carry only a small amount of goods will find it difficult to compete with the highly efficient systems of national and global distributors. These have been optimized from the perspective of resource consumption over decades and all parties have strived to reduce the number of miles driven per kilogram of goods and in other ways reduce the amount of resources used. But this will not be enough, because there are limits to how efficient the present large-scale systems can become. Local production and distribution systems have the potential of becoming much more efficient from a resource perspective, but they will be less efficient at first.

Sellers of locally produced goods are often farmers who sell their own products and sometimes the products of a few more producers on their farms or at markets. The small assortments and the relatively small sales volumes make it difficult to earn a living from sales, and the strategies and organizations are often not developed or run in a truly professional manner. Even if local systems involve shorter transport distances, it is likely to take time until the volumes and the efficiency of the local systems make them competitive against incumbents. Local and regional distribution systems also need to be developed in all regions, which means that the total investment will have to be very large. For the systems to work they will have to include distribution centres and distribution vehicles. In some cases, the systems can be built using existing warehouses and used trucks, but overall the new systems will have to be built in parallel with the national systems and they will for a number of years add resources and contribute to increasing resource consumption. It will not be until the new systems become competitive enough to take over substantial volumes of business from existing systems that resource consumption overall will start to go down. This fact needs to be noted, because many governments have decided to promote the circular economy as a way of reducing resource consumption in their countries. For reduced resource consumption to become a reality there is a need to invest in these systems so that they become efficient and save resources.

The Initial Steps

For the new systems to rapidly win volume from incumbent ones, change leaders need to inform consumers and corporate buyers about the need to transform and the ways in which this transformation needs to be driven forwards. Large numbers of consumers need to develop a preference for locally produced goods and existing food producers and manufacturers of other fast-moving merchandise need to support the growth of the systems by distributing their products through them to as large an extent as possible. Instead of buying beer and mineral water that have been produced on the opposite side of the globe, people need to buy the local alternatives and leave the imported ones on the shelves, and in order for this to happen consumers and buyers need help from wholesalers, retailers, legislators, investors, and governments to make apparent which products have been transported the shortest distances and also encourage entrepreneurs to establish new companies that cater to local markets.

There are many ways in which local products could be made to stand out from the ones that are distributed through national or global systems. There can be signs on shelves informing about local products or shops can organize sections where all the shelves are dedicated to local or regional producers. It would even be possible to create signage on shelves that signal the rough transport distances, indicating the products with less than 50 kilometres transport distance, the ones that have been transported between 51 and 150 kilometres, alternatives that have been transported from 151 to 500 kilometres, the ones that have travelled longer distances, and those that have been transported from the other side of the globe.

Such signage and other similar measures that can support the promotion of local and regional products would serve several important purposes. Firstly, they would help customers select products that have been transported the shortest distances, which is the primary goal of the activity. Secondly, they would send clear signals to customers that the times are a-changing and that they need to adopt new sets of values. In fact, this type of signage would remind customers every day, as they do their shopping, of the need to reduce resource consumption, and it would send a consistent message to all about one of the aspects of a sustainable society. Thirdly, convincing decision makers of such an important step would form a realistic and relevant goal, a quick win, or low-hanging fruit for change leaders to strive to accomplish. The fourth advantage would be that the measure will support local producers and encourage more entrepreneurs to start new companies with local and regional profiles. The step of promoting local and regional products merely implies a transfer of choices from some present products to some less resource-consuming alternatives. It would not imply any difficult sells, such as getting large parts of the population to reduce consumption. Compared to other alternatives it would be relatively unproblematic and a logical step to start with.

Companies with competitive business concepts can produce in several local markets and contribute to building local and regional distribution systems around their production. Instead of manufacturing all their products in Asia or in large facilities in Europe and the United States and shipping large volumes of clothes to western markets, as many fashion companies do, companies could produce in several locations closer to markets, in the way that is done by the fashion company Zara. This company builds its competitive advantage on the fact that they can introduce new garments several times during a season and respond quickly to fashion trends or changes in customer preferences. When many of their competitors produce in Asia, Zara bases its competitive advantage on production closer to markets, something that ought to be a sales argument to sustainability-minded customers. Companies that offer more durable and timeless garments produced close to markets could publicize the combined aspects of timelessness and short transport distances and win business advantages through this.

A brewery that has a small number of very large production units could instead produce in several smaller facilities, one in each region. Production cost would increase slightly, but resource consumption would go down substantially if many companies adopted this type of concept. In the car industry, just-in-time deliveries have forced first-tier suppliers to establish production within an hour's driving distance from car assembly plants. This is one example of how, in some industries, networks of local suppliers have been built up, and many times global companies have established facilities that serve each automotive plant with supplies. In the automotive industry second- and third-tier suppliers are located around the globe, but the truly regional systems of the future need to consist of supply chains where a large share of suppliers of all tiers will be located in the region.

Legislators need to find ways to support local production by making laws and regulations that make it increasingly difficult and costly to sell export goods in product groups where local alternatives are available and competitive. This may seem like an unnecessarily harsh measure, but some form of legislation to support local products would be a strong signal that the world is facing a new situation and that governments support transformation. It is true that the EU was founded to reduce trade barriers, but it was founded in the post-war period. In the present situation where the problem will not be that markets are not effective enough, but that a shortage of some resources, for example oil, is likely to emerge already in the next few years, probably with devastating consequences for the global economy, for jobs, and for the ability of families to make a decent living, it will be important to take measures that can start the change. There is no need for countries to exit the EU, but buying everything from the producer that offers the lowest price is not likely to be the formula for success for countries in the future. Collaboration needs to be built on other values, such as the goal of collaborating to build a sustainable and resilient society with sustainable and resilient supply chains.

It will be very difficult to make the EU, or any country, carbon neutral by 2050, and without strong measures it will be impossible. The situation that will develop as oil goes into decline will be similar to the reduction in supplies from China in the early part of 2020 as this country temporarily closed down in order to stop Covid-19 from spreading, only that it will be a permanent shortage of oil that will have disastrous consequences for countries without their own oil pro-duction, such as most European countries. Unlike coronavirus, the problem cannot be fought using temporary measures. Only a long-term reduction of the dependence on transportation and other uses of oil can reduce the woes caused by a shortage of fuel.

Similar to the coronavirus outbreak, this situation has neither been foreseen nor planned for by politicians, but at some point they will be forced to own up to their mistakes and make the turn-around of policies that will be needed to deal with the situation. The majority of politicians are not likely to do this without strong pressure from voters and some will not do it, regardless of the pressure, but it is important to start to put the facts on the table and demand an honest scrutiny by independent analysts. In the way that has been described above, there will be no silver bullet that can turn the situation back to normal. The reduction on the dependence on transportation and oil will require decades of hard work.

While I am convinced of this and of the fact that I have gone through the relevant evidence, my experience tells me that people will not be convinced until they themselves, or some of their most trusted peers, have gone through the material and come to similar conclusions. Initially, upon taking in the evidence, many will be inclined to draw the conclusion that the situation is not so very serious, and there will be a need for debate and discussion in order to settle on conclusions that most will be able to agree on. This is not surprising. It corresponds to what we have learned about human nature. Many people find it very difficult to change their minds and instead continue to hold the same beliefs, long after they have become obsolete.

Public Investment and Support

Private financing will not cover all the financing needs and there is not likely to be enough capital available, considering the situation that is likely to emerge, for market-based investment to pave the way for the change. The main constraining factor will be the early stage of develop- ment of the technologies and the heavy competition from incumbent products and services that will be experienced by change leaders who will try to promote resource-efficient supply chains, and as the economic development becomes increasingly uncertain investors and consumers are likely to become increasingly risk averse. Public financing will have to focus on the most prioritized areas of change, the ones that will be necessary to secure the supply of food, clothing, and other necessities for citizens.

To administrate the investments, large transformation programmes will have to be started. In a similar situation, during the Second World War, the United States Congress invested very large sums of money for the transformation of the country's industry to war production. President Roosevelt started a new government agency with the task of administrating the production system, mapping resources, procuring materials, and placing production orders for everything from uniforms and boots to rifles, tanks, freight vessels, fighters, and bombers. Most of American industry and a large share of the population were engaged in this massive effort to turn the United States into "the Arsenal of Democracy". As mentioned previously, the manager of the agency, Donald Nelson, was, up until his appointment, procurement manager at the United States' leading catalogue retailer, Sears & Roebuck. In the first six months of 1942 the United States government placed orders for military equipment of 100 billion US dollars, which was more than the country's GDP in 1940. In *An Empire of Wealth: The Epic History of American Economic Power*, John Steele Gordon writes: "The United States accomplished this awesome feat of industry by turning the world's largest capitalist economy into a centrally planned one, virtually overnight." The feat was that of making 6,500 ships and boats, 296,400 airplanes, 86,330 tanks, 64,546 landing craft, 8.5 million trans- port vehicles, 53 million tons of cargo ships, 12 million rifles and machine guns, and millions of tons of uniforms, boots, medical supplies, and large volumes of numerous other items.[2]

While each situation is unique and no solution can be carbon-copied and used in exactly the same way, it is relatively clear, based on the magnitude of the transformation, that the change programmes that will have to be initiated in each country will be so complex that the projects will have to be managed in a manner similar to the one that was applied by Roosevelt during the Second World War. Another agency was founded after the war, to administrate the Marshall Plan, that offered support to help Europe recover. For the administration of the Apollo Programme there was a need to develop a number of new technologies to fulfil the challenge posed by President Kennedy. The programme was financed by the government, but development services were procured on the market from the most competitive bidders and the main challenge was to make the budget cover the activities that needed to be undertaken during the programme.

Each of these three transformation and development programmes included a number of different tools for planning, incentives, and administration that can be applied in the transformation to a sustainable society, but there will also, inevitably, be a need to develop new solutions and tools that need to be adapted to the challenge at hand. One example is the need to transform the global economy to a system that does not depend on constant growth and expectations of growth. The global economy could not function in the way it does at present without growth, and it is the expectation that growth will continue for the foreseeable future that creates an environment where people take risks and invest in building assets to provide security and revenue in the future. Without growth expectations fewer people would start companies, build houses, and invest in their own education—and in the process of building the sustainable and resilient society of the future there is a need for extreme amounts of entrepreneurship, while at the same time it will be impossible to secure economic growth for the long term. As has been mentioned before, the investments that will be necessary to build the new production and distribution systems will drive growth, but the decreasing efficiency that is likely to arise as a consequence of reducing the reliance on the global economy is likely to hinder it. Altogether, it will become increasingly difficult to achieve

---

2   John Steele Gordon, *An Empire of Wealth*, pp. 353–54.

economic growth in a world with an increasing share of production done locally and regionally.

Growth Expectations

Growth and growth expectations provide a direction, like the needle of a compass that indicates which route people should take to do well in the future. Without growth expectations, individuals will need to find other signals that can guide them. In modern society people receive thousands of signals every day that point out how we as individuals should live our lives, and most individuals have invested much in their life choices, developing value systems and lifestyles that correspond to their resources and ambitions. Due to the resource situation, many of the signals are rapidly becoming obsolete and we, as a society, need to develop new and updated signalling systems. The media is rife with signals that support the freedom of every individual to independently decide which lifestyle to adopt and what we as individuals should aspire to achieve in the future. The sky is known to be the limit and anyone who has enough drive can make their dreams come true and climb mountains in all corners of the world, fly into space, or dive in the most spectacular locations on the planet. Many of the goals and ambitions that people have been taught to aspire to will have to be replaced by new and less resource-demanding goals that are not likely to initially feel as important or relevant as the ones people need to leave behind. It will be a difficult task for change leaders, and ultimately for politicians and other decision makers, to build a society where people realize that it is not likely to be a realistic goal to aspire to fly to far-away countries and drive fast and gas guzzling cars and instead plan for bicycle rides and vacations close to home.

Apart from starting up activities that can contribute to reducing the world's dependence on resources, there is a need to communicate this need to people in all parts of society.

Systematic Transformation

As has been mentioned above, there will not be enough resources to transform everything at once. The visionaries who discuss e-mobility and the circular economy envision that in the next decades all transportation will be transformed to e-mobility, biofuels, or hydrogen fuel cells. The year 2030 is often used as a target by which substantial changes will have to be implemented. Some experts indicate that by this year a substantial share of road transportation will have been transformed to electric mobility. This is despite the fact that the world at present has only 0.5 per cent electric cars out of the 1.2 billion cars that make up the world's car fleets, and there is no competitive system that is ready to be implemented for the transformation of the world's truck fleets. In the past two decades the share of electric cars has increased from 0 per cent to 0.5 per cent. Yet, optimists without a foundation believe that in the next few years growth will "take off" and the curve is going to turn sharply upwards. This type of forecast is sometimes referred to as "hockey stick planning", because the shape of the curve resembles a hockey stick, and it is usually frowned upon as it is relatively seldom that the growth expectations become reality. In the absence of strong measures designed to increase the demand for electric vehicles it is unlikely that demand will increase dramatically in many countries at the same time. If the price of electric cars does not rapidly decline and the communication of the need to speed up the transformation does not reach large numbers of people in the next few years, it is difficult to see why the growth of e-mobility should take off to substantially reduce the time it will take to transform transportation.

When oil production starts to decline, countries with their own oil production are likely to keep an increasing share of their oil for themselves and decrease exports. This will reduce the volumes available in export markets. For the EU with no oil producing country as a member and two oil producing countries in the immediate vicinity (the UK and Norway), reducing the dependence on oil should be one of the most important priorities. Russia should not be counted upon as a reliable ally and the United States has often been late to support their European allies in crises—and the willingness to support their allies seems to have decreased with the Trump administration. In the First World War the United States joined the war in 1916, after two years of hostilities, and in the Second World War they joined in 1942, three years after the beginning of the war, when it became increasingly obvious that American interests were seriously threatened—but Franklin D. Roosevelt still had to use all his political skills to get congress to mobilize the necessary resources.

In the case of the circular economy, the situation is even more problematic. Despite the fact that some experts, such as Michael Braungart, claim that the transformation is well underway, less than one per cent of products in any important industry is produced through processes that can be labelled circular. The vast majority of products are the products of global or national supply chains that are completely dependent on oil for their functioning, and countries have to some extent become aware of the fragility of production through the coronavirus pandemic. In the event of a shortage, the fuel available may at some point not be sufficient to cover even transportation for the most critical purposes. A shortage of oil will not immediately mean that countries will receive no oil at all. The reduction is likely to be a gradual process, but it will be difficult for countries to muster the resources for transformation when they face a shortage of the world's most important fuel. Such a depletion is likely to reduce economic activity in a way similar to how the coronavirus pandemic has reduced economic activity in 2020. Oil geologists estimate that the decline in production will amount to between one and two per cent per year in the first years and then increase. As oil is transported on tankers, shortages will emanate from the fact that fewer tankers than usual arrive to the ports of Rotterdam or any of the other refinery cities across the world in a particular week. In weeks when the need is not filled it is likely that the shortfall will be larger than one or two per cent, while in other weeks the situation is likely to go back more or less to normal. As the decline in production progresses over the years, the shortfalls will become larger and more frequent. After a few years, ports are likely to experience that in some weeks only half as many tankers arrive and drivers, logistics companies, and companies in general will suffer the consequences of this development.

As the situation unfolds people will realize that efforts to expand the circular economy by promoting the use of small amounts of biological plastics, car sharing schemes, companies that offer repairs of clothes, or locally produced food products on a small scale have not contributed very much to improve the resilience of society. The entire system is dependent on the daily replenishment of stocks and the delivery of spare parts when machines break down. This is not likely to change rapidly after the coronavirus crisis, as it will require very large investment over many years to change supply chains in significant ways. One of the reasons behind the improvements in productivity in recent decades has been the application of principles such as just-in-time deliveries that have been implemented in order to reduce the need for companies, shops, and households to keep stock. While a large share of all oil is used by private companies and households, the public sector is in many countries responsible for emergency services and critical infrastructure and governments are responsible for the pro-tection of citizens against external shocks. War and terrorism are not the only problems that a modern society needs to prepare for, and pandemics are not the only unexpected challenges that are likely to occur. Most people know that oil is a finite resource and independent experts on oil production have for two decades warned that oil production will reach its peak and then go into decline.

When I discuss the prospects of oil production with Professor Mikael Höök at Uppsala University, he argues that there is still a significant risk that oil production will go into decline in the next few years. The increase in the production of shale oil that has driven production growth in the past decade may not continue, and the production of conventional oil is likely to go into decline in the coming years. Neither the coronavirus pandemic nor the new technologies developed for the extraction of shale oil have changed the fundamentals of the situation. The world is still dependent on conventional oil for the bulk of oil production, and the growth in the production of shale oil is not likely to cover the large reductions in oil production that will occur when OPEC and other major exporters see their production shrink. Governments are the only organizations with the resources to take an overview of the needs and the possible measures and start preparations for a situation when oil production starts to decline. The same is true for the preparations that will be necessary to meet the other challenges that await countries in the years to come.

Slow Progress

The circular economy is supposed to change production and distribution systems so that an increasing share of all products will be produced locally, and that circles of use, remanufacturing, and reuse become established for different types of wares. But this development has not yet reached significant volumes. Every year hundreds of billions of euro are invested in the global economy. Investments are made in global supply chains to make them more efficient and large volumes of production are moved to low-cost countries, primarily China. According to the Trade Markets site of the bank Santander, foreign investments in China in 2019 amounted to 141 billion dollars, an increase of two per cent compared to the previous year.[3] At the same time, relatively small investments are made in the development of the circular economy. Exact amounts are not known, but, for example, the European Regional Development Fund (ERDF) invested 350 billion euro in the period from 2014 to 2020 and only a fraction of this amount

---

[3] https://santandertrade.com/en/portal/establish-overseas/china/foreign-investment.

went to projects with the goal of developing the circular economy.[4] This means a total of 50 billion euro per year for all the different purposes that the ERDF funds, and the projects promoting the circular economy often have more indirect effects, compared to the investment in the growth of the global economy.

Through the investment in the global economy, companies move large shares of production and procurement to Asia and other low-cost regions with the clear intent of improving the competitiveness of their offerings, and customers around the globe respond to this by increasing purchases of the less expensive products. Efforts are guided by analyses of improvement opportunities made by world leading consulting companies and investment is dimensioned based on the amount required to accomplish ambitious goals. The investment that is made in circular projects is often made in publicly funded projects, where budgets are small compared to the magnitude of the transformation that will be needed. The EU finances many such projects via the European Regional Development Fund and other EU funds. While this in many ways is a commendable set-up, projects are uncoordinated. Organizations apply for financing for projects that they would like to go through with, and applications are usually submitted by a number of organizations from different countries in a partnership. Budgets may amount to a few hundred thousand euro per partner for a project period of three years. Results seldom contribute very much to the large-scale transformation of the most important areas in society, for example to reduce dependence on oil. Projects may spend three years organizing workshops, informing members of the project's target groups about the concepts included under the umbrella of the circular economy, and the project may include small pilot investments of a few hundred thousand euro per project—amounts that are not large enough to create significant results. Many times, after the project period is finished, the results are not maintained, and the long-term results of the project are very limited. Government agencies in various countries also finance circular economy projects. In addition to this, many private companies invest in the development of circular concepts in projects driven by, for example, the Ellen McArthur Foundation.

Building the new economy primarily on start-ups is likely to be impossible, as companies that have been recently started do not possess

---

4   https://www.europarl.europa.eu/factsheets/en/sheet/95/el-fondo-europeo-de-desarrollo-regional-feder-.

the financial resources or manpower that is needed and it will take a very long time to build new resources on a large scale so that new companies will be able to replace existing incumbents. The transformation has to be built on existing companies, by giving them incentives to develop circular offerings and business models with the ultimate goal of replacing current global models. This will also involve risks, as companies are likely to accept financing without any strong interest in cannibalizing their core business. After all, it is the emergence of Tesla in the car industry that has driven the expansion of electric car fleets to the level of six million cars. Making incumbents responsible for the transformation would be like making the Big Bad Wolf responsible for raising Little Red Riding Hood. Nevertheless, the challenge of financing the transformation should not be underestimated and driving it forwards on a large scale will be difficult, regardless of which model will be used. From a business perspective, the transformation of well-functioning supply systems, consisting of primarily financially strong companies with competitive business models, to a new sector of weaker companies with business models that have not been tried and tested may be tantamount to throwing good money after bad, but from the perspective of the survival of present society there is no alternative to large-scale transformation.

Nobody has considered how the revolution can be organized on a large scale or how companies and countries can be made to cannibalize tried and tested business models and the processes of economic growth that have been improving affluence across the world for more than a century. There is no foolproof method of building more resource-efficient production and distribution systems and there are no, or at least very few, investment bankers or economists that work with the development of such methods—and there are few investors that take an interest in investing in ventures that are built on circular business models. Richard Branson and other investors have highlighted the business opportunities created by the upcycling of waste, but a large number of creative approaches will be needed on a large scale as the idea of the circular economy is to prevent products from becoming waste and starting upcycling loops, for example by reusing products. Such efforts have been started in areas where this is relatively straight-forward and where reuse and upcycling of goods can be achieved on a small scale at relatively low cost and require small investment, such as in the case of office furniture, where designer furniture can be refurbished and sold at one third of the price of new products (which creates a very favourable proposition for customers and an opportunity for entrepreneurs to make healthy profits). The big wins in terms of resource savings are not likely to be made by upcycling furniture—it just happens to be an area where there is low-hanging fruit that can be picked by resourceful entrepreneurs.

The question is entirely how significant demand for the offerings can be built in volume industries, such as food and clothes, and resources need to be invested to achieve this in the next few years. There is also a need to secure the supply of other critical products, such as pharmaceuticals, consumables for the healthcare sector, and spare parts for society's critical infrastructure. From the perspective of the resilience and sustainability of society, it is more important to secure the local production of the bare necessities of life than to upcycle office furniture or use biological plastics to make packages, but it is tempting to start with "low-hanging fruit", projects where results can be easily achieved, rather than tackling the more important, larger, and more complex issues. As countries take on the challenge of developing a circular economy, it will be important that they tackle the most pressing challenges. In order to deal with the challenges, present generations need to find solutions to problems that have not been foreseen or planned for, and we need to realize that, although the difficulties cannot be observed yet, present generations will have to deal with them in the coming decade.

The change leaders that want to drive this revolution cannot continue to work with small-scale challenges, such as getting municipalities to buy more products made of biological plastics or getting governments to ban or put taxes on plastic bags. They and the government bodies and transnational organizations that finance projects need to turn their attention to the challenges of financing and driving change on a large scale. The change that will be needed is unprecedented and entirely new ways of driving the transformation forwards will have to be developed. Solutions need to involve many new management and control mechanisms of the type that were invented in the transformation of US production to military materials and equipment during the Second World War, the Marshall Plan, and the Apollo Programme.

The probability of success through the present uncoordinated and unfocused set-up with insufficient funding is very low and there is an urgent need to develop a structured approach. The tools for dealing with the challenges must be developed by teams of experts who are able to consider and discuss abstract issues. Business strategy and economic development are abstract subjects and they are difficult to approach for individuals who lack the training and experiences from business schools and from working in business environments. Industrial change is a complex matter and not only a case of driving small-scale technical development projects in the hope that the results will change the world. The success of a company with a superior business strategy can be observed when the company grows and makes large profits, but the strategy and the business practices that are based on it have to be developed by strategists who are able to conceive a strategy for a venture before it gets started. The fact that the vast majority of new and creative products, services, and business strategies fail and never make any profit for the companies that have invested in them testifies to the difficulty of business development, even within the traditional economy, where advancement is driven by the development of conventional offerings of lower prices and increased customer value. Change leaders need to stake out the way forwards for the development and lead others through the labyrinth of choices, where present generations need to rapidly find the best way forwards and avoid taking the number of wrong turns into blind alleys by selecting technologies and concepts that lack long-term promise.

There will be a need for change leaders to step forwards. They need to be individuals who have developed the ability to grasp abstract reasoning and draw the most relevant conclusions in a turmoil of ideas of varying relevance and consider alternative paths of development for our society. At first, before the decline in oil production starts, the challenges may seem abstract and difficult to grasp, but once the peak in oil production occurs and the decline begins the situation will become clearer. We can use the coronavirus situation as an example, where it rapidly became clear that governments had not prepared for such an event. It immediately became evident that governments had to procure face masks, ventilators, and other necessary products and that the closing down of entire sectors of the economy threatened to cause shortages of supplies for companies in many industries. When oil production starts to decline, the effects are likely to be broader and it will be more difficult to prioritize the most important mitigation activities, but the situation will become clearer than it is now, before the decline has started. The shortages will not be limited to one or two product categories and it will not be possible to simply order companies to produce some types of equipment. At that point it will be clear that for a long time there will be intermittent shortages of oil that cause queues at petrol stations and that gradually, as oil production continues to decline, turn into permanent shortages.

The actions that need to be taken will be less obvious. There will still be people who argue that the solution must be a conversion to biofuels and there will be proponents of small-scale activities who promote the development of a circular economy. There are at present only a few who have been reached by the information about the peak in oil production and who understand the magnitude of the change that needs to take place. Many believe in the information that has been spread in recent decades about the need to transform society on a small scale through the increased use of biological materials, sharing services, and other concepts that belong to the circular economy.

Most people are likely to, in the absence of strong leadership that points at a constructive and realistic way forwards, turn to familiar lines of reasoning and these are likely to be either of two alternatives — primarily the notion that market forces will drive the transformation to fossil-free transport systems and resource-efficient lifestyles, and the ideas based on the small-scale transformation activities that are driven under the banner of the circular economy and the change to electric mobility. At present it seems to be an impossible thought for most people, even those that have many years' experience as managers and experts, to consider that some types of situations cannot be handled by the market and that small-scale change may not be enough to meet large-scale challenges. It also seems to be very difficult to grasp that the present way of life is at stake and that future generations may not be offered all the opportunities enjoyed by present generations.

Many questions remain to be solved and it is not until experts start to engage with them that the difficulties will become apparent. The start of change projects is often described by showing a curve where the spirit of the team initially increases as they are assigned the task of working with a subject that many have discussed and prepared for mentally for a long time. Shortly after the project starts people start to analyse facts and challenges that have not been identified during the preparations when the project was treated as a slightly abstract matter, and the complexity and magnitude of the change is felt in the team. This is similar to the situation in the case of sustainability, where experts and politicians have communicated unrealistically optimistic projections of change and where the start of transformation activities will force participants to scrutinize the actual data, an activity that is likely to be daunting to many. At that point, the optimism often turns into a feeling of despair at the complexity and magnitude of the challenges that the team will have to encounter. This despair often remains for some time into the project as the challenges are tackled and dealt with one after another. One way of building morale and turning the feeling of despair into one of optimism is the ability to bring home quick wins that show that progress is possible and that seemingly impossible goals can be achieved if strategies are developed and focused activities are initiated. To achieve this transformation, activities need to be managed and they need to direct attention and resources to the most important focus areas. The curve showing the decline in spirit is often called "The Valley of Despair", and the concept has become almost proverbial among the participants in change projects, but as the challenges are taken on, and successfully handled, the curve usually turns towards optimism and fortitude.

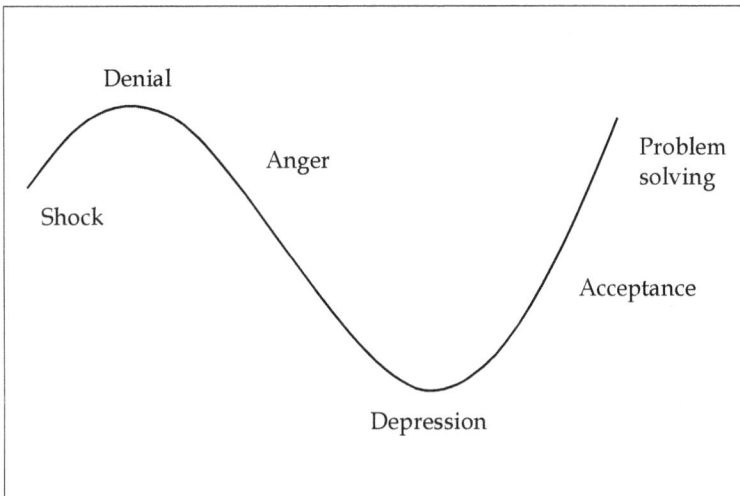

Figure 1. The Valley of Despair has become an important concept for under-standing large-scale change projects. The initial optimism is rapidly replaced by a feeling of despair, as the team realizes the magnitude and complexity of the task.

With the present naïve mind-set in society, experts do not engage with all the complex issues that are related to the transformation. It does not matter how intelligent the individuals are who discuss the matter, challenges will not be identified and solutions will not be developed until people start to work on the creation of a strategy and a plan for large-scale transformation. Then the challenges will be discovered, and experts and decision makers will start to realize that the transformation will require large-scale change efforts and investments. At this point it will also become apparent to all that change will be necessary on a massive scale. It usually happens in change projects that the feeling of despair turns into optimism once a few successes have been achieved and it becomes clear that the problems can be mastered. This feeling of optimism needs to be created for the transformation, but for this to happen citizens first need to familiarize themselves with the challenges and the process of coming to terms with them will take some time, since the change will not be a matter of transforming processes in a company, but changing society and the global economy.

Chapter Ten

Inventory of Local Building Blocks

The basis of future circular production and distribution systems needs to be local and regional production. This has been established in several reports on the circular economy. Resource efficiency improves with increasingly narrow circles of production, use, and reuse.[1] Thus, building local markets and local and regional production and distribution systems will be an important step towards reducing resource consumption, and the first step towards building these supply chains will be making an inventory of, for example:

- ...available resources that local production systems can be built on.
- ...resources that need to be acquired or built from scratch.
- ...the investment that will be needed to build local manufacture of products that cover most of the daily needs.

A Process with Many Challenges

The transformation to a circular economy will consist of many different types of activities and investments. Many resources are available locally in most places, but there are no supply chains that can manufacture and distribute large volumes of local and circular products to households and companies. Instead, most of what is produced is sent long distances from highly specialized manufacturers of materials to

---

[1] The fact that tighter geographical circles reduce resource consumption is, for example, one of the conclusions of the report by the Ellen MacArthur Foundation, "Towards the Circular Economy" from 2013. The report was written by the management consulting company McKinsey & Co, presented on page 30.

equally highly specialized producers of components and ingredients, to specialized plants for the manufacturing of final products that are eventually sold to customers. The majority of production is made for global or national markets, depending on the industry, and about 30 per cent of all manufacturing in the world is done in China. Additional volumes are produced in other countries in Asia and other parts of the world with low labour cost. People in Europe and North America increasingly work in service sectors and with research and development, which tends to pay better than manufacturing. Only a small share of the production of most industrial products is performed in Europe or North America. Food production is more national. The large volumes of food that are produced in centralized plants in each country are distributed through national supply systems to supermarkets and other outlets, and there are still very large flows of exports and imports. Especially northern countries are highly dependent on production in warmer climates. There are also large-scale flows of meat and other less climate-dependent products that move around the world.

There are many challenges that need to be dealt with in order to build a circular economy. Among them are the following:

– A growing share of individuals in developed economies aspire to work in well-paying and challenging positions in the growing service sectors. Fewer seem to be interested in working for local manufacturing companies or with the re-manufacturing of large volumes of furniture or clothes to sell them a second or a third time. More people need to turn their attention to the challenges related to local and regional production and to building local communities and supply chains.

– The reason behind the growing affluence in the world is the fact that people increasingly work with challenging and well-paid tasks as consultants or with the production of other high-end services. High salaries and wages contribute to increasing GDP levels and to the optimism and willingness to participate in economic exchange. Without economic growth and the optimism that this generates it will be difficult to invest large amounts of resources in the development of e-mobility and the circular economy, or continue to drive the development of digitization forwards in the way that has been done in the past. To develop an economy that can function without growth, a new global economic system needs to be developed. This is an extremely challenging task and it needs to be taken seriously.

- Very large investment needs to be made in the development of circular production and distribution systems. The idea is that all production and distribution will have to be transformed to circular systems, but no researcher has calculated the investment need or the change efforts that will be required to achieve this.

- The transformation will to a large extent be driven in the opposite direction compared to the development of recent decades. Changing buying preferences will be counter-intuitive to consumers and industrial buyers, and it will require a large amount of information and training to go through with this. Past practices have been driven in the direction of less expensive products and services, with the promise to consumers and investors that consumption can increase, and affluence can be improved. It has been easy to persuade people that what is good for them will be good for the economy and for society. To drive development in reverse people will have to realize that they can no longer increase consumption and that the economy cannot continue to grow for very long into the future. In the way that has been argued above, an increased use of services also requires large amounts of resources to be used, as services are often based on the use of hardware or real estate.

- Building circular practices and the systems of e-mobility will initially require more resources than the systems they will replace. This will be difficult to accept for proponents of the circular economy, who prefer to believe that circular production systems and business models will save resources from day one.

Regardless of this, the basis of circular production and distribution systems needs to be local and regional production. Building markets where as many as possible of everyday necessities are produced locally will be an important step towards reducing resource consumption, and the first step towards building these supply chains will be making an inventory of existing local reserves and the ones that need to be built up to expand local production.

Among the resources that will need to be acquired or built, the people who make the inventories are likely to identify the need for buildings, such as production facilities and distribution centres, and shops, machinery, computer systems for administration and production, and employees with relevant competence for the multitude of new jobs that will have to be filled. There will also be a need to inform people about the need to transform, for example in order to build demand for local products that can create markets for the multitude of new companies that need to be founded and for the transformation of many existing companies to circular business models, and there will be a need to manage this process. Clearly no change in history has ever been as dramatic or all-encompassing as the one that is suggested by the proponents of a circular economy, and it will go against the present direction of development of the economy. The change is tantamount to turning the flow of a river up-stream. To most mainstream economists the transformation of the economy in this way will be an act of madness, until they realize that the supply of oil is going to be reduced and that the need for new fuels and vehicles is too large for market forces to drive the transformation on their own.

Inventory of Local Resources

What are the resources that can be used to drive the transformation to create local production and distribution systems? Many resources can be used to build the local systems, but most of those that are needed are at present used for the production of goods and services for the global economy and it will be difficult to use them for other purposes, at least short term. Nevertheless, some resources can be utilized already to build the systems and others can be identified and earmarked for later stages of the transformation. An important aspect of making the inventory is to reduce the need for investment and instead, as far as possible, utilize existing assets.

We may start with an example taken from the region where I live, the Skåne region in southern Sweden. I live in the central part of this region around the small towns of Höör, Hörby, and Eslöv. This is an agricultural region with a large production of vegetables, livestock, and raw milk, but few of the products are distributed and sold locally. Instead, the output is delivered to large-scale storage facilities and processing plants, where vegetables are packed and distributed across Sweden and where raw milk is turned into dairy products, cheese, and then distributed to retailers across Sweden. In a similar way cattle, pigs, and chickens are raised on farms and sent to meat packers and processing plants for the manufacturing of products for the Swedish market. In the region there are also a large number of mechanical engineering and plastics companies that make components for packaging machines manufactured by Tetra Pak and other types of equipment made by other machine producers. Manufacturers that use wood make beds and other types of furniture for IKEA and other furniture companies to be sold in Sweden or internationally. Very few products are sent to local retailers or sold directly to local customers.

In principle, many products are made in the area, but there are virtually no distribution channels that make them available to local consumers or corporate customers. Instead, everything that is made in the area is integrated into global and national supply chains that are extremely efficient from a resource perspective, but the global economic system is built around the efficient use of manpower, which has become an expensive resource in developed countries. In the future the world needs to economize on other resources, such as fuel and materials, and this will require a major reorganization, not only within countries but across the globe.

As has been described above, the company En God Granne has identified local production and distribution of food as an emerging need and there is a substantial interest among supermarkets and customers to get more local products into shops. Despite this interest, growth has been difficult. This is because of the low number of small local producers that can compete with large manufacturers. Local producers often have a background in food processing or farming, and many are not aware of the strict requirements on, for example, packaging. For the small companies it is a relatively large investment to learn about the rules and develop the packaging required and use it for their small volumes of products. They also cannot afford to advertise products to create a large demand in the way that large companies can. The sales of the same brands and products nationally or all over the world create billion-euro markets and the resulting sales can finance large-scale advertising campaigns. Together with supermarkets who want to strengthen their profile as good citizens in the local community, En God Granne can advertise its brand and activities in the supermarkets that stock their products. Advantages of scale form the foundation of business and nowhere is this more apparent than in consumer goods industries, where there is a need for large brands to attract millions of customers on a daily basis. The transformation to circular business principles will need to involve a large-scale change of mind-set among consumers. Instead of making purchasing decisions based on which products are best known, most people need to start to demand local products and be ready to pay a premium to get them.

The inventory of local and regional resources needs to be based on the realization that eventually most production will have to be transformed to local supply chains. Different categories of resources need to be recognized:

- Producers that are already active in local and regional markets and that have started to build awareness and brands with customers.
- Producers that at present market nationally or globally, but that are located in the area and could start to distribute via local and regional distribution systems in the regions where they have production units. Such producers that already have strong brands and financial resources could form the backbone of new local production and distribution systems in their regions.
- Producers of raw materials, ingredients, or components that can form the basis of the local manufacture of finished products in the future.
- Production machinery, buildings, and stores where locally produced foodstuffs and other goods can be marketed and sold.
- Schools for the training of employees who can work with the production of food, clothes, and other consumer goods, and employees who can work with the building of the new supply chains, brands, and companies.
- Trained individuals who could start firms that produce or distribute locally manufactured wares or become employed by the local companies.

Short term, most companies and individuals have more to win from the continuation of present practices than from the adoption of new principles and the construction of new systems, but the need for change is real and everyone will need to contribute.

Financing and Risk Management

Two aspects that are often overlooked in books and reports about the circular economy are those of financing and risk management. Financial aspects are seldom discussed. It is usually taken for granted by experts on the circular economy that companies with circular business models will gradually take over most production and distribution and that financial resources will be created as companies grow. This is, however, an overly simplified vision of the process.

One of the most important advantages of incumbents in all industries is the financial strength of existing companies that have been in operation for decades. Many of these organizations have accumulated money and they have, through processes of trial and error, identified business principles that work in the countries and industries where they are present. It is important to emphasize the aspect of trial and error because innovation relies on experimentation—and most efforts fail, even for the strong global companies with large resources for analysis and operations development. The process of trial and error kills most fledgling ventures. Once a new company has made a few errors it is likely to run out of capital and is forced to declare bankruptcy or cease to do business. In many cases, ventures never grow to become big enough to make more than a few hundred thousand euro in revenues—and farm-based food producers often do not reach even that level of turnover. Many small companies close after a few years of operation when the owner finds that they will not be able to make enough profit to continue to run it. Only 30 per cent of all companies remain in operation after five years and very few have grown enough to make a turnover of, say, ten million euro or more.

These are important facts, because they illustrate the time it takes to build a new business sector. The difficulties are multiplied since the new companies will need to compete with highly efficient incumbents. This is especially the case in the circular economy and e-mobility. However, the slow growth of e-mobility illustrates how unlikely it is that incumbents will invest large amounts to drive the transformation as rapidly as possible. It was not until Tesla emerged on the scene that automotive companies started to take electric mobility seriously and it is largely because of Tesla that the transformation has arrived at the— still not so impressive—level of 0.5 per cent electric and hybrid cars out of the 1.2 billion in global fleets. Without Tesla, this number would have been substantially smaller.

Considering these circumstances, it will be impossible for the new companies and supply chains to replace the existing global systems based on organic growth and market-based allocation of resources. The resources necessary to invest in growth will not be available for small companies without extensive measures by governments. There is simply not enough time to wait and see and hope that the market will solve the problem, because the odds are stacked heavily against such a scenario.

The same is true for many of the new innovative products that are developed by large companies. In the absence of demand for significant volumes of new fossil-free materials, even large companies cannot afford to launch them and finance their growth. I interviewed one of the large Swedish pulp and paper companies that had developed a new cellulose-based material that can replace plastic for many products. When I conducted the interview the company had first spent a few years trying to launch it in the market for designer furniture, but it found that the volumes of designer furniture of the type their intended customers were producing are too small for this to become a viable strategy. Instead, they had started to focus their attention and marketing efforts on selling the material for the packaging of up-market products, such as electronics. While this may turn out to be a viable strategy, it requires the creation of new supply chains of companies that become converters of the new material into packages and that sell it to electronics companies. The establishment of production systems for the large-scale conversion of these new materials will require very large investment by the companies that are prepared to carry the financial risk of doing this. To achieve volume growth, the new materials must go down in price, and this will take time. While fossil-free packaging has become a sales argument for food products, this has not yet become the case in electronics. We may still have to wait some time until Apple, or some other electronics company, launches an advertising campaign with the message that they use fossil-free packages for all or some of their products, or that they have reduced the amount of plastics used by a significant amount. As has been mentioned above, however, the conversion of all plastics production to the use of biological feedstock will not be possible, since the volumes of plastics used are far too large. Too much agricultural land will have to be used, so the only alternative that is viable for the longer term will be to reduce the use of packaging materials overall.

The marketing of the new material, first to furniture producers, then to electronics companies, had been going on for a few years and sales had not even started, even though a large company had developed the material. A similar situation is present for clothes made from cellulose. In a similar way, the technology to make fabric from wood fibres and replace cotton has existed for a number of years and both consumers and corporate buyers know that cotton production is very demanding of water. It may take 10,000 litres of water to make one kilo of cotton fabric. This is especially alarming as cotton is grown in dry climates where water is often scarce. Trees are grown in more temperate climates where water tends to be less of a problem. Despite these two important new uses for wood they have not yet caused an additional demand for wood. The use of oil and natural gas for plastics production is so large that if a significant share of all plastics were to be made from cellulose the forests of the world would not last for many years. Because of this, changing to cellulose for plastics and fabric on a large scale is not viable in the long run. The examples illustrate the time frame of these types of transformation and the need to take an approach that speeds up the process.

Experimentation, the building of capital, and a long-term presence in their markets, in combination with large investment in advertising to build brands, have rendered incumbents strong brands and the strength of these brands and the reliability of the products that are endorsed by them can seldom be matched by local producers. Major brands offer superior products at very competitive prices, while local producers make unique products that are seldom adapted to the tastes of broad customer groups. Standardized consumer products are made in large volumes and sold at low prices to consumers. Local products tend to have more specialized flavours or other special qualities that cater to narrow groups of customers or are adapted to be used on special occasions. Small producers find it difficult to compete against the standard varieties of strawberry jam or orange marmalade offered by large companies, and they may instead offer rhubarb and liquorice jam or fig marmalade. For such products they can charge a premium price, but they are not likely to be able to compete with large brands for everyday use.

One of the factors that is needed in order for small local producers and distributors to expand is financing, but there will be a need for very large amounts of financing to build local or regional producers and supply chains for all major product categories in every region. New production and distribution systems will not only have to be built once in each country, the systems will have to be replicated in every region and each system will be slightly different compared to the rest, because of regional differences. The development of an entirely new sector of consumer goods industries will inevitably require very large investment. In order to develop local and regional suppliers there is a need to build small-scale production resources for meat, processed meat, bread, cereals, fruit and vegetables that can be grown in local greenhouses, jams and pickled vegetables and other canned products, dairy products, clothes, and spare parts for critical urban infrastructures, such as sewage, water systems, and waste management systems.

This is of course a very tall order and the development of such systems will be a very risky proposition, considering the low level of awareness that is present today among consumers and corporate buyers regarding if and why this transformation will become necessary. The first prerequisite for substantially reducing energy consumption that needs to be established will be information to consumers about the need, which will be necessary to establish a demand for locally produced products. The next step needs to be aspects related to financing the transformation and containing the business risks involved.

When the challenge is described in this way it becomes obvious that a strategy needs to be developed for the change. It is very unlikely that demand will reach a high enough level so that regional supply chains grow based on market forces alone. There will be a need for stimuli to establish the new production and distribution systems, but to implement support systems there is a need for knowledge. And overall, the question remains how long it is likely to take, even at the best of times, for the new systems to lead to resource savings. In the way that has been mentioned above, for a long time the new systems will inevitably represent an additional use of resources, and while they are in the process of being expanded and until the technologies and business principles become mature, they are not likely to contribute to savings. For this to change, the transformation needs to be planned and structured so that the speed increases and the new systems rapidly reach maturity. Typically, the knowledge of sustainability experts does not cover the most important aspects related to the organization or financing of the transformation. The process must be led by experienced business managers and consultants who understand business development and change management and they need to work with strong support from governments and the leaders of large companies. Sustainability experts also need to participate, but it is unlikely that they will be able to master all the competencies that will become necessary to drive the transformation to large-scale change. This should not be taken as a terribly rude statement. Business experts are seldom the right persons to build bridges or skyscrapers. Complex and demanding tasks need to be led by people with training in and experience of the relevant areas.

Efficiency Challenges

The development of local and regional supply chains will be difficult, but it will be necessary. It is not likely to be possible for much longer to continue to run global and national supply chains to the extent that is done today. Politicians and business leaders have already agreed that the present linear economy will have to be replaced by a circular economy built to a large extent on local production, but no strategy has been created for the transformation. Based on the above account someone may draw the conclusion that the food industry may be the ideal sector to start with, as other large industries, such as the car industry or telecoms, will be even more difficult and costly to reform than food. Food is produced in every region and food is a low-tech industry, even if many modern production plants are highly automated and technically advanced. Products like sausages and yoghurt can be produced at home or on a small scale in industrial facilities, if people have the time and equipment.

The challenge is not the actual production, but the efficiency and competitiveness of both production and distribution in the eyes of customers. In the past, food was produced on a small scale on farms and most people were involved in agriculture and food production, but this situation is not possible to go back to. To take current society into the future, a high level of efficiency of production and distribution needs to be maintained, while at the same time supply chains must be made less resource intensive. This is a very difficult problem, and the decision makers who have agreed that it needs to be done are probably not aware of the extent of the challenges.

To go through with the plans of developing a circular economy, governments need to contribute large amounts of financing and project management. It cannot be achieved through independent activities and investment by large numbers of public and private players in collaboration. There is also no alternative but to face the challenge of transforming the production of food and other necessities to local supply systems, as declining oil production poses a risk of shortages of the bare necessities of human life. There is no point in making any part of car production slightly more sustainable if people will not have enough food and clothes to keep them from starving and freezing. Unfortunately, development in recent decades has to a large extent been focused on the realization of the potential of individuals, the highest level of Maslow's hierarchy of needs. Most people take it for granted that their basic needs will forever be satisfied, and that affluence will continue to improve. Despite vehement warnings put forward by sustainability experts, few—probably including many of the activists themselves—are insightful enough to realize that this may not be the case and that even the satisfaction of the basic needs may be threatened. Because of the lack of insight, too few resources have been spent preparing for the challenges of the future.

Chapter Eleven

The Basis of a Transformation Programme

The coronavirus situation has weakened the economies of countries and of their citizens and this will force upon people a reduction of consumption and investment, as large sums of money have been spent on the mitigation of the effects of Covid-19. The effects of this spending will remain and will weaken the economies of countries for a long time. Reduced consumption is a necessary step towards reducing the use of resources to develop a circular economy. The unexpected arrival of the coronavirus pandemic has forced countries to jump-start a few aspects of the development to increase the production of some necessities within their borders. For several reasons, reduced consumer spending is not a pleasant thought. One reason is that people have become accustomed to enjoying increasing wealth and more affluent lifestyles, and the message that we need to cut down on consumption is not likely to be quietly received and adhered to. Reduced consumption will also lead to increasing unemployment as many industries are hard hit by the switch to sustainability, and it is likely to take many years for them and the economy to fully recover. Politicians and their supporters will need to start transformation programmes aimed at rebuilding the economies of countries, but they also need to become more resilient. Change leaders need to be prepared to communicate unexpected truths and not just put forward information and arguments that are politically correct based on the situation in society that has prevailed up until now.

Normally, this type of process would continue over decades and the competitiveness of electric cars would be improved incrementally and quite slowly, while most other things remain the same as today. In some cases in recent decades, the penetration of new technologies has gone relatively fast, because they have created significant new value for users and many users have been affluent enough and willing to pay the relatively high price at the initial stage of development and put up with the low initial level of user-friendliness of the new products. At present we see examples of some sectors financing the transformation of others. The development of electric cars and trucks is financed by automotive companies through the sale of petrol and diesel cars that are still the cash cows of the automotive industry. Governments help finance the transformation through the support of different development activities. This development is an investment for the future but, without the revenue that is created by the petrol and diesel cars and the efficiency that is created in other sectors of the economy, it would not be possible to finance the advancement of electric cars. In the case of a large-scale transformation, the sectors that currently finance the small-scale change that is going on will have to be transformed as well.

Inevitably the production and sale of petrol and diesel cars will have to be phased out. The automotive industry is one of the largest industries in many countries, and there are parts of Europe where the automotive industry accounts for 20 per cent of employment. With a large-scale transformation to electric mobility there is no guarantee that most automotive production can be maintained. China and the United States have taken the lead in battery production and there is a risk that new entrants into the car market take over a significant share of sales. The foreseeable changes and the probable additional forces that are going to form the future automotive industry will inevitably be strong, and large numbers of people will have to be retrained and find new jobs. In addition to the challenges that this transformation will pose for individuals and companies, it will be a tough challenge for society and for national governments. So far, insignificant preparations have been made for this change and few decision makers and people in general are prepared for the strains that the development will put on society. No other transformation in history has required an adjustment of a large share of production in all countries. The most urgent insight that is necessary is that preparations cannot wait until problems arise, because when this happens events are likely to unfold at a quick pace. As uncomfortable as this may be, change leaders and decision makers need to start to rapidly come to terms with this development to be able to immediately start to make the right decisions.

There is no alternative to large-scale change. There is, however, a necessary complement. As there is no way that humanity can rebuild society, almost from the ground up, over the course of one or two decades, the only opportunity is to reduce consumption.

Facing Facts

Having to face a crisis is not a palatable proposition to put forward for politicians and business leaders, and the question that immediately arises is who is responsible for failing to inform the public about this. This is a very difficult issue that is probably best responded to by saying that a very large number of people have been less receptive to negative news than they should have been—and that many have been more eager to promote positive aspects of an unlikely future than the negative aspects of a more probable one. In recent decades there have been few politicians with the courage of Winston Churchill who dared tell the British people "I have nothing to offer but blood, toil, tears, and sweat". Instead, politicians have tried to convince themselves that the problem of transformation will go away or that it will be solved automatically by market forces as soon as oil prices increase to a high enough level. Like Neville Chamberlain, the optimists, who have no foundation for their belief, now need to step aside and let the realists in, those who understand the transformation and will be able to lead people through it.

As I have tried to inform several hundred decision makers, experts, and journalists about the need to transform transport and distribution systems to sustainability, my reasoning has been met with nods and favourable remarks, but few seem to have understood that I will not be able to achieve the transformation on my own, or that I cannot inform the entire Swedish or global society by myself and set up the transformation programmes that will be necessary. Greta Thunberg has been given substantial opportunities to spread her message, but her message has been familiar, and she has not been forced to go into detail. Instead, she has reiterated information that people have heard for many years from other experts and activists. She has added the fact that a young person puts forward these arguments and speaks on behalf of all the children in the world, but she does not bring any new information into play. Followers support my activities on social media and a number help in promoting the idea of a large-scale transformation programme through project initiatives, but most do not seem to notice the difference between what I am trying to convey and what Greta Thunberg and other experts put forward. Thus, the magnitude and the systemic aspects have gone unnoticed.

The inability of most people to understand that the present approach by governments and the EU will not lead to significant results probably emanates from different factors. There is clearly a fear among experts to take strong positions and stand out from their peers by putting forward arguments that may be criticized and that may make them look foolish in case they may have misunderstood some aspect of the argument or presented it in the wrong way. Most people who are involved in the sustainability sector have no business experience and some distrust companies and business managers. Some have been brought up in an environment where the ideas of investment and profits have been frowned upon and where the idea that local communities will be able to drive the entire process of change has been prominent—and where people have argued that society needs to go back towards a higher degree of self-sufficiency. This is to some extent true, but it will be impossible for families in cities to grow their own vegetables, and moving into the countryside is not possible as there are not enough homes and jobs available in rural areas.

In sustainability circles it is seldom mentioned that the transformation will require large investment in building the new production systems and that this investment will have to be made either by the government, companies, or by individual households. Many seem to take it for granted that, because the change is necessary and beneficial to society, it does not need to be discussed or dissected. Instead, it must be accepted as something that will inevitably take place by everyone who is in favour of the transformation. I have participated in discussion groups on the internet that have been dominated by persons with a sustainability background, and I found that participants with penetrating arguments and a willingness to discuss the details of transformation, such as myself, have been counteracted by participants who have tried to suppress uncomfortable ideas, for example by immediately posting trivial remarks on top of any attempt to start a serious discussion of the transition before too many of the participants on the forum had had the opportunity to read the posting.

The lack of a serious discussion of the different aspects of a switch to e-mobility or the circular economy hinders both a serious debate and development of the details of change. When the discussion is led by people who lack an understanding of the concept and process of change—and who are not used to ironing out the details of complex development and change processes—the discourse may serve some political purpose, but it also effectively prohibits progress. Without the opportunity to raise important issues, the leaders at different levels of the sustainability movement manage to give participants the impression that the movement towards sustainability is on the right track and that there are no significant obstacles in the way of change. They also manage to preserve the impression that business knowledge and experience will not be necessary to succeed. The majority of members of the sustainability movement seem to subscribe to the idea that the transformations to e-mobility and the circular economy will be driven at the necessary speed once the price of oil or other key resources increase to high enough levels.

In business, most leaders seem to subscribe to a similar worldview, which is understandable. Companies operate in markets where they have to take into account the competitive situation and they make investments only when doing so makes business sense. Most are forced by the stock market or by private owners to make a profit every year, and in most cases the only acceptable reason for a low profit one year is that investment has been made that will increase profits the next year. Many take pride in their ability to understand markets and customers and it then seems like a natural step to also attribute to markets the power to drive innovation from the first steps of innovation of a technology to the later stages when it—and the products and services that are spawned from it—has reached maturity. The fact that the idea of market-driven development applies only to the later stages of development and that activities in the early stages are heavily depend-ent on government financing to proceed at speed is not obvious, and it is a difficult aspect to figure out for people who have not studied numerous examples of technology development from the past. People who study technology and business development since the 1990s are not likely to observe the role that government investment has had for the advancement of technologies and systems during the entire twentieth century up until then. Governments have invested large amounts in technology development in recent decades as well, but not in the focused and systematic way they did throughout the early stages of the evolution of technologies like ICT, power, aviation, space, fresh water and sewage systems, and many other instances of technology innovation. Long-term and large-scale government financing has been a cornerstone, without which the development could not have succeeded. But as the need for government involvement has not been highlighted by the blind guardians of ignorance, or their followers, few have understood that different players in the economy need to take on different roles in the process.

Politicians work on behalf of both constituencies, environmentalists, and more business minded and conservative individuals, and there are in many countries parties for both these ideologies. Despite the fact that the need for change that is proclaimed by environmentalists amounts to a complete transformation of transportation, industry, and supply chains, the environmental issues of government tend to be handled by a Minister for the Environment, while industrial policies are taken care of by a Minister of Industry. This way of organizing environmental and industrial politics as entirely separate aspects contributes to the separation of the two hemispheres of business and the environment — and this separation contributes to creating the impression that it will both be possible to create continuous economic growth and at the same time create a sustainable society without letting the transformation have a negative impact on growth. If the head of the Ministry of Industry clearly states that economic growth will continue and explains how this is going to be achieved, and the Minister heading the Ministry of the Environment argues that countries are going to transform society to sustainability and resilience, people will believe that they know what they are talking about.

Even citizens that are relatively knowledgeable about these things are likely to be confused and think that the government may know something that other experts do not, but this is not the case. The ministers act as blind guardians of ignorance by remaining oblivious to the devastating effects of separating the two spheres and giving the impression that the change can be driven while at the same time companies and public organizations continue to do business as usual. Citizens believe that their governments monitor the development in the economy and in the world at large and base their activities and organizational structure on realistic forecasts of economic and business development, and most would never dream that governments could fail to spot a need to update their ways of organizing ministries or change the rhetoric of politicians in order to match the more realistic and less optimistic forecasts for the future that are developed as the most relevant facts and figures are included into forecasts.

In a reasonable world both Ministers of the Environment and Industry would sing from the same hymn sheet and admit that the only realistic forecast for the future is that citizens will have to cut down on consumption and that governments need to find ways to support this change so that the reduction and transition will be as orderly as possible. In the present situation neither the people responsible for industrial development, nor their counterparts who are responsible for the march towards sustainability seem to realize that there is something wrong with the rhetoric and that these two areas have something to do with each other. Almost everybody on this planet seems to live and work in a bubble where they do not question the rhetoric that the future will bring more affluence and prosperity to the coming generations.

Create Excitement

An important driver of development is the excitement individuals find in the various alternative paths forwards that are available. For a long time, the world of international business has attracted competent people with a drive to see the world and take on challenging tasks in business management and technology development. This interest has strengthened the belief in the market as a key tool for allocating resources. People have been able to observe that the market has created opportunities for them, and the aspects of development that the market cannot handle have seldom been discussed. Now, change leaders will have to communicate the excitement and the challenges of the transformation and make people realize that the development of a sustainable and resilient society is the most important task for humanity at present. But the story of the future must be told in a truthful way and the challenges cannot continue to be swept under the carpet. Leaders need to emulate Winston Churchill, who, during the Second World War, gave his people truthful accounts of the situation, yet visions that they could believe in and work towards. It is no great pleasure to be the person who has to tell people that the party's over[1] and that we cannot continue to consume in the way we have done in the past, but someone has to do it. Experts on oil production have been arguing this for a long time. I am offering a structured approach to the transformation process.

Based on the present insight that the transformation to sustainability will require large amounts of resources and that the failure to succeed may mean that the entire present society is endangered — as countries

---

[1]   I first learned about the imminent peak in oil production from the book *The Party's Over* by Richard Heinberg, which in 2003 was one of the early texts to explore this subject. I thought the book was very enlightening, but I considered the conclusion — that there is nothing countries can do to succeed with the transformation, because of its magnitude — was a little too pessimistic. With experience from business development and change management I believed that it may be possible to transform the economy to sustainability, but that there is a need for strategy, planning, and collective action.

are likely to suffer shortages of fuel and industrial raw materials—governments need to act forcefully. One of the reasons why the idea of sustainability has been so easy for decision makers to adopt and incorporate into present structures is because sustainability offers an alternative job market for individuals who are unsatisfied with the market- and financially-driven logic of business. With the adaptation to sustainability, people who have felt that they wanted to work towards a more utilitarian goal than the one of increasing the profitability of their employer have been offered a large and growing job opportunity with a relatively large diversity of jobs to choose from. This opportunity was less obvious in the 1960s and 1970s when large numbers of young people in different ways revolted against society, which in its most violent forms resulted in terrorism and violent crimes against business magnates in Germany, Italy, and other countries.

At present, most people seem to work towards the same goal, that of improving present society in small and very diverse steps, and few people see a need to revolt against the prevailing world order. Compared to the 1970s, the present situation is peaceful, and affluence is gradually improving. The term "political correctness" has been created to describe arguments that are acceptable in society and political life. The willingness of every person to keep to arguments that are politically correct seems to indicate that people believe that the present direction and speed of development is in general creating the society that people want, and individuals hesitate to raise the alarm and instead continue as usual. Few people possess the necessary facts and knowledge to put forward an argument that is critical against current policies, and few have an incentive to risk their jobs and their positions by going against the political current of the times. As the present political formula of opening up markets to competition and allowing technology development to drive society forwards has led to the unprecedented improvements of living standards that people have experienced in the past, people assume that a continuation of the same policies will lead to similar results in the future.

As communities have not yet realized the magnitude of change that is awaiting us, most see no other opportunity than to continue present behaviours and contribute to the development in society that is driven by companies and public organizations.

There are two main paths to choose from for young individuals who want to contribute to the development of society at large. There is the business approach, which is the one that attracts the vast majority of the world's resources—people who want to continue to develop the efficiency and competitiveness of the global economy, that so far has increased the world's dependence on large-scale transportation. The other path is the one of sustainability, which also encompasses companies and business, but on a smaller scale. In clean-tech and other sustainability sectors profit is emphasized to a lesser degree and the need to make business and society at large more sustainable is given the strongest emphasis. People who work in growing sustainability sectors tend to argue that the circular economy is soon to become the norm in most industries and that circular business principles are about to replace the practices of the global, or "linear", economy, but this is a mistake. Global companies are still growing rapidly, and increasing volumes of goods are transported through the supply chains of most large industries. This trend can be observed through the continuous growth of the transport sector, the demand for trucks, airplanes, ships, and cars, the construction of hotels, distribution centres, conference halls, resorts, and theme parks, and the growth of wholesalers and retailers that distribute and sell products that are produced by supply chains that are becoming increasingly global in nature. The aspect that can be changed at short notice is the opportunity for people to reduce business travel, because the systems for this, in the form of ICT and communication infrastructures, have been built and expanded over recent decades so the investment in the technologies for digital meetings has already been made. In the case of the development of the other systems needed for the transformation to sustainability, they still remain to be expanded to replace existing ones, something that is likely to take decades. In most cases there are no sustainable systems in existence that can start to take over business volumes and grow.

Very large amounts of resources are required to grow the circular economy so that it will encompass the entire society and replace the highly competitive products, services, and business concepts of the global economy. This is an important insight: there is a need for large volumes of resources to build the new resource-saving systems!

Chapter Twelve

Developing a Strategy

When put forward in the way above, the transformation may seem daunting, but necessary. Without suitable tools many tasks seem impossible. It is not very likely that someone will develop a simple and straightforward method for transforming present society to less resource intensive production and distribution systems for most goods and services if nobody has drawn a map of the terrain or if the goal has been stated in an imprecise or irrelevant way.

After the Second World War, the task of rebuilding Europe in terms of housing and production resources in agriculture and industry must have seemed impossible. In the years after the war, people were starving because there were no jobs and there was too little food. Production and distribution systems had been blown to pieces through bombings and battles during the war. In many parts of Europe people had to get by on less than 1,500 calories per day.[1] Factories, homes, and office buildings had been bombed and the rubble had to be removed to construct new buildings. In the turmoil following the war, United States Secretary of State George Marshall realized that there was a danger that Europe may not get out of this precarious situation, that unemployment and starvation may become permanent, and that most countries may be taken over by the Soviet Union, in the same way that the eastern parts of Europe already had been. Leaders in the United States also realized that the countries of western Europe could become important markets for American products, if only the purchasing power of their populations could be restored. Marshall managed to convince Congress that the United States' government should help finance the rebuilding of Europe through a large-scale programme of humanitarian and industrial aid, the Marshall Plan.

---

[1]   In *The Most Noble Adventure* Greg Behrman describes the background and implementation of the Marshall Plan.

The programme was supposed to run for four years, from 1948 to 1951, but owing to the aid European recovery went faster than expected and the plan could be discontinued one year before its intended end. From 1947 to 1951 the aggregate gross national products of the recipient countries grew from 120 billion to 160 billion dollars. In 1951 the industrial production of western Europe had increased by 35 per cent compared to the situation before the war, a much bigger result than had been expected.[2]

Via the plan the United States invested 17 billion dollars (corresponding to 202 billion in 2019 terms) in the reconstruction of Europe, and it helped get European industry back on a growth track. By rebuilding Europe, the United States also built a market with a strong demand for American products. This and other examples of large-scale transformation endeavours show that it is possible to achieve very ambitious goals if tasks are approached in a systematic way with relevant funding and resources. In the present situation, governments need to develop strategies with the potential of achieving large-scale results in a short space of time—and it is impossible to know what can be achieved before the transformation has been planned and started. What we can be completely certain of, however, is that if countries do not try to achieve ambitious goals, they will never be able to reach them.

The example of the Marshall Plan illustrates how a tremendous task can be managed if only resources are dedicated to analysing the problem and focused activities are put in place to solve it. As no resources have been spent analysing and understanding the challenges of transformation to less resource intensive production and distribution systems, very little is known about the details of the challenge and the possible solutions. This may sound strange, as work has been going on for decades to develop new transport solutions and sustainable materials and production systems.

The challenge of the transformation to sustainability and resilience is to focus resources on the transformation of the most important sectors of society and use these as good examples and encouragement to drive the rest of the transformation forwards.

The question is whether it will at all be possible to start change on a large scale so that we have a chance of taking society up to a level of significant sustainability. This cannot be done by trying to do a little of

---

[2]   Greg Behrman, *The Most Noble Adventure*, p. 333.

everything at the same time. The present approach is similar to building a large number of houses in parallel without the significant resources that are needed to finalize each one. With that approach, none of the buildings will become ready to live in any time soon and a lot of resources will be wasted on building houses that will never be finished. In order for the new systems to save resources, they need to be developed to a significant level of efficiency, because when they are unfinished and remain at early stages of development the existence of many systems that serve the same purpose increases resource consumption and the transformation is not likely to reach critical mass in any one area. It will be much more efficient to build one system or a few systems at the time and finish them. Even though there is a need to change everything at once, this cannot be done with any realistic chance of success.

The Double Hamster Wheel

The current situation is like a pair of hamster wheels. Humanity is in this case the hamster and we are increasingly aware of only the small wheel that we can observe in our daily lives. The two wheels represent the development that is going on in society, and the size of the wheels illustrate the time frame of development. The small one represents the business cycle and the short-term growth that is created as mature technologies help boost economic growth, new products and service offerings are developed, and new job opportunities arise as affluence is gradually improved. The large wheel represents the longer cycles of technical and economic development that emanate from the growth and maturity of technologies, and the peaks and troughs of the business cycle that occur through the transitions between the growth cycles of different technologies. The speed of the small wheel is the level of growth of the economy short term, and the speed of the large wheel represents how much effort present generations invest in building favourable economic circumstances for coming generations.

The media, literature, and films give the impression that only the small wheel exists and that digitization and the different developments that are related to this are the only technological advancements that are relevant. This impression is supported by analyses of economic growth by many economists. Reports focus primarily on short-term aspects. Similarly, experts on different technologies report the progress of technical development, and TV shows like Top Gear reinforce these types of information by sending strong emotional signals that communicate the feeling that humanity can continue to use inordinate amounts of resources, for pure pleasure—something that the available data tells us will not be possible. Most people seem to assume that if the inner wheel is running without glitches, the outer wheel is driven by the momentum of the inner wheel and future generations will be fine. Sustainability activists and experts like Greta Thunberg argue vaguely that leaders are not doing enough to combat climate change, that the future is at risk, and that the environmental footprint of humanity is too large. What these experts are saying is that present generations do not pay enough attention to the large wheel.

Even if all attention is paid to the workings of the inner wheel, most individuals seem to think that the outer wheel will continue to generate new opportunities that benefit future generations, but this is not the case. The inner wheel and the outer wheel are driven by entirely different activities and both need to be managed for short-term and long-term development to go smoothly. Most of this book has been the story of the interdependencies between the inner and the outer wheel and how the consequences of a widespread blindness to the outer wheel threatens to cause severe problems in the functioning of the inner wheel as soon as the next decade. Because, if present generations do not focus enough resources on keeping the outer wheel in motion, the inner wheel is likely to break down sometime in the future. Keeping the outer wheel in shape is not only a matter of avoiding environmental disasters. It is also a matter of making sure that there are enough resources to sustain society long term and that there are technologies that are about to mature and drive economic growth in the future.

The inner wheel can be driven by the resource allocation of market forces because it is driven by mature technologies. The outer wheel needs to be tended to via political decisions and conscious allocation of resources to long-term development projects. Projects that have developed the technologies that have driven economic growth in recent decades have not been started with that objective in mind. In fact, previous generations have not quite understood how far the development of computers and communication technologies would take us. The decision makers who decided to finance projects for the development of mainframe computers, the internet, and radio telephony did not envision that these innovations would result in a future where almost everybody would carry mobile computers in their pockets. In the 1970s the CEO of Digital Corporation, Ken Olsen, argued that it would never become relevant for people to have computers in their homes, and in the early 1990s economist Robert Solow discovered the, so-called, IT paradox by saying that computers could be seen every-where, except in the productivity statistics.

Now, in the early twenty-first century, we have a much better understanding of development. We know that it can be possible to transform transport systems to electric mobility and that it is possible to reorganize production and distribution in systems that are both sustainable and resilient. We will have to reduce consumption, but we believe that we can develop an economy that can make this possible. We just have not discovered how to do it and we have not really, as a society, realized that we need to devise the strategies and plans that will be necessary to take present society and its inhabitants into the future. An increasing share of the focus in society is fixed on the issue of getting the inner wheel to run smoother and faster. The outer wheel is something that is neither seen nor experienced every day. We per-ceive it more like Halley's Comet and other comets, phenomena that appear in the sky at intervals, but our collective genius has not been able to grasp what guides the appearances and disappearances of the issues related to the functioning of the wheels, whether there are regularities or if events are predictable, at least to some extent.

Some decision makers and experts argue that there is no outer wheel and that neither people nor decision makers need to worry about anything, except keeping up consumption and investment, and then everything will turn out for the best. These people are in this book referred to as the blind guardians of ignorance. There are also people who argue that we need to care more about some aspects of the outer wheel, such as resource consumption, but are oblivious to the activities that are needed in order to rebuild both the inner and outer wheels so that they can take humanity into the future. They also become blind guardians of ignorance, as they fail to see the complexity and magni-tude of the investment that will be necessary. The entire set of wheels, representing the global economy, is the most complex system that has been developed by mankind. It is so complex that very few understand how it works.

The inner wheel is all that people experience most of the time. Once in a while, like Halley's Comet, an unexpected recession reminds us that there are also longer cycles of development and that countries need to prepare for "unexpected" events. The significant disturbances to the inner wheel that have been caused by the Covid-19 pandemic tell us that many people who have been responsible for the outer wheel have failed to set aside resources for preparations for pandemics, even though pandemics are known to regularly strike our global society, and modern lifestyles make countries increasingly vulnerable to these events. In the case of the peak in oil production and the recession that will inevitably follow this, this indicates that there may also be very long cycles that end when important resources reach their peak and there are no new sources of resources that are ready to replace them. If the people responsible for the outer wheel do not prepare for a decline in oil production well in advance of the start of the decrease, the inner wheel will suffer because the inner wheel to a large extent is driven by oil as the main fuel for transportation on road, air, sea, and a share of trains around the world.

Economic historians have for a long time studied the short-term and long-term cycles of the economy and noted that there are cycles that run over a few years, longer ones that run over twenty years, and really long cycles that run over half a century. These have been studied in detail and have been given names like Kondratiev Waves, that are supposed to have a wave-length of some fifty years. Sometimes there have been severe recessions at the end of one cycle before a new one has started. One of the examples of this was the stagflation period in the 1970s and 1980s that economists ascribe to the transition between the technologies that had driven growth after the Second World War and the technologies that have driven growth since the 1980s. Investment in the development of the latter technologies started at a later point and their advancement had not made enough progress for them to drive growth in the 1970s.

The recession that must be expected as oil production goes into decline is likely to be very different from the long and short economic cycles that have already been mentioned. The decline in oil production will not be a temporary development that will be present for a few years as humanity learns how to utilize new forms of energy, such as replacing petroleum-based fuels with electricity. The decline in oil production will be permanent and there are no new fuels or transport systems available that have been developed through activities in the outer wheel to the point where they can be implemented on a large scale and thus make the transformation of fuels for the inner wheel smooth. This means that the recession that will be caused by the expected decline in oil production is not likely to be temporary. Instead, the decline will continue for a long time and there will be no new fuel ready to replace it. Governments and individuals will have to convert vehicles to the use of electricity or reduce the need for transportation by better coordinating distribution and using the available fuels more efficiently. They will also have to promote an increase of local production. It will be a challenge for countries and the global economy to cope with a declining supply of fuel, and governments are likely to take unexpected measures to avoid for as long as possible forcing reduced consumption and use of resources on their citizens.

The large hamster wheel is driven by large-scale and long-term investment, the type of investment that has been responsible for the development of innovations like information technology, communication technology, materials and production technologies, and vehicle technologies to their present level, and it will be difficult to invest enough in this type of development to take new technologies to maturity when the inner wheel next slows down. This conundrum will be a very unexpected challenge and politicians and business leaders are not likely to immediately understand how the situation could at all arise or how it needs to be dealt with. Change leaders need to be there and tell them what is going on.

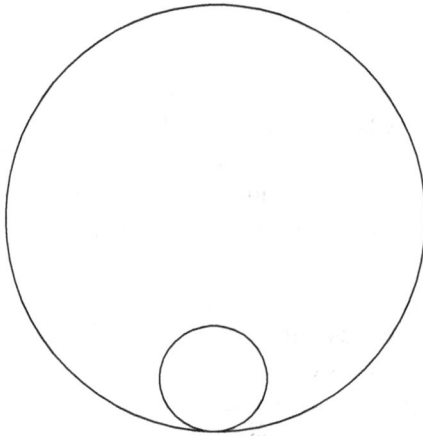

Figure 2. An illustration of the double hamster wheel. People are aware primarily of the smaller wheel, which seems to revolve faster and faster, while at the same time the larger wheel is going slower as less money than is needed is invested in the development of the technologies and business principles underlying the circular economy and e-mobility.

Change leaders need to take the challenges seriously and start to pay attention to the outer wheel, the one that is responsible for the long-term development of our society. Up until a few decades ago, governments invested enough money and resources into long-term development projects to keep the inner wheel running smoothly for a few decades, but over recent decades it has been assumed that market forces — which are primarily focused on the short-term operation of the economy — could also be made responsible for the long-term advancement of society and the global economy. Through the coronavirus pandemic, we can now observe that this is not the case. The market does not take responsibility for anything, it only allocates resources to alternatives that are competitive short-term, and new technologies and developments never attract the resources necessary to drive them through the early stages of innovation. Governments and citizens will discover this in the coming decades, and countries will have to manage the emerging situation in the best way they can. The present book has provided some key tools for change leaders, governments, and ordinary citizens to handle the situation as it unfolds. Above all, future development will require collaboration on all levels of society and between countries on a scale that has not been experienced before. In the next few years, the blind guardians of ignorance need to become change leaders who can lead humanity into the next phase of global development, or the blind guardians and present leaders need to step out of the way and make room for leaders who understand the challenges and know how to cope with them.

Literature

Aleklett, K. (2012) *Peeking at Peak Oil*, New York: Springer.

Behrman, G. (2007) *The Most Noble Adventure*, New York: Free Press.

Brynjolfsson, E. & McAfee, A. (2016) *The Second Machine Age*, New York: W.W. Norton & Company.

Crowley, R. (2011) *City of Fortune*, London: Faber and Faber.

Daly, H.E. (1996) *Beyond Growth*, Boston: Beacon Press.

Ford, M. (2015) *The Rise of the Robots*, London: Oneworld Publications.

Gordon, J.S. (2004) *An Empire of Wealth*, New York: Harper Perennial.

Hammer, M. & Champy, J. (1993) *Reengineering the Corporation*, New York: Nicholas Brealey Publishing.

Harari, Y.N. (2018) *21 Lessons for the 21st Century*, London: Penguin Random House.

Heinberg, R. (2014) *Snake Oil*, West Houthly: Clearview Books.

Honogsbaum, M. (2019) *The Pandemic Century*, New York: W.W. Norton & Company.

Kelly, K. (2016) *The Inevitable*, New York: Penguin Books.

Larsson, M. (2005) *The Limits of Business Development and Economic Growth*, Basingstoke: Palgrave Macmillan.

Larsson, M. (2009) *Global Energy Transformation*, Basingstoke: Palgrave Macmillan.

Larsson, M. (2012) *The Business of Global Energy Transformation*, Basingstoke: Palgrave Macmillan.

Larsson, M. (2018) *Circular Business Models*, Basingstoke: Palgrave Macmillan.

McDonough, W. & Braungart, M. (2013) *The Upcycle*, New York: North Point Press.

Moore, G.A. (1991) *Crossing the Chasm*, New York: Harper Collins.

Murray, C. & Bly Cox, C. (2004) *Apollo*, Burkittsville: South Mountain Books.

Olsen, B. (2010) *Pandemi*, Stockholm: Norstedts.

Orloff, R.W. & Harland, D.M. (2006) *Apollo*, New York: Springer.

Pfeiffer, D.A. (2006) *Eating Fossil Fuels*, Gabriola Island: New Society Publishers.

Ruttan, V.W. (2006) *Is War Necessary for Economic Growth?*, Oxford: Oxford University Press.

Simmons, M.R. (2005) *Twilight in the Desert*, New York: John Wiley and Sons.

Susskind, J. (2018) *Future Politics*, Oxford: Oxford University Press.

Svensmark, H. & Calder, N. (2007) *The Chilling Stars*, London: Icon Books.

Tainter, J.A. (1988) *The Collapse of Complex Societies*, Cambridge: Cambridge University Press.

Thunberg, G. (2019) *No One Is Too Small to Make a Difference*, London: Penguin Random House.

Uddenfeldt, T. (2016) *Gratislunchen*, Stockholm: Albert Bonniers Förlag.

Weckesser, T. (2019) *The EV's Are Coming*, Frederiksberg: Dansk Energi.

Westergård, R. (2016) *Ett jordklot räcker*, Stockholm: Calidris Förlag.

Worldwatch Institute (2007) *Biofuels for Transport*, London: Earthscan.